Practical symfony

Create professional web applications with PHP and symfony 1.3 & 1.4

symfony 1.3 & 1.4 | Doctrine

Fabien Potencier

Practical symfony | symfony 1.3 & 1.4 | Doctrine | version *jobeet-1.4-doctrine-en-2009-11-19*

© 2007-2010 Fabien Potencier

ISBN-13: 978-2-918390-16-9

Editor: Fabien Potencier
Cover: Julien Madelin, Franck Bodiot
Index: Nicolas Perriault
Icons: DocBook XSL stylesheets

Sensio SA

92-98, boulevard Victor Hugo
92 115 Clichy
France
info@sensio.com

The information in this book is distributed on an "as is" basis, without warranty. Although every precaution has been taken in the preparation of this work, neither the author(s) nor Sensio shall have any liability to any person or entity with respect to any loss or damage caused or alleged to be caused directly or indirectly by the information contained in this work.

If you find typos or errors, feel free to report them by creating a ticket on the symfony ticketing system (*http://trac.symfony-project.org/register*). Based on tickets and users feedback, this book is continuously updated.

You can contact the author about this book, symfony and Open-Source at *fabien.potencier@symfony-project.com* or for training, consulting, application development, or business related questions at *fabien.potencier@sensio.com*.

To Lucas, Thomas, and Hélène —

Contents at a Glance

Table of Contents

About the Author

Fabien Potencier discovered the Web in 1994, at a time when connecting to the Internet was still associated with the harmful strident sounds of a modem. Being a developer by passion, he immediately started to build websites with Perl. But with the release of PHP 5, he decided to switch focus to PHP, and created the symfony framework project in 2004 to help his company leverage the power of PHP for its customers.

Fabien is a serial-entrepreneur, and among other companies, he created Sensio, a services and consulting company specialized in web technologies and Internet marketing, in 1998.

Fabien is also the creator of several other Open-Source projects, a writer, a blogger, a speaker at international conferences, and a happy father of two wonderful kids.

His Website: *http://fabien.potencier.org/*

On Twitter: *http://www.twitter.com/fabpot*

About Sensio Labs

Sensio Labs is a services and consulting company specialized in Open-Source Web technologies and Internet marketing.

Founded in 1998 by Fabien Potencier, Gregory Pascal, and Samuel Potencier, Sensio benefited from the Internet growth of the late 1990s and situated itself as a major player for building complex web applications. It survived the Internet bubble burst by applying professional and industrial methods to a business where most players seemed to reinvent the wheel for each project. Most of Sensio's clients are large corporations, who hire its teams to deal with small- to middle-scale projects with strong time-to-market and innovation constraints.

Sensio Labs develops interactive web applications, both for dot-com and traditional companies. Sensio Labs also provides auditing, consulting, and training on Internet technologies and complex application deployment. It helps define the global Internet strategy of large-scale industrial players. Sensio Labs has projects in France and abroad.

For its own needs, Sensio Labs develops the symfony framework and sponsors its deployment as an Open-Source project. This means that symfony is built from experience and is employed in many web applications, including those of large corporations.

Since its beginnings eleven years ago, Sensio has always based its strategy on strong technical expertise. The company focuses on Open-Source technologies, and as for dynamic scripting languages, Sensio offers developments in all LAMP platforms. Sensio acquired strong experience on the best frameworks using these languages, and often develops web applications in Django, Rails, and, of course, symfony.

Sensio Labs is always open to new business opportunities, so if you ever need help developing a web application, learning symfony, or evaluating a symfony development, feel free to contact us at fabien.potencier@sensio.com. The consultants, project managers, web designers, and developers of Sensio can handle projects from A to Z.

Which symfony Version?

This book has been written for both symfony 1.3 and symfony 1.4. As writing a single book for two different versions of a software is quite unusual, this section explains what are the main differences between the two versions, and how to make the best choice for your projects.

Both symfony 1.3 and symfony 1.4 versions have been released at about the same time (at the end of 2009). As a matter of fact, they both have the **exact same feature set**. The only difference between the two versions is on how they support backward compatibility with older symfony versions.

Symfony 1.3 is the release you want to use if you need to upgrade a legacy project that uses an older symfony version (1.0, 1.1, or 1.2). It has a backward compatibility layer and all the features that have been deprecated during the 1.3 development period are still available. It means that upgrading is easy, simple, and safe.

But if you start a new project today, you should use symfony 1.4. This version has the same feature set as symfony 1.3 but all the deprecated features and the compatibility layer has been removed. This version is cleaner and also a bit faster than symfony 1.3. Another big advantage of using symfony 1.4 is its longer support. Being a Long Term Support release, it is maintained by the symfony core team for three years (until November 2012).

Of course, you can migrate your projects to symfony 1.3 and then slowly update your code to remove the deprecated features and eventually move to symfony 1.4 to benefit from the long term support. You have plenty of time to plan the move as symfony 1.3 is supported for a year (until November 2010).

As this book does not describe deprecated features, all examples work equally well on both versions.

Day 1

Starting up the Project

Introduction

The symfony[1] framework has been an Open-Source project for more than four years and has become one of the most popular PHP frameworks thanks to its great features and great documentation.

This book describes the creation of a web application with the symfony framework, step-by-step from the specifications to the implementation. It is targeted at beginners who want to learn symfony, understand how it works, and also learn about the best web development practices.

The application to be designed could have been yet another blog engine. But we want to use symfony on a useful project. The goal is to demonstrate that symfony can be used to develop professional applications with style and little effort.

We will keep the content of the project secret for another day as we already have much to do today. However, let's give it a name: **Jobeet**.

Each chapter of this book is meant to last between one and two hours, and will be the occasion to learn symfony by coding a real website, from start to finish. Every day, new features will be added to the application, and we'll take advantage of this development to introduce you to new symfony functionalities as well as good practices in symfony web development.

---

1. `http://www.symfony-project.org/`

This Book is different

Remember the early days of PHP4. Ah, la Belle Epoque[2]! PHP was one of the first languages dedicated to the web and one of the easiest to learn.

But as web technologies evolve at a very fast pace, web developers need to keep up with the latest best practices and tools. The best way to learn is of course by reading blogs, tutorials, and books. We have read a lot of these, be they written for PHP, Python, Java, Ruby, or Perl, and many of them fall short when the author starts giving snippets of codes as examples.

You are probably used to reading warnings like:

"For a real application, don't forget to add validation and proper error handling."

or

"Security is left as an exercise to the reader."

or

"You will of course need to write tests."

What? These things are serious business. They are perhaps the most important part of any piece of code. And as a reader, you are left alone. Without these concerns taken into account, the examples are much less useful. You cannot use them as a good starting point. That's bad! Why? Because security, validation, error handling, and tests, just to name a few, take care to code right.

In this book, you will never see statements like those as we will write tests, error handling, validation code, and be sure we develop a secure application. That's because symfony is about code, but also about best practices and how to develop professional applications for the enterprise. We will be able to afford this luxury because symfony provides all the tools needed to code these aspects easily without writing too much code.

Validation, error handling, security, and tests are first-class citizens in symfony, so it won't take us too long to explain. This is just one of many reasons why to use a framework for "real life" projects.

All the code you will read in this book is code you could use for a real project. We encourage you to copy and paste snippets of code or steal whole chunks.

---

2. http://en.wikipedia.org/wiki/Belle_Époque

What for Today?

We won't write PHP code today. But even without writing a single line of code, you will start understanding the benefits of using a framework like symfony, just by bootstrapping a new project.

The objective of this chapter is to setup the development environment and display a page of the application in a web browser. This includes installation of symfony, creation of an application, and web server configuration.

As this book will mostly focus on the symfony framework, we will assume that you already have a solid knowledge of PHP 5 and Object Oriented programming.

Prerequisites

Before installing symfony, you need to check that your computer has everything installed and configured correctly. Take the time to conscientiously read this chapter and follow all the steps required to check your configuration, as it may save your day further down the road.

Third-Party Software

First of all, you need to check that your computer has a friendly working environment for web development. At a minimum, you need a web server (Apache, for instance), a database engine (MySQL, PostgreSQL, SQLite, or any PDO[3]-compatible database engine), and PHP 5.2.4 or later.

Command Line Interface

The symfony framework comes bundled with a command line tool that automates a lot of work for you. If you are a Unix-like OS user, you will feel right at home. If you run a Windows system, it will also work fine, but you will just have to type a few commands at the **cmd** prompt.

 Unix shell commands can come in handy in a Windows environment. If you would like to use tools like **tar**, **gzip** or **grep** on Windows, you can install Cygwin[4]. The adventurous may also like to try Microsoft's Windows Services for Unix[5].

---

3. `http://www.php.net/PDO`
4. `http://cygwin.com/`
5. `http://technet.microsoft.com/en-gb/interopmigration/bb380242.aspx`

PHP Configuration

As PHP configurations can vary a lot from one OS to another, or even between different Linux distributions, you need to check that your PHP configuration meets the symfony minimum requirements.

First, ensure that you have PHP 5.2.4 at a minimum installed by using the **phpinfo()** built-in function or by running **php -v** on the command line. Be aware that on some configurations, you might have two different PHP versions installed: one for the command line, and another for the web.

Then, download the symfony configuration checker script at the following URL:

Listing 1-1
```
http://sf-to.org/1.4/check.php
```

Save the script somewhere under your current web root directory.

Launch the configuration checker script from the command line:

Listing 1-2
```
$ php check_configuration.php
```

If there is a problem with your PHP configuration, the output of the command will give you hints on what to fix and how to fix it.

You should also execute the checker from a browser and fix the issues it might discover. That's because PHP can have a distinct **php.ini** configuration file for these two environments, with different settings.

 Don't forget to remove the file from your web root directory afterwards.

Symfony Installation

Initializing the Project Directory

Before installing symfony, you first need to create a directory that will host all the files related to Jobeet:

Listing 1-3
```
$ mkdir -p /home/sfprojects/jobeet
$ cd /home/sfprojects/jobeet
```

Or on Windows:

```
c:\> mkdir c:\development\sfprojects\jobeet
c:\> cd c:\development\sfprojects\jobeet
```

Listing
1-4

 Windows users are advised to run symfony and to setup their new project in a path which contains no spaces. Avoid using the Documents and Settings directory, including anywhere under My Documents.

 If you create the symfony project directory under the web root directory, you won't need to configure your web server. Of course, for production environments, we strongly advise you to configure your web server as explained in the web server configuration section.

Choosing the Symfony Version

Now, you need to install symfony. As the symfony framework has several stable versions, you need to choose the one you want to install by reading the installation page[6] on the symfony website.

This book assumes you want to install symfony 1.3 or symfony 1.4.

Choosing the Symfony Installation Location

You can install symfony globally on your machine, or embed it into each of your project. The latter is the recommended one as projects will then be totally independent from each others. Upgrading your locally installed symfony won't break some of your projects unexpectedly. It means you will be able to have projects on different versions of symfony, and upgrade them one at a time as you see fit.

As a best practice, many people install the symfony framework files in the lib/vendor project directory. So, first, create this directory:

```
$ mkdir -p lib/vendor
```

Listing
1-5

---

6. http://www.symfony-project.org/installation

Installing Symfony

Installing from an Archive

The easiest way to install symfony is to download the archive for the version you choose from the symfony website. Go to the installation page for the version you have just chosen, symfony 1.4[7] for instance.

Under the "**Source Download**" section, you will find the archive in `.tgz` or in `.zip` format. Download the archive, put it under the freshly created `lib/vendor/` directory, un-archive it, and rename the directory to `symfony`:

Listing
1-6
```
$ cd lib/vendor
$ tar zxpf symfony-1.4.0.tgz
$ mv symfony-1.4.0 symfony
$ rm symfony-1.4.0.tgz
```

Under Windows, unzipping the zip file can be achieved using Windows Explorer. After you rename the directory to `symfony`, there should be a directory structure similar to `c:\dev\sfprojects\jobeet\lib\vendor\symfony`.

Installing from Subversion (recommended)

If you use Subversion, it is even better to use the `svn:externals` property to embed symfony into your project in the `lib/vendor/` directory:

Listing
1-7
```
$ svn pe svn:externals lib/vendor/
```

 Importing your project in a new Subversion repository is explained at the end of this chapter.

If everything goes well, this command will run your favorite editor to give you the opportunity to configure the external Subversion sources.

 On Windows, you can use tools like TortoiseSVN[8] to do everything without the need to use the console.

If you are conservative, tie your project to a specific release (a subversion tag):

Listing
1-8
```
symfony http://svn.symfony-project.com/tags/RELEASE_1_4_0
```

---

7. http://www.symfony-project.org/installation/1_4
8. http://tortoisesvn.net/

Whenever a new release comes out (as announced on the symfony blog[9]), you will need to change the URL to the new version.

If you want to go the bleeding-edge route, use the 1.4 branch:

```
symfony http://svn.symfony-project.com/branches/1.4/
```
Listing 1-9

Using the branch makes your project benefits from the bug fixes automatically whenever you run a **svn update**.

Installation Verification

Now that symfony is installed, check that everything is working by using the symfony command line to display the symfony version (note the capital **V**):

```
$ cd ../..
$ php lib/vendor/symfony/data/bin/symfony -V
```
Listing 1-10

On Windows:

```
c:\> cd ..\..
c:\> php lib\vendor\symfony\data\bin\symfony -V
```
Listing 1-11

The **-V** option also displays the path to the symfony installation directory, which is stored in **config/ProjectConfiguration.class.php**.

If the path to symfony is an absolute one (which should not be by default if you follow the above instructions), change it so it reads like follows for better portability:

```
// config/ProjectConfiguration.class.php
require_once dirname(__FILE__).'/../lib/vendor/symfony/lib/autoload/
sfCoreAutoload.class.php';
```
Listing 1-12

That way, you can move the project directory anywhere on your machine or another one, and it will just work.

 If you are curious about what this command line tool can do for you, type **symfony** to list the available options and tasks:

```
$ php lib/vendor/symfony/data/bin/symfony
```
Listing 1-13

On Windows:

---

9. http://www.symfony-project.org/blog/

`c:\> php lib\vendor\symfony\data\bin\symfony`

The symfony command line is the developer's best friend. It provides a lot of utilities that improve your productivity for day-to-day activities like cleaning the cache, generating code, and much more.

Project Setup

In symfony, **applications** sharing the same data model are regrouped into **projects**. For most projects, you will have two different applications: a frontend and a backend.

Project Creation

From the **sfprojects/jobeet** directory, run the symfony **generate:project** task to actually create the symfony project:

`$ php lib/vendor/symfony/data/bin/symfony generate:project jobeet`

On Windows:

`c:\> php lib\vendor\symfony\data\bin\symfony generate:project jobeet`

The **generate:project** task generates the default structure of directories and files needed for a symfony project:

Directory	Description
`apps/`	Hosts all project applications
`cache/`	The files cached by the framework
`config/`	The project configuration files
`lib/`	The project libraries and classes
`log/`	The framework log files
`plugins/`	The installed plugins
`test/`	The unit and functional test files
`web/`	The web root directory (see below)

Why does symfony generate so many files? One of the main benefits of using a full-stack framework is to standardize your developments. Thanks to symfony's default structure of files and directories, any developer with some symfony knowledge can take over the maintenance of any symfony project. In a matter of minutes, he will be able to dive into the code, fix bugs, and add new features.

The **generate:project** task has also created a **symfony** shortcut in the project root directory to shorten the number of characters you have to write when running a task.

So, from now on, instead of using the fully qualified path to the symfony program, you can use the **symfony** shortcut.

Application Creation

Now, create the frontend application by running the **generate:app** task:

```
$ php symfony generate:app frontend
```

Listing 1-17

 Because the symfony shortcut file is executable, Unix users can replace all occurrences of '**php symfony**' by '**./symfony**' from now on.

On Windows you can copy the '**symfony.bat**' file to your project and use '**symfony**' instead of '**php symfony**':

```
c:\> copy lib\vendor\symfony\data\bin\symfony.bat .
```

Listing 1-18

Based on the application name given as an *argument*, the **generate:app** task creates the default directory structure needed for the application under the **apps/frontend/** directory:

Directory	Description
config/	The application configuration files
lib/	The application libraries and classes
modules/	The application code (MVC)
templates/	The global template files

Directory Structure Rights

Before trying to access your newly created project, you need to set the write permissions on the **cache/** and **log/** directories to the appropriate levels, so that your web server can write to them:

Listing 1-19

```
$ chmod 777 cache/ log/
```

Web Server Configuration: The ugly Way

If you have created the project directory it somewhere under the web root directory of your web server, you can already access the project in a web browser.

Of course, as there is no configuration, it is very fast to set up, but try to access the **config/databases.yml** file in your browser to understand the bad consequences

---

10. http://en.wikipedia.org/wiki/Cross-site_scripting
11. http://en.wikipedia.org/wiki/CSRF

of such a lazy attitude. If the user knows that your website is developed with symfony, he will have access to a lot of sensitive files.

Never ever use this setup on a production server, and read the next section to learn how to configure your web server properly.

Web Server Configuration: The secure Way

A good web practice is to put under the web root directory only the files that need to be accessed by a web browser, like stylesheets, JavaScripts and images. By default, we recommend to store these files under the **web/** sub-directory of a symfony project.

If you have a look at this directory, you will find some sub-directories for web assets (**css/** and **images/**) and the two front controller files. The front controllers are the only PHP files that need to be under the web root directory. All other PHP files can be hidden from the browser, which is a good idea as far as security is concerned.

Web Server Configuration

Now it is time to change your Apache configuration, to make the new project accessible to the world.

Locate and open the **httpd.conf** configuration file and add the following configuration at the end:

Listing 1-20

```
# Be sure to only have this line once in your configuration
NameVirtualHost 127.0.0.1:8080

# This is the configuration for your project
Listen 127.0.0.1:8080

<VirtualHost 127.0.0.1:8080>
  DocumentRoot "/home/sfprojects/jobeet/web"
  DirectoryIndex index.php
  <Directory "/home/sfprojects/jobeet/web">
    AllowOverride All
    Allow from All
  </Directory>

  Alias /sf /home/sfprojects/jobeet/lib/vendor/symfony/data/web/sf
  <Directory "/home/sfprojects/jobeet/lib/vendor/symfony/data/web/sf">
    AllowOverride All
    Allow from All
```

```
</Directory>
</VirtualHost>
```

 The /sf alias gives you access to images and javascript files needed to properly display default symfony pages and the web debug toolbar|Web Debug Toolbar.

On Windows, you need to replace the **Alias** line with something like:

Listing 1-21
```
Alias /sf "c:\dev\sfprojects\jobeet\lib\vendor\symfony\data\web\sf"
```

And **/home/sfprojects/jobeet/web** should be replaced with:

Listing 1-22
```
c:\dev\sfprojects\jobeet\web
```

This configuration makes Apache listen to port **8080** on your machine, so the website will be accessible at the following URL:

Listing 1-23
```
http://localhost:8080/
```

You can change **8080** to any number, but favour numbers greater than **1024** as they do not require administrator rights.

If you are an administrator on your machine, it is better to setup virtual hosts instead of adding a new port each time you start a new project. Instead of choosing a port and add a **Listen** statement, choose a domain name (for instance the real domain name with **.localhost** added at the end) and add a **ServerName** statement:

```
# This is the configuration for your project
<VirtualHost 127.0.0.1:80>
  ServerName www.jobeet.com.localhost
  <!-- same configuration as before -->
</VirtualHost>
```

Listing 1-24

The domain name **www.jobeet.com.localhost** used in the Apache configuration has to be declared locally. If you run a Linux system, it has to be done in the **/etc/hosts** file. If you run Windows XP, this file is located in the **C:\WINDOWS\system32\drivers\etc** directory.

Add in the following line:

```
127.0.0.1 www.jobeet.com.localhost
```

Listing 1-25

Test the New Configuration

Restart Apache, and check that you now have access to the new application by opening a browser and typing **http://localhost:8080/index.php/**, or **http://www.jobeet.com.localhost/index.php/** depending on the Apache configuration you chose in the previous section.

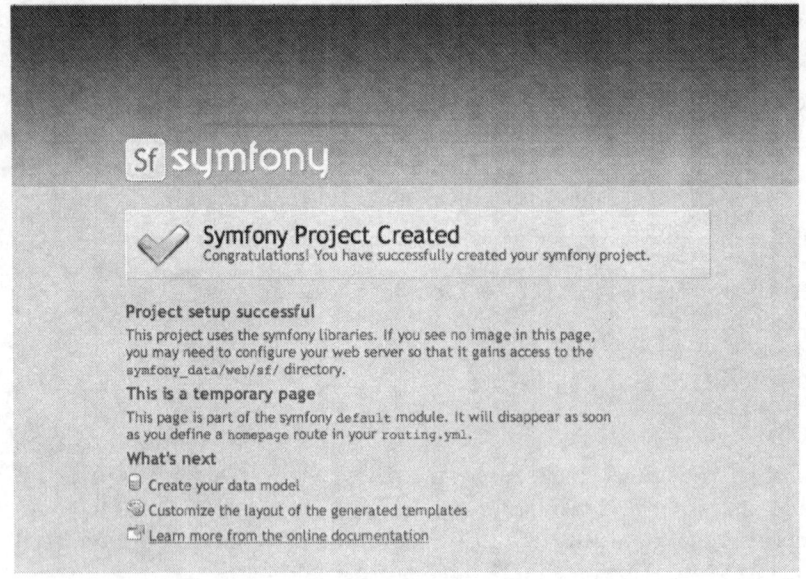

 If you have the Apache **mod_rewrite** module installed, you can remove the **index.php/** part of the URL. This is possible thanks to the rewriting rules configured in the **web/.htaccess** file.

You should also try to access the application in the development environment (see the next section for more information about environments). Type in the following URL:

Listing 1-26
```
http://www.jobeet.com.localhost/frontend_dev.php/
```

The web debug toolbar should show in the top right corner, including small icons proving that your **sf/** alias configuration is correct.

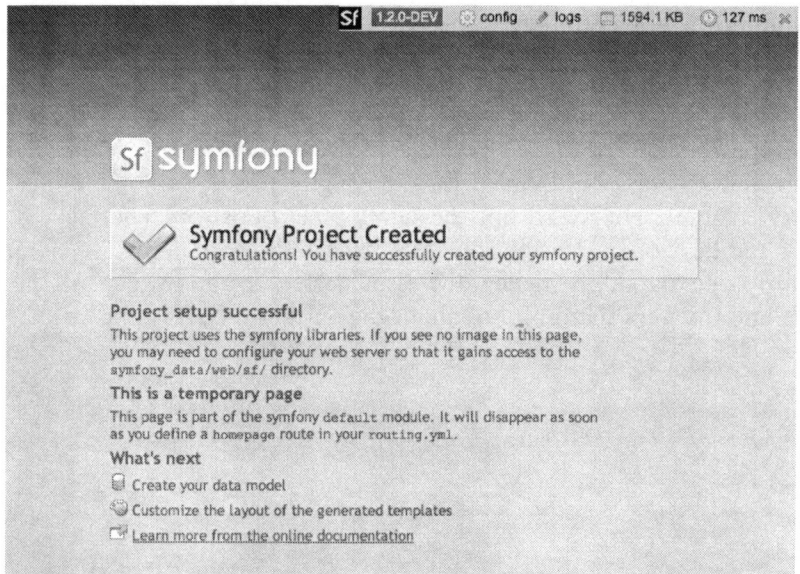

 The setup is a little different if you want to run symfony on an IIS server in a Windows environment. Find how to configure it in the related tutorial[12].

The Environments

If you have a look at the web/ directory, you will find two PHP files: index.php and frontend_dev.php. These files are called **front controllers**; all requests to the application are made through them. But why do we have two front controllers for each application?

Both files point to the same application but for different **environments**. When you develop an application, except if you develop directly on the production server, you need several environments:

- The **development environment**: This is the environment used by **web developers** when they work on the application to add new features, fix bugs, ...

- The **test environment**: This environment is used to automatically test the application.

- The **staging environment**: This environment is used by the **customer** to test the application and report bugs or missing features.

---

12. http://www.symfony-project.com/cookbook/1_0/web_server_iis

- The **production environment**: This is the environment **end users** interact with.

What makes an environment unique? In the development environment for instance, the application needs to log all the details of a request to ease debugging, but the cache system must be disabled as all changes made to the code must be taken into account right away. So, the development environment must be optimized for the developer. The best example is certainly when an exception occurs. To help the developer debug the issue faster, symfony displays the exception with all the information it has about the current request right into the browser:

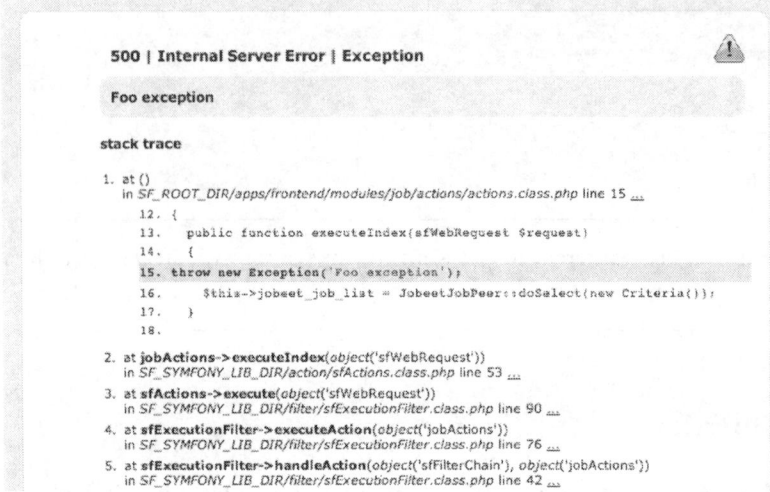

But on the production environment, the cache layer must be activated and, of course, the application must display customized error messages instead of raw exceptions. So, the production environment must be optimized for performance and the user experience.

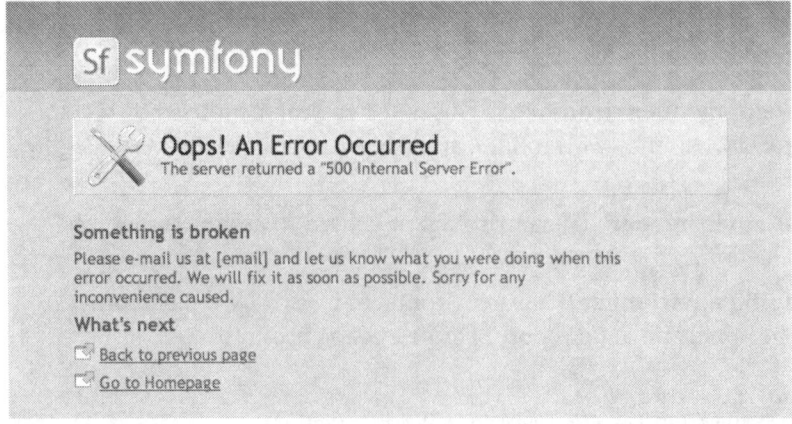

If you open the front controller files, you will see that their content is the same except for the environment setting:

Listing
1-27

```
// web/index.php
<?php

require_once(dirname(__FILE__).'/../config/
ProjectConfiguration.class.php');

$configuration =
ProjectConfiguration::getApplicationConfiguration('frontend',
'prod', false);
sfContext::createInstance($configuration)->dispatch();
```

The web debug toolbar is also a great example of the usage of environment. It is present on all pages in the development environment and gives you access to a lot of information by clicking on the different tabs: the current application configuration, the logs for the current request, the SQL statements executed on the database engine, memory information, and time information.

Subversion

It is a good practice to use source version control when developing a web application. Using a source version control allows us to:

- work with confidence
- revert to a previous version if a change breaks something
- allow more than one person to work efficiently on the project
- have access to all the successive versions of the application

In this section, we will describe how to use Subversion[13] with symfony. If you use another source code control tool, it must be quite easy to adapt what we describe for Subversion.

We assume you have already access to a Subversion server and can access it via HTTP.

 If you don't have a Subversion server at your disposal, you can create a repository for free on Google Code[14] or just type "free subversion repository" in Google to have a lot more options.

---

13. http://subversion.tigris.org/

First, create a repository for the **jobeet** project on the repository server:

Listing
1-28
```
$ svnadmin create /path/to/jobeet/repository
```

On your machine, create the basic directory structure:

Listing
1-29
```
$ svn mkdir -m "created default directory structure"
  ➥ http://svn.example.com/jobeet/trunk
  ➥ http://svn.example.com/jobeet/tags
  ➥ http://svn.example.com/jobeet/branches
```

And checkout the empty **trunk/** directory:

Listing
1-30
```
$ cd /home/sfprojects/jobeet
$ svn co http://svn.example.com/jobeet/trunk/ .
```

Then, remove the content of the **cache/** and **log/** directories as we don't want to put them into the repository.

Listing
1-31
```
$ rm -rf cache/* log/*
```

Now, make sure to set the write permissions on the cache and logs directories to the appropriate levels so that your web server can write to them:

Listing
1-32
```
$ chmod 777 cache/ log/
```

Now, import all the files and directories:

Listing
1-33
```
$ svn add *
```

As we will never want to commit files located in the **cache/** and **log/** directories, you need to specify an ignore list:

Listing
1-34
```
$ svn propedit svn:ignore cache
```

The default text editor configured for SVN should launch. Subversion must ignore all the content of this directory:

Listing
1-35
```
*
```

Save and quit. You're done.

Repeat the procedure for the **log/** directory:

---

14. http://code.google.com/hosting/

```
$ svn propedit svn:ignore log
```
Listing
1-36

And enter:

```
*
```
Listing
1-37

Finally, commit these changes to the repository:

```
$ svn import -m "made the initial import" .
  ↳ http://svn.example.com/jobeet/trunk
```
Listing
1-38

 Windows users can use the great TortoiseSVN[15] client to manage their subversion repository.

See you Tomorrow

Well, time is over for today! Even if we have not yet started talking about symfony, we have setup a solid development environment, we have talked about web development best practices, and we are ready to start coding.

Tomorrow, we will reveal what the application will do and talk about the requirements we need to implement for Jobeet.

---

15. http://tortoisesvn.tigris.org/

Day 2

The Project

We have not written a single line of PHP yet, but yesterday, we setup the environment, created an empty symfony project, and made sure we started with some good security defaults. If you followed along, you have been looking at your screen delightedly since then, as it displays the beautiful default symfony page for new applications.

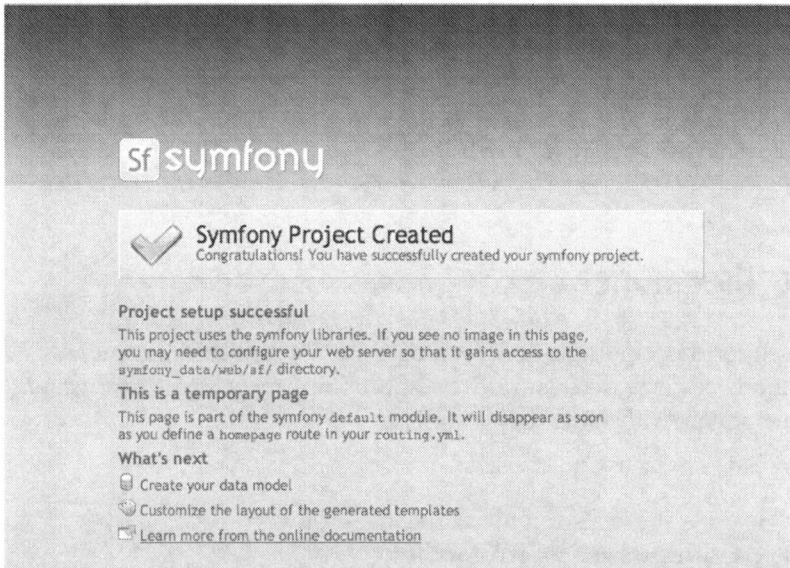

But you want more. You want to learn all the nitty gritty details of symfony application development. So, let's resume our trip to symfony development nirvana.

Today, we will take the time to describe the requirements of the Jobeet project with some basic mockups.

The Project Pitch

Everybody is talking about the crisis nowadays. Unemployment is rising again.

I know, symfony developers are not really concerned and that's why you want to learn symfony in the first place. But it is also quite difficult to find good symfony developers.

Where can you find a symfony developer? Where can you advertise your symfony skills?

You need to find a good job board. Monster you say? Think again. You need a focused job board. One where you can find the best people, the experts. One where it is easy, fast, and fun to look for a job, or to propose one.

Search no more. Jobeet is the place. **Jobeet is Open-Source job board software** that only does one thing, but does it well. It is easy to use, customize, extend, and embed into your website. It supports multiple languages out of the box, and of course uses the latest Web 2.0 technologies to enhance user experience. It also provides feeds and an API to interact with it programatically.

Does it already exist? As as user, you will find a lot of job boards like Jobeet on the Internet. But try to find one which is Open-Source, and as feature-rich as what we propose here.

 If you are really looking for a symfony job or want to hire a symfony developer, you can go to the symfonians[16] website.

The Project User Stories

Before diving into the code head-first, let's describe the project a bit more. The following sections describe the features we want to implement in the first version/ iteration of the project with some simple stories.

The Jobeet website has four kind of users:

- **admin**: He owns the website and has the magic power
- **user**: He visits the website to look for a job
- **poster**: He visits the website to post a job
- **affiliate**: He re-publishes some jobs on his website

---

16. http://symfonians.net/

The project has two applications: the **frontend** (stories F1 to F7, below), where the users interact with the website, and the **backend** (stories B1 to B3), where admins manage the website.

The backend application is secured and requires credentials to access.

Story F1: On the homepage, the user sees the latest active jobs

When a user comes to the Jobeet website, he sees a list of active jobs. The jobs are sorted by category and then by publication date (newer jobs first). For each job, only the location, the position, and the company are displayed.

For each category, the list only shows the first 10 jobs and a link allows to list all the jobs for a given category (*Story F2*).

On the homepage, the user can refine the job list (*Story F3*), or post a new job (*Story F5*).

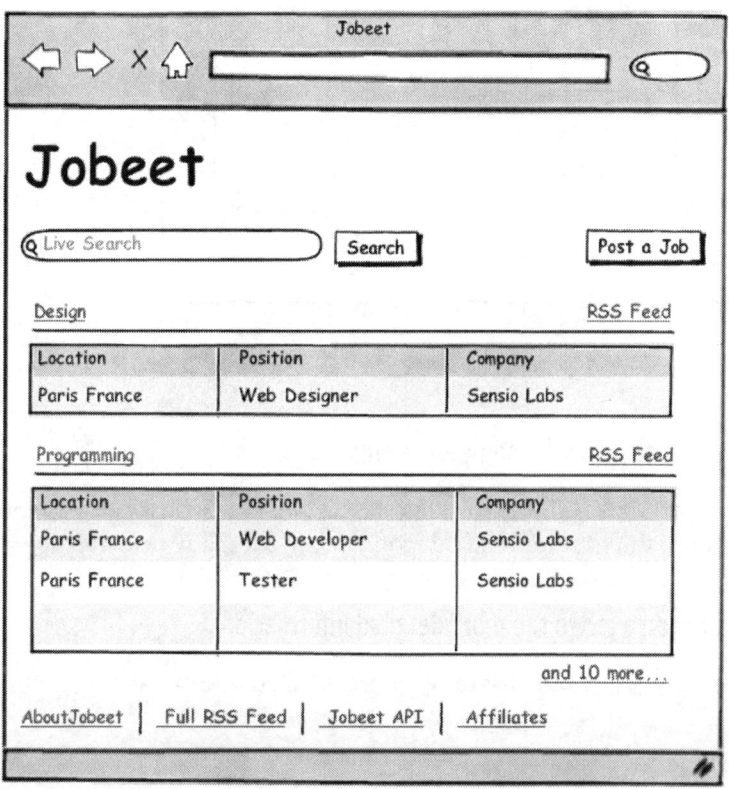

Story F2: A user can ask for all the jobs in a given category

When a user clicks on a category name or on a "more jobs" link on the homepage, he sees all the jobs for this category sorted by date.

The list is paginated with 20 jobs per page.

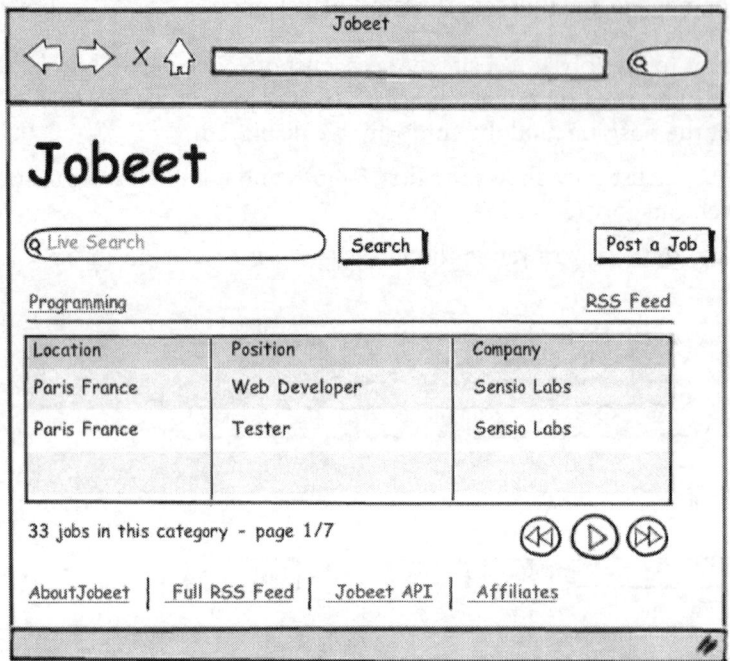

Story F3: A user refines the list with some keywords

The user can enter some keywords to refine his search. Keywords can be words found in the location, the position, the category, or the company fields.

Story F4: A user clicks on a job to see more detailed information

The user can select a job from the list to see more detailed information.

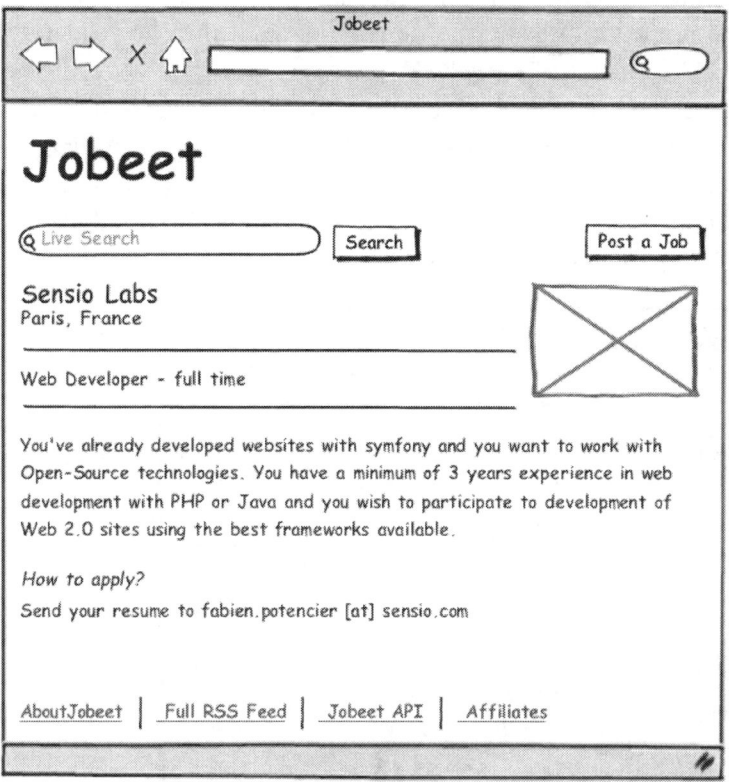

Story F5: A user posts a job

A user can post a job. A job is made of several pieces of information:

- Company
- Type (full-time, part-time, or freelance)
- Logo (optional)
- URL (optional)
- Position
- Location
- Category (the user chooses in a list of possible categories)
- Job description (URLs and emails are automatically linked)
- How to apply (URLs and emails are automatically linked)
- Public (whether the job can also be published on affiliate websites)
- Email (email of the poster)

There is no need to create an account to post a job.

The process is straightforward with only two steps: first, the user fills in the form with all the needed information to describe the job, then he validates the information by previewing the final job page.

Even if the user has no account, a job can be modified afterwards thanks to a specific URL (protected by a token given to the user when the job is created).

Each job post is online for 30 days (this is configurable by the admin - see *Story B2*). A user can come back to re-activate or extend the validity of the job ad for an extra 30 days but only when the job expires in less than 5 days.

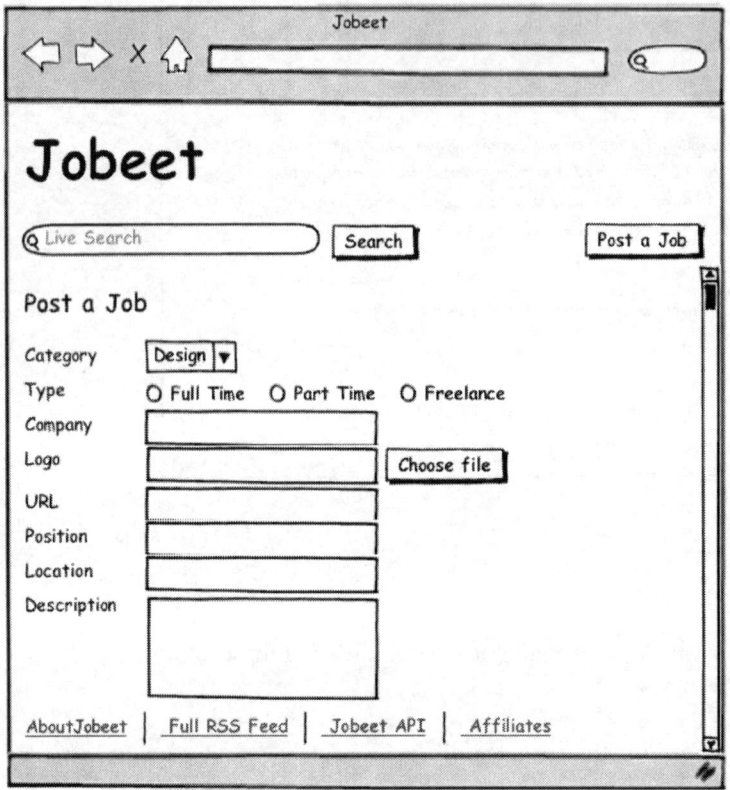

Story F6: A user applies to become an affiliate

A user needs to apply to become an affiliate and be authorized to use the Jobeet API. To apply, he must give the following information:

- Name
- Email
- Website URL

The affiliate account must be activated by the admin (*Story B3*). Once activated, the affiliate receives a token to use with the API via email.

When applying, the affiliate can also choose to get jobs from a sub-set of the available categories.

Story F7: An affiliate retrieves the current active job list

An affiliate can retrieve the current job list by calling the API with his affiliate token. The list can be returned in the XML, JSON or YAML format.

The list contains the public information available for a job.

The affiliate can also limit the number of jobs to be returned, and refine his query by specifying a category.

Story B1: An admin configures the website

An admin can edit the categories available on the website.

Story B2: An admin manages the jobs

An admin can edit and remove any posted job.

Story B3: An admin manages the affiliates

The admin can create or edit affiliates. He is responsible for activating an affiliate and can also disable one.

When the admin activates a new affiliate, the system creates a unique token to be used by the affiliate.

See you Tomorrow

As for any web development, you never start coding the first day. You need to gather the requirements first and work on a mockup design. That's what we have done today.

Day 3

The Data Model

Those of you itching to open your text editor and lay down some PHP will be happy to know today's tutorial will get us into some development. We will define the Jobeet data model, use an ORM to interact with the database, and build the first module of the application. But as symfony does a lot of the work for us, we will have a fully functional web module without writing too much PHP code.

The Relational Model

The user stories we have written yesterday describe the main objects of our project: jobs, affiliates, and categories. Here is the corresponding entity relationship diagram:

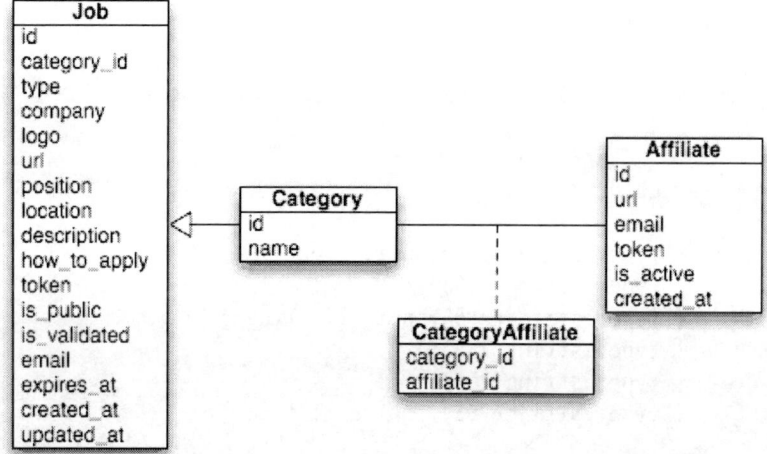

In addition to the columns described in the stories, we have also added a created_at field to some tables. Symfony recognizes such fields and sets the value to the current system time when a record is created. That's the same for updated_at fields: Their value is set to the system time whenever the record is updated.

The Schema

To store the jobs, affiliates, and categories, we obviously need a relational database.

But as symfony is an Object-Oriented framework, we like to manipulate objects whenever we can. For example, instead of writing SQL statements to retrieve records from the database, we'd rather prefer to use objects.

The relational database information must be mapped to an object model. This can be done with an ORM tool[17] and thankfully, symfony comes bundled with two of them: Propel[18] and Doctrine[19]. In this tutorial, we will use Doctrine.

The ORM needs a description of the tables and their relationships to create the related classes. There are two ways to create this description schema: by introspecting an existing database or by creating it by hand.

As the database does not exist yet and as we want to keep Jobeet database agnostic, let's create the schema file by hand by editing the empty config/doctrine/schema.yml file:

Listing 3-1

```
# config/doctrine/schema.yml
JobeetCategory:
  actAs: { Timestampable: ~ }
  columns:
    name: { type: string(255), notnull: true, unique: true }

JobeetJob:
  actAs: { Timestampable: ~ }
  columns:
    category_id:  { type: integer, notnull: true }
    type:         { type: string(255) }
    company:      { type: string(255), notnull: true }
    logo:         { type: string(255) }
    url:          { type: string(255) }
    position:     { type: string(255), notnull: true }
```

17. http://en.wikipedia.org/wiki/Object-relational_mapping
18. http://propel.phpdb.org/
19. http://www.doctrine-project.org/

```
    location:      { type: string(255), notnull: true }
    description:   { type: string(4000), notnull: true }
    how_to_apply: { type: string(4000), notnull: true }
    token:         { type: string(255), notnull: true, unique: true }
    is_public:     { type: boolean, notnull: true, default: 1 }
    is_activated: { type: boolean, notnull: true, default: 0 }
    email:         { type: string(255), notnull: true }
    expires_at:    { type: timestamp, notnull: true }
  relations:
    JobeetCategory: { onDelete: CASCADE, local: category_id, foreign:
id, foreignAlias: JobeetJobs }

JobeetAffiliate:
  actAs: { Timestampable: ~ }
  columns:
    url:        { type: string(255), notnull: true }
    email:      { type: string(255), notnull: true, unique: true }
    token:      { type: string(255), notnull: true }
    is_active: { type: boolean, notnull: true, default: 0 }
  relations:
    JobeetCategories:
      class: JobeetCategory
      refClass: JobeetCategoryAffiliate
      local: affiliate_id
      foreign: category_id
      foreignAlias: JobeetAffiliates

JobeetCategoryAffiliate:
  columns:
    category_id:  { type: integer, primary: true }
    affiliate_id: { type: integer, primary: true }
  relations:
    JobeetCategory:  { onDelete: CASCADE, local: category_id, foreign:
id }
    JobeetAffiliate: { onDelete: CASCADE, local: affiliate_id,
foreign: id }
```

 If you have decided to create the tables by writing SQL statements, you can generate the corresponding **schema.yml** configuration file by running the **doctrine:build-schema** task:

```
$ php symfony doctrine:build-schema
```

Listing 3-2

The above task requires that you have a configured database in **databases.yml**. We show you how to configure the database in a later step. If you try and run this task now it won't work as it doesn't know what database to build the schema for.

The schema is the direct translation of the entity relationship diagram in the YAML format.

The YAML Format

According to the official YAML[20] website, YAML is "a human friendly data serialization standard for all programming languages"

Put another way, YAML is a simple language to describe data (strings, integers, dates, arrays, and hashes).

In YAML, structure is shown through indentation, sequence items are denoted by a dash, and key/value pairs within a map are separated by a colon. YAML also has a shorthand syntax to describe the same structure with fewer lines, where arrays are explicitly shown with [] and hashes with {}.

If you are not yet familiar with YAML, it is time to get started as the symfony framework uses it extensively for its configuration files. A good starting point is the symfony YAML component documentation[21].

There is one important thing you need to remember when editing a YAML file: **indentation must be done with one or more spaces, but never with tabulations**.

The **schema.yml** file contains the description of all tables and their columns. Each column is described with the following information:

- **type**: The column type (**boolean**, **integer**, **float**, **decimal**, **string**, **array**, **object**, **blob**, **clob**, **timestamp**, **time**, **date**, **enum**, **gzip**)
- **notnull**: Set it to **true** if you want the column to be required
- **unique**: Set it to **true** if you want to create a unique index for the column.

 The **onDelete** attribute defines the **ON DELETE** behavior of foreign keys, and Doctrine supports **CASCADE**, **SET NULL**, and **RESTRICT**. For instance, when a **job** record is deleted, all the **jobeet_category_affiliate** related records will be automatically deleted by the database.

---

20. http://yaml.org/
21. http://components.symfony-project.org/yaml/documentation

The Database

The symfony framework supports all PDO-supported databases (MySQL, PostgreSQL, SQLite, Oracle, MSSQL, ...). PDO[22] is the database abstraction layer bundled with PHP.

Let's use MySQL for this tutorial:

```
$ mysqladmin -uroot -p create jobeet
Enter password: mYsEcret ## The password will echo as ********
```

Listing
3-3

  Feel free to choose another database engine if you want. It won't be difficult to adapt the code we will write as we will use the ORM will write the SQL for us.

We need to tell symfony to use this database for the Jobeet project:

```
$ php symfony configure:database
  ➥ "mysql:host=localhost;dbname=jobeet" root mYsEcret
```

Listing
3-4

The **configure:database** task takes three arguments: the PDO DSN[23], the username, and the password to access the database. If you don't need a password to access your database on the development server, just omit the third argument.

  The **configure:database** task stores the database configuration into the **config/databases.yml** configuration file. Instead of using the task, you can edit this file by hand.

  Passing the database password on the command line is convenient but insecure[24]. Depending on who has access to your environment, it might be better to edit the **config/databases.yml** to change the password. Of course, to keep the password safe, the configuration file access mode should also be restricted.

---

22. http://www.php.net/PDO
23. http://www.php.net/manual/en/pdo.drivers.php
24. http://dev.mysql.com/doc/refman/5.1/en/password-security.html

The ORM

Thanks to the database description from the `schema.yml` file, we can use some Doctrine built-in tasks to generate the SQL statements needed to create the database tables:

First in order to generate the SQL you must build your models from your schema files.

Listing
3-5
```
$ php symfony doctrine:build --model
```

Now that your models are present you can generate and insert the SQL.

Listing
3-6
```
$ php symfony doctrine:build-sql
```

The `doctrine:build-sql` task generates SQL statements in the `data/sql/` directory, optimized for the database engine we have configured:

Listing
3-7
```
# snippet from data/sql/schema.sql
CREATE TABLE jobeet_category (id BIGINT AUTO_INCREMENT, name
VARCHAR(255)
NOT NULL COMMENT 'test', created_at DATETIME, updated_at DATETIME, slug
VARCHAR(255), UNIQUE INDEX sluggable_idx (slug), PRIMARY KEY(id))
ENGINE = INNODB;
```

To actually create the tables in the database, you need to run the `doctrine:insert-sql` task:

Listing
3-8
```
$ php symfony doctrine:insert-sql
```

As the task drops the current tables before re-creating them, you are required to confirm the operation. You can also add the `--no-confirmation` option to bypass the question, which is useful if you want to run the task from within a non-interactive batch:

Listing
3-9
```
$ php symfony doctrine:insert-sql --no-confirmation
```

 As for any command line tool, symfony tasks can take arguments and options. Each task comes with a built-in help message that can be displayed by running the `help` task:

Listing
3-10
```
$ php symfony help doctrine:insert-sql
```

The help message lists all the possible arguments and options, gives the default values for each of them, and provides some useful usage examples.

The ORM also generates PHP classes that map table records to objects:

```
$ php symfony doctrine:build-model
```

Listing
3-11

The **doctrine:build-model** task generates PHP files in the **lib/model/** directory that can be used to interact with the database.

By browsing the generated files, you have probably noticed that Doctrine generates three classes per table. For the **jobeet_job** table:

- **JobeetJob**: An object of this class represents a single record of the **jobeet_job** table. The class is empty by default.

- **BaseJobeetJob**: The parent class of **JobeetJob**. Each time you run **doctrine:build --model**, this class is overwritten, so all customizations must be done in the **JobeetJob** class.

- **JobeetJobTable**: The class defines methods that mostly return collections of **JobeetJob** objects. The class is empty by default.

The column values of a record can be manipulated with a model object by using some accessors (**get*()** methods) and mutators (**set*()** methods):

```
$job = new JobeetJob();
$job->setPosition('Web developer');
$job->save();

echo $job->getPosition();

$job->delete();
```

Listing
3-12

You can also define foreign keys directly by linking objects together:

```
$category = new JobeetCategory();
$category->setName('Programming');

$job = new JobeetJob();
$job->setCategory($category);
```

Listing
3-13

The **doctrine:build-all** task is a shortcut for the tasks we have run in this section and some more. So, run this task now to generate forms and validators for the Jobeet model classes:

Listing
3-14
```
$ php symfony doctrine:build-all --no-confirmation
```

You will see validators in action at the end of the day and forms will be explained in great details on day 10.

 A symfony task is made of a namespace and a task name. Each one can be shortened as much as there is no ambiguity with other tasks. So, the following commands are equivalent to `doctrine:build-model`:

Listing
3-15
```
$ php symfony doctrine:build-mo
$ php symfony doc:build-mo
```

The Initial Data

The tables have been created in the database but there is no data in them. For any web application, there are three types of data:

- **Initial data**: Initial data are needed for the application to work. For example, Jobeet needs some initial categories. If not, nobody will be able to submit a job. We also need an admin user to be able to login to the backend.
- **Test data**: Test Data are needed for the application to be tested. As a developer, you will write tests to ensure that Jobeet behaves as described in the user stories, and the best way is to write automated tests. So, each time you run your tests, you need a clean database with some fresh data to test on.
- **User data**: User data are created by the users during the normal life of the application.

Each time symfony creates the tables in the database, all the data are lost. To populate the database with some initial data, we could create a PHP script, or execute some SQL statements with the `mysql` program. But as the need is quite common, there is a better way with symfony: create YAML files in the **data/fixtures/** directory and use the **doctrine:data-load** task to load them into the database.

First, create the following fixture files:

Listing
3-16
```
# data/fixtures/categories.yml
JobeetCategory:
  design:
```

```
    name: Design
  programming:
    name: Programming
  manager:
    name: Manager
  administrator:
    name: Administrator

# data/fixtures/jobs.yml
JobeetJob:
  job_sensio_labs:
    JobeetCategory: programming
    type:          full-time
    company:       Sensio Labs
    logo:          sensio-labs.gif
    url:           http://www.sensiolabs.com/
    position:      Web Developer
    location:      Paris, France
    description:   |
      You've already developed websites with symfony and you want to
work
      with Open-Source technologies. You have a minimum of 3 years
      experience in web development with PHP or Java and you wish to
      participate to development of Web 2.0 sites using the best
      frameworks available.
    how_to_apply:  |
      Send your resume to fabien.potencier [at] sensio.com
    is_public:     true
    is_activated:  true
    token:         job_sensio_labs
    email:         job@example.com
    expires_at:    '2010-10-10'

  job_extreme_sensio:
    JobeetCategory:  design
    type:          part-time
    company:       Extreme Sensio
    logo:          extreme-sensio.gif
    url:           http://www.extreme-sensio.com/
    position:      Web Designer
    location:      Paris, France
    description:   |
      Lorem ipsum dolor sit amet, consectetur adipisicing elit, sed do
      eiusmod tempor incididunt ut labore et dolore magna aliqua. Ut
      enim ad minim veniam, quis nostrud exercitation ullamco laboris
```

```
    nisi ut aliquip ex ea commodo consequat. Duis aute irure dolor
    in reprehenderit in.

    Voluptate velit esse cillum dolore eu fugiat nulla pariatur.
    Excepteur sint occaecat cupidatat non proident, sunt in culpa
    qui officia deserunt mollit anim id est laborum.
how_to_apply: |
    Send your resume to fabien.potencier [at] sensio.com
is_public:    true
is_activated: true
token:        job_extreme_sensio
email:        job@example.com
expires_at:   '2010-10-10'
```

 The job fixture file references two images. You can download them
(http://www.symfony-project.org/get/jobeet/sensio-labs.gif,
http://www.symfony-project.org/get/jobeet/extreme-sensio.gif) and
put them under the web/uploads/jobs/ directory.

A fixtures file is written in YAML, and defines model objects, labelled with a
unique name (for instance, we have defined two jobs labelled job_sensio_labs
and job_extreme_sensio). This label is of great use to link related objects without
having to define primary keys (which are often auto-incremented and cannot be
set). For instance, the job_sensio_labs job category is programming, which is the
label given to the 'Programming' category.

 In a YAML file, when a string contains line breaks (like the description
column in the job fixture file), you can use the pipe (|) to indicate that the
string will span several lines.

Although a fixture file can contain objects from one or several models, we have
decided to create one file per model for the Jobeet fixtures.

 Propel requires that the fixtures files be prefixed with numbers to determine
the order in which the files will be loaded. With Doctrine this is not required
as all fixtures will be loaded and saved in the correct order to make sure foreign
keys are set properly.

In a fixture file, you don't need to define all columns values. If not, symfony
will use the default value defined in the database schema. And as symfony uses
Doctrine to load the data into the database, all the built-in behaviors (like

automatically setting the **created_at** or **updated_at** columns) and the custom behaviors you might have added to the model classes are activated.

Loading the initial data into the database is as simple as running the **doctrine:data-load** task:

```
$ php symfony doctrine:data-load
```

Listing
3-17

 The **doctrine:build-all-reload** task is a shortcut for the **doctrine:build-all** task followed by the **doctrine:data-load** task.

Run the **doctrine:build --all --and-load** task to make sure everything is generated from your schema. This will generate your forms, filters, models, drop your database and re-create it with all the tables.

```
$ php symfony doctrine:build --all --and-load
```

Listing
3-18

See it in Action in the Browser

We have used the command line interface a lot but that's not really exciting, especially for a web project. We now have everything we need to create Web pages that interact with the database.

Let's see how to display the list of jobs, how to edit an existing job, and how to delete a job. As explained during day 1, a symfony project is made of applications. Each application is further divided into **modules**. A module is a self-contained set of PHP code that represents a feature of the application (the API module for example), or a set of manipulations the user can do on a model object (a job module for example).

Symfony is able to automatically generate a module for a given model that provides basic manipulation features:

```
$ php symfony doctrine:generate-module --with-show
    ➥ --non-verbose-templates frontend job JobeetJob
```

Listing
3-19

The **doctrine:generate-module** generates a **job** module in the **frontend** application for the **JobeetJob** model. As with most symfony tasks, some files and directories have been created for you under the **apps/frontend/modules/job/** directory:

Directory	Description
actions/	The module actions

Directory	Description
`templates/`	The module templates

The `actions/actions.class.php` file defines all the available **action** for the `job` module:

Action name	Description
`index`	Displays the records of the table
`show`	Displays the fields and their values for a given record
`new`	Displays a form to create a new record
`create`	Creates a new record
`edit`	Displays a form to edit an existing record
`update`	Updates a record according to the user submitted values
`delete`	Deletes a given record from the table

You can now test the job module in a browser:

Listing 3-20 `http://jobeet.localhost/frontend_dev.php/job`

Edit Job

If you try to edit a job, you will notice the Category id drop down has a list of all the category names. The value of each option is gotten from the __toString() method.

Doctrine will try and provide a base __toString() method by guessing a descriptive column name like, **title**, **name**, **subject**, etc. If you want something custom then you will need to add your own __toString() methods like below. The **JobeetCategory** model is able to guess the __toString() method by using the **name** column of the **jobeet_category** table.

Listing
3·21

```php
// lib/model/doctrine/JobeetJob.class.php
class JobeetJob extends BaseJobeetJob
{
  public function __toString()
  {
    return sprintf('%s at %s (%s)', $this->getPosition(),
      $this->getCompany(), $this->getLocation());
  }
}

// lib/model/doctrine/JobeetAffiliate.class.php
class JobeetAffiliate extends BaseJobeetAffiliate
{
  public function __toString()
  {
    return $this->getUrl();
  }
}
```

You can now create and edit jobs. Try to leave a required field blank, or try to enter an invalid date. That's right, symfony has created basic validation rules by introspecting the database schema.

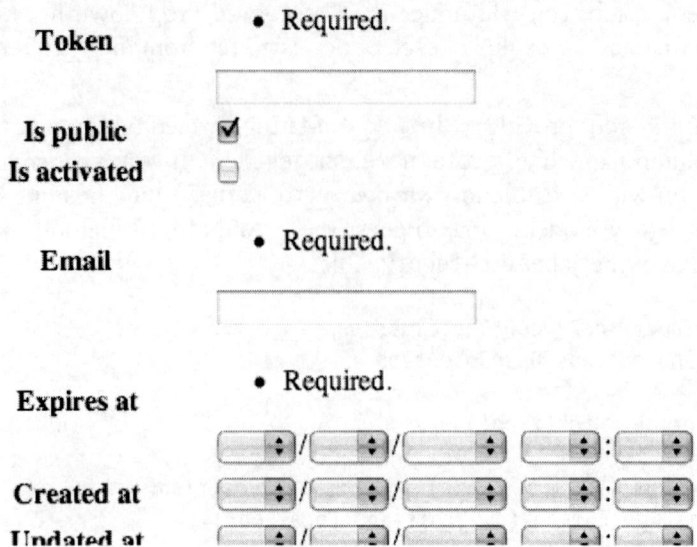

See you Tomorrow

That's all for today. I have warned you in the introduction. Today, we have barely written PHP code but we have a working web module for the job model, ready to be tweaked and customized. Remember, no PHP code also means no bugs!

If you still have some energy left, feel free to read the generated code for the module and the model and try to understand how it works. If not, don't worry and sleep well, as tomorrow, we will talk about one of the most used paradigm in web frameworks, the MVC design pattern[25].

25. http://en.wikipedia.org/wiki/Model-view-controller

Day 4

The Controller and the View

Yesterday, we explored how symfony simplifies database management by abstracting the differences between database engines, and by converting the relational elements to nice object oriented classes. We have also played with Doctrine to describe the database schema, create the tables, and populate the database with some initial data.

Today, we are going to customize the basic **job** module we created yesterday. The **job** module already has all the code we need for Jobeet:

- A page to list all jobs
- A page to create a new job
- A page to update an existing job
- A page to delete a job

Although the code is ready to be used as is, we will refactor the templates to match closer to the Jobeet mockups.

The MVC Architecture

If you are used to developing PHP websites without a framework, you probably use the one PHP file per HTML page paradigm. These PHP files probably contain the same kind of structure: initialization and global configuration, business logic related to the requested page, database records fetching, and finally HTML code that builds the page.

You may use a templating engine to separate the logic from the HTML. Perhaps you use a database abstraction layer to separate model interaction from business logic. But most of the time, you end up with a lot of code that is a nightmare to maintain. It was fast to build, but over time, it's more and more difficult to make changes, especially because nobody except you understands how it is built and how it works.

As with every problem, there are nice solutions. For web development, the most common solution for organizing your code nowadays is the **MVC design pattern**[26]. In short, the MVC design pattern defines a way to organize your code according to its nature. This pattern separates the code into **three layers**:

- The **Model** layer defines the business logic (the database belongs to this layer). You already know that symfony stores all the classes and files related to the Model in the `lib/model/` directory.

- The **View** is what the user interacts with (a template engine is part of this layer). In symfony, the View layer is mainly made of PHP templates. They are stored in various `templates/` directories as we will see later on today.

- The **Controller** is a piece of code that calls the Model to get some data that it passes to the View for rendering to the client. When we installed symfony the first day, we saw that all requests are managed by front controllers (`index.php` and `frontend_dev.php`). These front controllers delegate the real work to **actions**. As we saw yesterday, these actions are logically grouped into **modules**.

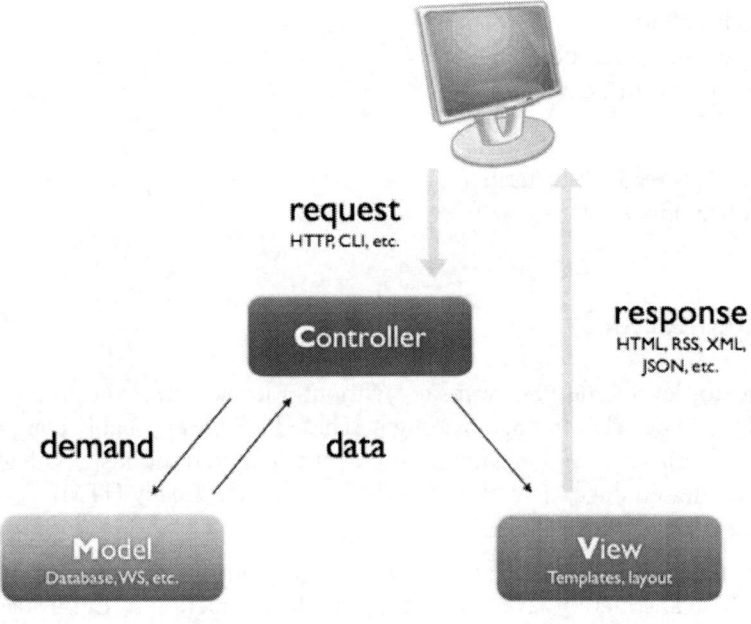

---

26. `http://en.wikipedia.org/wiki/Model-view-controller`

Today, we will use the mockup defined in day 2 to customize the homepage and the job page. We will also make them dynamic. Along the way, we will tweak a lot of things in many different files to demonstrate the symfony directory structure and the way to separate code between layers.

The Layout

First, if you have a closer look at the mockups, you will notice that much of each page looks the same. You already know that code duplication is bad, whether we are talking about HTML or PHP code, so we need to find a way to prevent these common view elements from resulting in code duplication.

One way to solve the problem is to define a header and a footer and include them in each template:

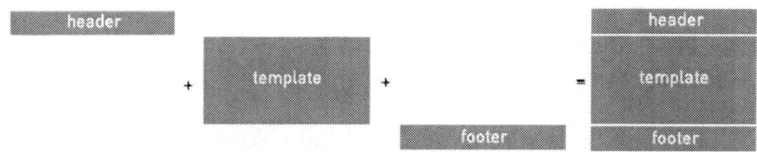

But here the header and the footer files do not contain valid HTML. There must be a better way. Instead of reinventing the wheel, we will use another design pattern to solve this problem: the decorator design pattern[27]. The decorator design pattern resolves the problem the other way around: the template is decorated after the content is rendered by a global template, called a **layout** in symfony:

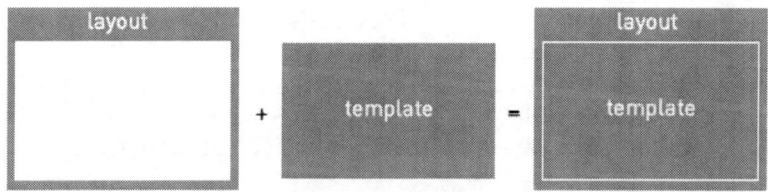

The default layout of an application is called **layout.php** and can be found in the **apps/frontend/templates/** directory. This directory contains all the global templates for an application.

Replace the default symfony layout with the following code:

```
<!-- apps/frontend/templates/layout.php -->
<!DOCTYPE html PUBLIC "-//W3C//DTD XHTML 1.0 Transitional//EN"
  "http://www.w3.org/TR/xhtml1/DTD/xhtml1-transitional.dtd">
```

Listing 4-1

27. http://en.wikipedia.org/wiki/Decorator_pattern

```
<html xmlns="http://www.w3.org/1999/xhtml" xml:lang="en" lang="en">
  <head>
    <title>Jobeet - Your best job board</title>
    <link rel="shortcut icon" href="/favicon.ico" />
    <?php include_javascripts() ?>
    <?php include_stylesheets() ?>
  </head>
  <body>
    <div id="container">
      <div id="header">
        <div class="content">
          <h1><a href="<?php echo url_for('job/index') ?>">
            <img src="http://www.symfony-project.org/images/logo.jpg"
alt="Jobeet Job Board" />
          </a></h1>

          <div id="sub_header">
            <div class="post">
              <h2>Ask for people</h2>
              <div>
                <a href="<?php echo url_for('job/index') ?>">Post a
Job</a>
              </div>
            </div>

            <div class="search">
              <h2>Ask for a job</h2>
              <form action="" method="get">
                <input type="text" name="keywords"
                  id="search_keywords" />
                <input type="submit" value="search" />
                <div class="help">
                  Enter some keywords (city, country, position, ...)
                </div>
              </form>
            </div>
          </div>
        </div>
      </div>

      <div id="content">
        <?php if ($sf_user->hasFlash('notice')): ?>
          <div class="flash_notice">
            <?php echo $sf_user->getFlash('notice') ?>
          </div>
```

```php
    <?php endif; ?>

    <?php if ($sf_user->hasFlash('error')): ?>
      <div class="flash_error">
        <?php echo $sf_user->getFlash('error') ?>
      </div>
    <?php endif; ?>

    <div class="content">
      <?php echo $sf_content ?>
    </div>
  </div>

  <div id="footer">
    <div class="content">
      <span class="symfony">
        <img src="http://www.symfony-project.org/images/
jobeet-mini.png" />
        powered by <a href="http://www.symfony-project.org/">
        <img src="http://www.symfony-project.org/images/
symfony.gif" alt="symfony framework" />
        </a>
      </span>
      <ul>
        <li><a href="">About Jobeet</a></li>
        <li class="feed"><a href="">Full feed</a></li>
        <li><a href="">Jobeet API</a></li>
        <li class="last"><a href="">Affiliates</a></li>
      </ul>
    </div>
  </div>
    </div>
  </body>
</html>
```

A symfony template is just a plain PHP file. In the layout template, you see calls to PHP functions and references to PHP variables. ~$sf_content~ is the most interesting variable: it is defined by the framework itself and contains the HTML generated by the action.

If you browse the job module (http://jobeet.localhost/frontend_dev.php/job), you will see that all actions are now decorated by the layout.

The Stylesheets, Images, and JavaScripts

As this tutorial is not about web design, we have already prepared all the needed assets we will use for Jobeet: download the image files[28] archive and put them into the **web/images/** directory; download the stylesheet files[29] archive and put them into the **web/css/** directory.

 In the layout, we have included a *favicon*. You can download the Jobeet one[30] and put it under the **web/** directory.

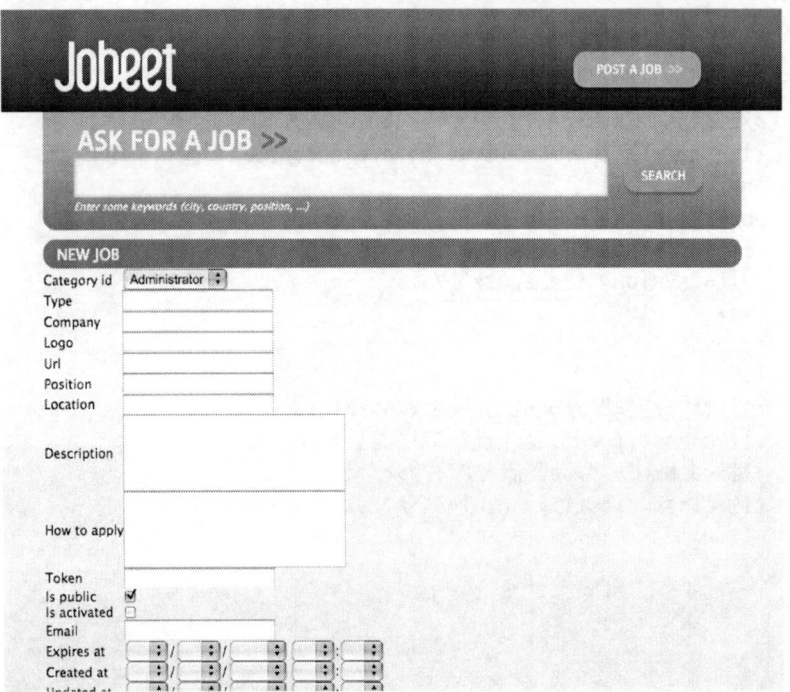

 By default, the **generate:project** task has created three directories for the project assets: **web/images/** for images, **web/css/** for stylesheets, and **web/js/** for JavaScripts. This is one of the many conventions defined by symfony, but you can of course store them elsewhere under the **web/** directory.

---

28. `http://www.symfony-project.org/get/jobeet/images.zip`
29. `http://www.symfony-project.org/get/jobeet/css.zip`
30. `http://www.symfony-project.org/get/jobeet/favicon.ico`

The astute reader will have noticed that even if the `main.css` file is not mentioned anywhere in the default layout, it is definitely present in the generated HTML. But not the other ones. How is this possible?

The stylesheet file has been included by the `include_stylesheets()` function call found within the layout `<head>` tag. The `include_stylesheets()` function is called a **helper**. A helper is a function, defined by symfony, that can take parameters and returns HTML code. Most of the time, helpers are time-savers, they package code snippets frequently used in templates. The `include_stylesheets()` helper generates `<link>` tags for stylesheets.

But how does the helper know which stylesheets to include?

The View layer can be configured by editing the `view.yml` configuration file of the application. Here is the default one generated by the `generate:app` task:

Listing
4-2

```
# apps/frontend/config/view.yml
default:
  http_metas:
    content-type: text/html

  metas:
    #title:        symfony project
    #description:  symfony project
    #keywords:     symfony, project
    #language:     en
    #robots:       index, follow

  stylesheets:   [main.css]

  javascripts:   []

  has_layout:    true
  layout:        layout
```

The `view.yml` file configures the **default** settings for all the templates of the application. For instance, the **stylesheets** entry defines an array of stylesheet files to include for every page of the application (the inclusion is done by the `include_stylesheets()` helper).

 In the default `view.yml` configuration file, the referenced file is `main.css`, and not `/css/main.css`. As a matter of fact, both definitions are equivalent as symfony prefixes relative paths with `/css/`.

If many files are defined, symfony will include them in the same order as the definition:

Listing
4-3 `stylesheets:    [main.css, jobs.css, job.css]`

You can also change the **media** attribute and omit the **.css** suffix:

Listing
4-4 `stylesheets:    [main.css, jobs.css, job.css, print: { media: print }]`

This configuration will be rendered as:

Listing
4-5
```
<link rel="stylesheet" type="text/css" media="screen"
   href="/css/main.css" />
<link rel="stylesheet" type="text/css" media="screen"
   href="/css/jobs.css" />
<link rel="stylesheet" type="text/css" media="screen"
   href="/css/job.css" />
<link rel="stylesheet" type="text/css" media="print"
   href="/css/print.css" />
```

 The **view.yml** configuration file also defines the default layout used by the application. By default, the name is **layout**, and so symfony decorates every page with the **layout.php** file. You can also disable the decoration process altogether by switching the **has_layout** entry to **false**.

It works as is but the **jobs.css** file is only needed for the homepage and the **job.css** file is only needed for the job page. The **view.yml** configuration file can be customized on a per-module basis. Change the stylesheets key of the application **view.yml** file to only contain the **main.css** file:

Listing
4-6
```
# apps/frontend/config/view.yml
stylesheets:    [main.css]
```

To customize the view for the **job** module, create a **view.yml** file in the **apps/frontend/modules/job/config/** directory:

Listing
4-7
```
# apps/frontend/modules/job/config/view.yml
indexSuccess:
  stylesheets: [jobs.css]

showSuccess:
  stylesheets: [job.css]
```

Under the **indexSuccess** and **showSuccess** sections (they are the template names associated with the **index** and **show** actions, as we will see later on), you can customize any entry found under the **default** section of the application **view.yml**.

All specific entries are merged with the application configuration. You can also define some configuration for all actions of a module with the special **all** section.

Configuration Principles in symfony

For many symfony configuration files, the same setting can be defined at different levels:

- The default configuration is located in the framework
- The global configuration for the project (in **config/**)
- The local configuration for an application (in **apps/APP/config/**)
- The local configuration restricted to a module (in **apps/APP/ modules/MODULE/config/**)

At runtime, the configuration system merges all the values from the different files if they exist and caches the result for better performance.

As a rule of thumb, when something is configurable via a configuration file, the same can be accomplished with PHP code. Instead of creating a **view.yml** file for the **job** module for instance, you can also use the **use_stylesheet()** helper to include a stylesheet from a template:

```
<?php use_stylesheet('main.css') ?>
```

Listing 4-8

You can also use this helper in the layout to include a stylesheet globally.

Choosing between one method or the other is really a matter of taste. The **view.yml** file provides a way to define things for all actions of a module, which is not possible in a template, but the configuration is quite static. On the other hand, using the **use_stylesheet()** helper is more flexible and moreover, everything is in the same place: the stylesheet definition and the HTML code. For Jobeet, we will use the **use_stylesheet()** helper, so you can remove the **view.yml** we have just created and update the **job** templates with the **use_stylesheet()** calls:

```
<!-- apps/frontend/modules/job/templates/indexSuccess.php -->
<?php use_stylesheet('jobs.css') ?>

<!-- apps/frontend/modules/job/templates/showSuccess.php -->
<?php use_stylesheet('job.css') ?>
```

Listing 4-9

 Symmetrically, the JavaScript configuration is done via the **javascripts** entry of the **view.yml** configuration file and the **use_javascript()** helper defines JavaScript files to include for a template.

The Job Homepage

As seen in day 3, the job homepage is generated by the **index** action of the **job** module. The **index** action is the Controller part of the page and the associated template, **indexSuccess.php**, is the View part:

Listing 4-10

```
apps/
  frontend/
    modules/
      job/
        actions/
          actions.class.php
        templates/
          indexSuccess.php
```

The Action

Each action is represented by a method of a class. For the job homepage, the class is **jobActions** (the name of the module suffixed by **Actions**) and the method is **executeIndex()** (**execute** suffixed by the name of the action). It retrieves all the jobs from the database:

Listing 4-11

```php
// apps/frontend/modules/job/actions/actions.class.php
class jobActions extends sfActions
{
  public function executeIndex(sfWebRequest $request)
  {
    $this->jobeet_job_list = Doctrine::getTable('JobeetJob')
      ->createQuery('a')
      ->execute();
  }

  // ...
}
```

Let's have a closer look at the code: the **executeIndex()** method (the Controller) calls the Table **JobeetJob** to create a query to retrieve all the jobs. It returns a **Doctrine_Collection** of **JobeetJob** objects that are assigned to the **jobeet_job_list** object property.

All such object properties are then automatically passed to the template (the View). To pass data from the Controller to the View, just create a new property:

Listing 4-12

```
public function executeFooBar(sfWebRequest $request)
{
  $this->foo = 'bar';
  $this->bar = array('bar', 'baz');
}
```

This code will make $foo and $bar variables accessible in the template.

The Template

By default, the template name associated with an action is deduced by symfony thanks to a convention (the action name suffixed by **Success**).

The **indexSuccess.php** template generates an HTML table for all the jobs. Here is the current template code:

Listing
4-13

```
<!-- apps/frontend/modules/job/templates/indexSuccess.php -->
<?php use_stylesheet('jobs.css') ?>

<h1>Job List</h1>

<table>
  <thead>
    <tr>
      <th>Id</th>
      <th>Category</th>
      <th>Type</th>
<!-- more columns here -->
      <th>Created at</th>
      <th>Updated at</th>
    </tr>
  </thead>
  <tbody>
    <?php foreach ($jobeet_job_list as $jobeet_job): ?>
    <tr>
      <td>
        <a href="<?php echo url_for('job/
show?id='.$jobeet_job->getId()) ?>">
          <?php echo $jobeet_job->getId() ?>
        </a>
      </td>
      <td><?php echo $jobeet_job->getCategoryId() ?></td>
      <td><?php echo $jobeet_job->getType() ?></td>
<!-- more columns here -->
      <td><?php echo $jobeet_job->getCreatedAt() ?></td>
```

```
      <td><?php echo $jobeet_job->getUpdatedAt() ?></td>
    </tr>
    <?php endforeach; ?>
  </tbody>
</table>

<a href="<?php echo url_for('job/new') ?>">New</a>
```

In the template code, the **foreach** iterates through the list of **Job** objects (**$jobeet_job_list**), and for each job, each column value is output. Remember, accessing a column value is as simple as calling an accessor method which name begins with **get** and the camelCased column name (for instance the **getCreatedAt()** method for the **created_at** column).

Let's clean this up a bit to only display a sub-set of the available columns:

Listing 4-14

```
<!-- apps/frontend/modules/job/templates/indexSuccess.php -->
<?php use_stylesheet('jobs.css') ?>

<div id="jobs">
  <table class="jobs">
    <?php foreach ($jobeet_job_list as $i => $job): ?>
      <tr class="<?php echo fmod($i, 2) ? 'even' : 'odd' ?>">
        <td class="location"><?php echo $job->getLocation() ?></td>
        <td class="position">
          <a href="<?php echo url_for('job/show?id='.$job->getId())
?>">
            <?php echo $job->getPosition() ?>
          </a>
        </td>
        <td class="company"><?php echo $job->getCompany() ?></td>
      </tr>
    <?php endforeach; ?>
  </table>
</div>
```

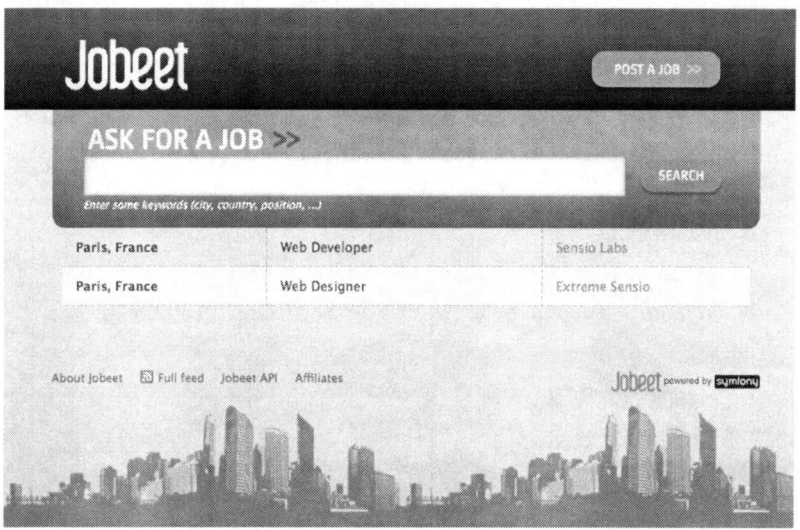

The url_for() function call in this template is a symfony helper that we will discuss tomorrow.

The Job Page Template

Now let's customize the template of the job page. Open the showSuccess.php file and replace its content with the following code:

Listing 4-15

```
<!-- apps/frontend/modules/job/templates/showSuccess.php -->
<?php use_stylesheet('job.css') ?>
<?php use_helper('Text') ?>

<div id="job">
  <h1><?php echo $job->getCompany() ?></h1>
  <h2><?php echo $job->getLocation() ?></h2>
  <h3>
    <?php echo $job->getPosition() ?>
    <small> - <?php echo $job->getType() ?></small>
  </h3>

  <?php if ($job->getLogo()): ?>
    <div class="logo">
      <a href="<?php echo $job->getUrl() ?>">
        <img src="http://www.symfony-project.org/uploads/jobs/<?php
echo $job->getLogo() ?>"
          alt="<?php echo $job->getCompany() ?> logo" />
      </a>
```

```
    </div>
  <?php endif; ?>

  <div class="description">
    <?php echo simple_format_text($job->getDescription()) ?>
  </div>

  <h4>How to apply?</h4>

  <p class="how_to_apply"><?php echo $job->getHowToApply() ?></p>

  <div class="meta">
    <small>posted on <?php echo
$job->getDateTimeObject('created_at')->format('m/d/Y') ?></small>
  </div>

  <div style="padding: 20px 0">
    <a href="<?php echo url_for('job/edit?id='.$job->getId()) ?>">
      Edit
    </a>
  </div>
</div>
```

This template uses the **$job** variable passed by the action to display the job information. As we have renamed the variable passed to the template from **$jobeet_job** to **$job**, you need to also make this change in the **show** action (be careful, there are two occurrences of the variable):

Listing 4-16
```
// apps/frontend/modules/job/actions/actions.class.php
public function executeShow(sfWebRequest $request)
{
  $this->job = Doctrine::getTable('JobeetJob')->
    ➥ find($request->getParameter('id'));
  $this->forward404Unless($this->job);
}
```

Notice that date columns can be converted to PHP DateTime object instances. As we have defined the **created_at** column as a timestamp, you can convert the column value to a DateTime object by using the **getDateTimeObject()** method and then call the **format()** method which takes a date formatting pattern as its first argument:

Listing 4-17
```
$job->getDateTimeObject('created_at')->format('m/d/Y');
```

The job description uses the `simple_format_text()` helper to format it as HTML, by replacing carriage returns with `<br />` for instance. As this helper belongs to the **Text** helper group, which is not loaded by default, we have loaded it manually by using the `use_helper()` helper.

Slots

Right now, the title of all pages is defined in the `<title>` tag of the layout:

```
<title>Jobeet - Your best job board</title>
```

Listing 4-18

But for the job page, we want to provide more useful information, like the company name and the job position.

In symfony, when a zone of the layout depends on the template to be displayed, you need to define a slot:

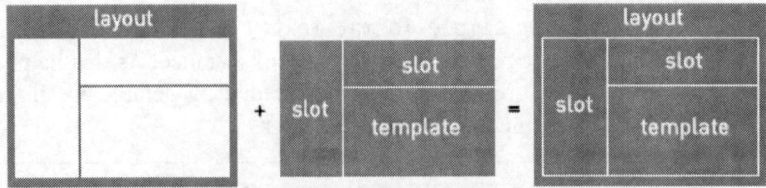

Add a slot to the layout to allow the title to be dynamic:

Listing
4-19

```
// apps/frontend/templates/layout.php
<title><?php include_slot('title') ?></title>
```

Each slot is defined by a name (`title`) and can be displayed by using the `include_slot()` helper. Now, at the beginning of the `showSuccess.php` template, use the `slot()` helper to define the content of the slot for the job page:

Listing
4-20

```
// apps/frontend/modules/job/templates/showSuccess.php
<?php slot(
  'title',
  sprintf('%s is looking for a %s', $job->getCompany(),
$job->getPosition())))
?>
```

If the title is complex to generate, the `slot()` helper can also be used with a block of code:

Listing
4-21

```
// apps/frontend/modules/job/templates/showSuccess.php
<?php slot('title') ?>
  <?php echo sprintf('%s is looking for a %s', $job->getCompany(),
$job->getPosition()) ?>
<?php end_slot(); ?>
```

For some pages, like the homepage, we just need a generic title. Instead of repeating the same title over and over again in templates, we can define a default title in the layout:

Listing
4-22

```
// apps/frontend/templates/layout.php
<title>
  <?php include_slot('title', 'Jobeet - Your best job board') ?>
</title>
```

The second argument of the `include_slot()` method is the default value for the slot if it has not been defined. If the default value is longer or has some HTML tags, you can also defined it like in the following code:

```
// apps/frontend/templates/layout.php
<title>
  <?php if (!include_slot('title')): ?>
    Jobeet - Your best job board
  <?php endif; ?>
</title>
```

Listing
4-23

The include_slot() helper returns **true** if the slot has been defined. So, when you define the **title** slot content in a template, it is used; if not, the default title is used.

 We have already seen quite a few helpers beginning with include_. These helpers output the HTML and in most cases have a get_ helper counterpart to just return the content:

```
<?php include_slot('title') ?>
<?php echo get_slot('title') ?>

<?php include_stylesheets() ?>
<?php echo get_stylesheets() ?>
```

Listing
4-24

The Job Page Action

The job page is generated by the **show** action, defined in the **executeShow()** method of the **job** module:

```
class jobActions extends sfActions
{
  public function executeShow(sfWebRequest $request)
  {
    $this->job = Doctrine::getTable('JobeetJob')->
      ➥ find($request->getParameter('id'));
    $this->forward404Unless($this->job);
  }

  // ...
}
```

Listing
4-25

As in the **index** action, the **JobeetJob** table class is used to retrieve a job, this time by using the **find()** method. The parameter of this method is the unique identifier of a job, its primary key. The next section will explain why the **$request->getParameter('id')** statement returns the job primary key.

If the job does not exist in the database, we want to forward the user to a 404 page, which is exactly what the **forward404Unless()** method does. It takes a Boolean as its first argument and, unless it is true, stops the current flow of execution. As the forward methods stops the execution of the action right away by throwing a **sfError404Exception**, you don't need to return afterwards.

As for exceptions, the page displayed to the user is different in the **prod** environment and in the **dev** environment:

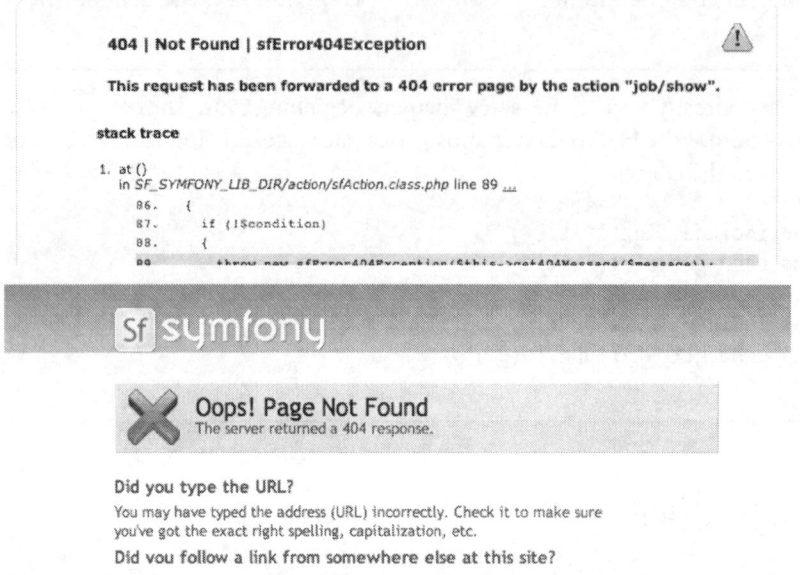

 Before you deploy the Jobeet website to the production server, you will learn how to customize the default 404 page.

The forward404Unless call is actually equivalent to:

```
$this->forward404If(!$this->job);
```

Listing 4-26

which is also equivalent to:

```
if (!$this->job)
{
  $this->forward404();
}
```

Listing 4-27

The forward404() method itself is just a shortcut for:

```
$this->forward('default', '404');
```

Listing 4-28

The forward() method forwards to another action of the same application; in the previous example, to the **404** action of the **default** module. The **default** module is bundled with symfony and provides default actions to render 404, secure, and login pages.

The Request and the Response

When you browse to the /job or /job/show/id/1 pages in your browser, your are initiating a round trip with the web server. The browser is sending a **request** and the server sends back a **response**.

We have already seen that symfony encapsulates the request in a **sfWebRequest** object (see the **executeShow()** method signature). And as symfony is an Object-Oriented framework, the response is also an object, of class **sfWebResponse**. You can access the response object in an action by calling $this->getResponse().

These objects provide a lot of convenient methods to access information from PHP functions and PHP global variables.

 Why does symfony wrap existing PHP functionalities? First, because the symfony methods are more powerful than their PHP counterpart. Then, because when you test an application, it is much more easier to simulate a request or a response object than trying to fiddle around with global variables or work with PHP functions like header() which do too much magic behind the scene.

The Request

The sfWebRequest class wraps the ~$_SERVER~, ~$_COOKIE~, ~$_GET~, ~$_POST~, and ~$_FILES~ PHP global arrays:

Method name	PHP equivalent
getMethod()	$_SERVER['REQUEST_METHOD']
getUri()	$_SERVER['REQUEST_URI']
getReferer()	$_SERVER['HTTP_REFERER']
getHost()	$_SERVER['HTTP_HOST']
getLanguages()	$_SERVER['HTTP_ACCEPT_LANGUAGE']
getCharsets()	$_SERVER['HTTP_ACCEPT_CHARSET']
isXmlHttpRequest()	$_SERVER['X_REQUESTED_WITH'] == 'XMLHttpRequest'
getHttpHeader()	$_SERVER
getCookie()	$_COOKIE
isSecure()	$_SERVER['HTTPS']
getFiles()	$_FILES
getGetParameter()	$_GET
getPostParameter()	$_POST
getUrlParameter()	$_SERVER['PATH_INFO']
getRemoteAddress()	$_SERVER['REMOTE_ADDR']

We have already accessed request parameters by using the getParameter() method. It returns a value from the $_GET or $_POST global variable, or from the PATH_INFO variable.

If you want to ensure that a request parameter comes from a particular one of these variables, you need use the getGetParameter(), getPostParameter(), and getUrlParameter() methods respectively.

 When you want to restrict an action for a specific HTTP method, for instance when you want to ensure that a form is submitted as a POST, you can use the isMethod() method: $this->forwardUnless($request->isMethod('POST'));.

The Response

The **sfWebResponse** class wraps the **header()** and **setrawcookie()** PHP methods:

Method name	PHP equivalent
setCookie()	setrawcookie()
setStatusCode()	header()
setHttpHeader()	header()
setContentType()	header()
addVaryHttpHeader()	header()
addCacheControlHttpHeader()	header()

Of course, the **sfWebResponse** class also provides a way to set the content of the response (**setContent()**) and send the response to the browser (**send()**).

Earlier today we saw how to manage stylesheets and JavaScripts in both the **view.yml** file and in templates. In the end, both techniques use the response object **addStylesheet()** and **addJavascript()** methods.

 The **sfAction**[31], **sfRequest**[32], and **sfResponse**[33] classes provide a lot of other useful methods. Don't hesitate to browse the API documentation[34] to learn more about all symfony internal classes.

See you Tomorrow

Today, we have described some design patterns used by symfony. Hopefully the project directory structure now makes more sense. We have played with the templates by manipulating the layout and the template files. We have also made them a bit more dynamic thanks to slots and actions.

Tomorrow, we will learn more about the **url_for()** helper we have used today, and the routing sub-framework associated with it.

---

31. http://www.symfony-project.org/api/1_4/sfAction
32. http://www.symfony-project.org/api/1_4/sfRequest
33. http://www.symfony-project.org/api/1_4/sfResponse
34. http://www.symfony-project.org/api/1_4/

Day 5

The Routing

If you've completed day 4, you should now be familiar with the MVC pattern and it should be feeling like a more and more natural way of coding. Spend a bit more time with it and you won't look back. To practice a bit yesterday, we customized the Jobeet pages and in the process, also reviewed several symfony concepts, like the layout, helpers, and slots.

Today we will dive into the wonderful world of the symfony routing framework.

URLs

If you click on a job on the Jobeet homepage, the URL looks like this: `/job/show/id/1`. If you have already developed PHP websites, you are probably more accustomed to URLs like `/job.php?id=1`. How does symfony make it work? How does symfony determine the action to call based on this URL? Why is the **id** of the job retrieved with `$request->getParameter('id')`? Today, we will answer all these questions.

But first, let's talk about URLs and what exactly they are. In a web context, a URL is the unique identifier of a web resource. When you go to a URL, you ask the browser to fetch a resource identified by that URL. So, as the URL is the interface between the website and the user, it must convey some meaningful information about the resource it references. But "traditional" URLs do not really describe the resource, they expose the internal structure of the application. The user does not care that your website is developed with the PHP language or that the job has a certain identifier in the database. Exposing the internal workings of your application is also quite bad as far as security is concerned: What if the user tries to guess the URL for resources he does not have access to? Sure, the developer must secure them the proper way, but you'd better hide sensitive information.

URLs are so important in symfony that it has an entire framework dedicated to their management: the **routing** framework. The routing manages internal URIs and external URLs. When a request comes in, the routing parses the URL and converts it to an internal URI.

You have already seen the internal URI of the job page in the showSuccess.php template:

Listing 5-1
```
'job/show?id='.$job->getId()
```

The url_for() helper converts this internal URI to a proper URL:

Listing 5-2
```
/job/show/id/1
```

The internal URI is made of several parts: job is the module, show is the action and the query string adds parameters to pass to the action. The generic pattern for internal URIs is:

Listing 5-3
```
MODULE/ACTION?key=value&key_1=value_1&...
```

As the symfony routing is a two-way process, you can change the URLs without changing the technical implementation. This is one of the main advantages of the front-controller design pattern.

Routing Configuration

The mapping between internal URIs and external URLs is done in the routing.yml configuration file:

Listing 5-4
```
# apps/frontend/config/routing.yml
homepage:
  url:   /
  param: { module: default, action: index }

default_index:
  url:   /:module
  param: { action: index }

default:
  url:   /:module/:action/*
```

The routing.yml file describes routes. A route has a name (homepage), a pattern (/:module/:action/*), and some parameters (under the param key).

When a request comes in, the routing tries to match a pattern for the given URL. The first route that matches wins, so the order in `routing.yml` is important. Let's take a look at some examples to better understand how this works.

When you request the Jobeet homepage, which has the `/job` URL, the first route that matches is the `default_index` one. In a pattern, a word prefixed with a colon (`:`) is a variable, so the `/:module` pattern means: Match a `/` followed by something. In our example, the `module` variable will have `job` as a value. This value can then be retrieved with `$request->getParameter('module')` in the action. This route also defines a default value for the `action` variable. So, for all URLs matching this route, the request will also have an `action` parameter with `index` as a value.

If you request the `/job/show/id/1` page, symfony will match the last pattern: `/:module/:action/*`. In a pattern, a star (*) matches a collection of variable/value pairs separated by slashes (`/`):

Request parameter	Value
module	job
action	show
id	1

 The `module` and `action` variables are special as they are used by symfony to determine the action to execute.

The `/job/show/id/1` URL can be created from a template by using the following call to the `url_for()` helper:

```
url_for('job/show?id='.$job->getId())
```

Listing 5-5

You can also use the route name by prefixing it by `@`:

```
url_for('@default?module=job&action=show&id='.$job->getId())
```

Listing 5-6

Both calls are equivalent but the latter is much faster as the routing does not have to parse all routes to find the best match, and it is less tied to the implementation (the module and action names are not present in the internal URI).

Route Customizations

For now, when you request the `/` URL in a browser, you have the default congratulations page of symfony. That's because this URL matches the **homepage** route. But it makes sense to change it to be the Jobeet homepage. To make the change, modify the **module** variable of the **homepage** route to **job**:

Listing 5-7
```
# apps/frontend/config/routing.yml
homepage:
  url:   /
  param: { module: job, action: index }
```

We can now change the link of the Jobeet logo in the layout to use the **homepage** route:

Listing 5-8
```
<!-- apps/frontend/templates/layout.php -->
<h1>
  <a href="<?php echo url_for('@homepage') ?>">
    <img src="http://www.symfony-project.org/images/logo.jpg"
alt="Jobeet Job Board" />
  </a>
</h1>
```

That was easy!

 When you update the routing configuration, the changes are immediately taken into account in the development environment. But to make them also work in the production environment, you need to clear the cache by calling the **cache:clear** task.

For something a bit more involved, let's change the job page URL to something more meaningful:

Listing 5-9
```
/job/sensio-labs/paris-france/1/web-developer
```

Without knowing anything about Jobeet, and without looking at the page, you can understand from the URL that Sensio Labs is looking for a Web developer to work in Paris, France.

 Pretty URLs are important because they convey information for the user. It is also useful when you copy and paste the URL in an email or to optimize your website for search engines.

The following pattern matches such a URL:

Listing 5-10
```
/job/:company/:location/:id/:position
```

Edit the `routing.yml` file and add the `job_show_user` route at the beginning of the file:

Listing
5-11

```
job_show_user:
  url:   /job/:company/:location/:id/:position
  param: { module: job, action: show }
```

If you refresh the Jobeet homepage, the links to jobs have not changed. That's because to generate a route, you need to pass all the required variables. So, you need to change the `url_for()` call in `indexSuccess.php` to:

Listing
5-12

```
url_for('job/show?id='.$job->getId().'&company='.$job->getCompany().
  '&location='.$job->getLocation().'&position='.$job->getPosition())
```

An internal URI can also be expressed as an array:

Listing
5-13

```
url_for(array(
  'module'   => 'job',
  'action'   => 'show',
  'id'       => $job->getId(),
  'company'  => $job->getCompany(),
  'location' => $job->getLocation(),
  'position' => $job->getPosition(),
))
```

Requirements

During the first day tutorial, we talked about validation and error handling for good reasons. The routing system has a built-in validation feature. Each pattern variable can be validated by a regular expression defined using the **requirements** entry of a route definition:

Listing
5-14

```
job_show_user:
  url:   /job/:company/:location/:id/:position
  param: { module: job, action: show }
  requirements:
    id: \d+
```

The above **requirements** entry forces the **id** to be a numeric value. If not, the route won't match.

Route Class

Each route defined in **routing.yml** is internally converted to an object of class **sfRoute**[35]. This class can be changed by defining a **class** entry in the route definition. If you are familiar with the HTTP protocol, you know that it defines several "methods", like GET, POST, ~HEAD|HEAD (HTTP Method)~, DELETE, and PUT. The first three are supported by all browsers, while the other two are not.

To restrict a route to only match for certain request methods, you can change the route class to **sfRequestRoute**[36] and add a requirement for the virtual **sf_method** variable:

Listing 5-15
```
job_show_user:
  url:   /job/:company/:location/:id/:position
  class: sfRequestRoute
  param: { module: job, action: show }
  requirements:
    id: \d+
    sf_method: [get]
```

 Requiring a route to only match for some HTTP methods is not totally equivalent to using **sfWebRequest::isMethod()** in your actions. That's because the routing will continue to look for a matching route if the method does not match the expected one.

Object Route Class

The new internal URI for a job is quite long and tedious to write (**url_for('job/show?id='.$job->getId().'&company='.$job->getCompany().'&location='.$job->getLocation().'&position='.$job->getPosition())**), but as we have just learned in the previous section, the route class can be changed. For the **job_show_user** route, it is better to use **sfDoctrineRoute**[37] as the class is optimized for routes that represent Doctrine objects or collections of Doctrine objects:

Listing 5-16
```
job_show_user:
  url:     /job/:company/:location/:id/:position
```

---

35. http://www.symfony-project.org/api/1_4/sfRoute
36. http://www.symfony-project.org/api/1_4/sfRequestRoute
37. http://www.symfony-project.org/api/1_4/sfDoctrineRoute

```
class:    sfDoctrineRoute
options: { model: JobeetJob, type: object }
param:    { module: job, action: show }
requirements:
  id: \d+
  sf_method: [get]
```

The **options** entry customizes the behavior of the route. Here, the **model** option defines the Doctrine model class (**JobeetJob**) related to the route, and the **type** option defines that this route is tied to one object (you can also use **list** if a route represents a collection of objects).

The **job_show_user** route is now aware of its relation with **JobeetJob** and so we can simplify the **url_for()** call to:

```
url_for(array('sf_route' => 'job_show_user', 'sf_subject' => $job))
```
Listing 5-17

or just:

```
url_for('job_show_user', $job)
```
Listing 5-18

 The first example is useful when you need to pass more arguments than just the object.

It works because all variables in the route have a corresponding accessor in the **JobeetJob** class (for instance, the **company** route variable is replaced with the value of **getCompany()**).

If you have a look at generated URLs, they are not quite yet as we want them to be:

```
http://jobeet.localhost/frontend_dev.php/job/Sensio+Labs/
Paris%2C+France/1/Web+Developer
```
Listing 5-19

We need to "slugify" the column values by replacing all non ASCII characters by a -. Open the **JobeetJob** file and add the following methods to the class:

```
// lib/model/doctrine/JobeetJob.class.php
public function getCompanySlug()
{
  return Jobeet::slugify($this->getCompany());
}

public function getPositionSlug()
{
  return Jobeet::slugify($this->getPosition());
```
Listing 5-20

```
  }

  public function getLocationSlug()
  {
    return Jobeet::slugify($this->getLocation());
  }
```

Then, create the **lib/Jobeet.class.php** file and add the **slugify** method in it:

Listing
5-21
```
// lib/Jobeet.class.php
class Jobeet
{
  static public function slugify($text)
  {
    // replace all non letters or digits by -
    $text = preg_replace('/\W+/', '-', $text);

    // trim and lowercase
    $text = strtolower(trim($text, '-'));

    return $text;
  }
}
```

 In this tutorial, we never show the opening **<?php** statement in the code examples that only contain pure PHP code to optimize space and save some trees. You should obviously remember to add it whenever you create a new PHP file. Just remember to not add it to template files.

We have defined three new "virtual" accessors: **getCompanySlug()**, **getPositionSlug()**, and **getLocationSlug()**. They return their corresponding column value after applying it the **slugify()** method. Now, you can replace the real column names by these virtual ones in the **job_show_user** route:

Listing
5-22
```
job_show_user:
    url:     /job/:company_slug/:location_slug/:id/:position_slug
    class:   sfDoctrineRoute
    options: { model: JobeetJob, type: object }
    param:   { module: job, action: show }
    requirements:
      id: \d+
      sf_method: [get]
```

You will now have the expected URLs:

```
http://jobeet.localhost/frontend_dev.php/job/sensio-labs/paris-france/
1/web-developer
```
Listing
5-23

But that's only half the story. The route is able to generate a URL based on an object, but it is also able to find the object related to a given URL. The related object can be retrieved with the **getObject()** method of the route object. When parsing an incoming request, the routing stores the matching route object for you to use in the actions. So, change the **executeShow()** method to use the route object to retrieve the **Jobeet** object:

Listing
5-24

```
class jobActions extends sfActions
{
  public function executeShow(sfWebRequest $request)
  {
    $this->job = $this->getRoute()->getObject();

    $this->forward404Unless($this->job);
  }

  // ...
}
```

If you try to get a job for an unknown **id**, you will see a 404 error page but the error message has changed:

404 | Not Found | sfError404Exception

**Unable to find the JobeetJobPeer object with the following parameters "array (
'company_as_slug' => 'extreme-sensio', 'location_as_slug' => 'paris-france', 'id'
=> '888', 'position_as_slug' => 'web-designer',)").**

stack trace

```
1. at ()
   in SF_SYMFONY_LIB_DIR/routing/sfObjectRoute.class.php line 111 ...
     108.    // check the related object
     109.    if (is_null($this->object = $this->getObjectForParameters($this->paramet
```

That's because the 404 error has been thrown for you automatically by the **getRoute()** method. So, we can simplify the **executeShow** method even more:

Listing
5-25

```
class jobActions extends sfActions
{
  public function executeShow(sfWebRequest $request)
  {
    $this->job = $this->getRoute()->getObject();
  }
```

```
// ...
}
```

 If you don't want the route to generate a 404 error, you can set the **allow_empty** routing option to **true**.

 The related object of a route is lazy loaded. It is only retrieved from the database if you call the **getRoute()** method.

Routing in Actions and Templates

In a template, the **url_for()** helper converts an internal URI to an external URL. Some other symfony helpers also take an internal URI as an argument, like the **link_to()** helper which generates an **<a>** tag:

Listing
5-26
```
<?php echo link_to($job->getPosition(), 'job_show_user', $job) ?>
```

It generates the following HTML code:

Listing
5-27
```
<a href="/job/sensio-labs/paris-france/1/web-developer">Web
Developer</a>
```

Both **url_for()** and **link_to()** can also generate absolute URLs:

Listing
5-28
```
url_for('job_show_user', $job, true);

link_to($job->getPosition(), 'job_show_user', $job, true);
```

If you want to generate a URL from an action, you can use the **generateUrl()** method:

Listing
5-29
```
$this->redirect('job_show_user', $job);
```

Collection Route Class

For the **job** module, we have already customized the **show** action route, but the URLs for the others methods (**index**, **new**, **edit**, **create**, **update**, and **delete**) are still managed by the **default** route:

```
default:
  url: /:module/:action/*
```

Listing *5-30*

The **default** route is a great way to start coding without defining too many routes. But as the route acts as a "catch-all", it cannot be configured for specific needs.

As all **job** actions are related to the **JobeetJob** model class, we can easily define a custom **sfDoctrineRoute** route for each as we have already done for the **show** action. But as the **job** module defines the classic seven actions possible for a model, we can also use the **sfDoctrineRouteCollection**[38] class. Open the **routing.yml** file and modify it to read as follows:

```
# apps/frontend/config/routing.yml
job:
  class:   sfDoctrineRouteCollection
  options: { model: JobeetJob }

job_show_user:
  url:     /job/:company_slug/:location_slug/:id/:position_slug
  class:   sfDoctrineRoute
  options: { model: JobeetJob, type: object }
  param:   { module: job, action: show }
  requirements:
    id: \d+
    sf_method: [get]
```

Listing *5-31*

---

38. http://www.symfony-project.org/api/1_4/sfDoctrineRouteCollection

```
# default rules
homepage:
  url:   /
  param: { module: job, action: index }

default_index:
  url:   /:module
  param: { action: index }

default:
  url:   /:module/:action/*
```

The **job** route above is really just a shortcut that automatically generate the following seven **sfDoctrineRoute** routes:

Listing 5-32

```
job:
  url:       /job.:sf_format
  class:     sfDoctrineRoute
  options: { model: JobeetJob, type: list }
  param:     { module: job, action: index, sf_format: html }
  requirements: { sf_method: get }

job_new:
  url:       /job/new.:sf_format
  class:     sfDoctrineRoute
  options: { model: JobeetJob, type: object }
  param:     { module: job, action: new, sf_format: html }
  requirements: { sf_method: get }

job_create:
  url:       /job.:sf_format
  class:     sfDoctrineRoute
  options: { model: JobeetJob, type: object }
  param:     { module: job, action: create, sf_format: html }
  requirements: { sf_method: post }

job_edit:
  url:       /job/:id/edit.:sf_format
  class:     sfDoctrineRoute
  options: { model: JobeetJob, type: object }
  param:     { module: job, action: edit, sf_format: html }
  requirements: { sf_method: get }

job_update:
```

```
  url:     /job/:id.:sf_format
  class:   sfDoctrineRoute
  options: { model: JobeetJob, type: object }
  param:   { module: job, action: update, sf_format: html }
  requirements: { sf_method: put }

job_delete:
  url:     /job/:id.:sf_format
  class:   sfDoctrineRoute
  options: { model: JobeetJob, type: object }
  param:   { module: job, action: delete, sf_format: html }
  requirements: { sf_method: delete }

job_show:
  url:     /job/:id.:sf_format
  class:   sfDoctrineRoute
  options: { model: JobeetJob, type: object }
  param:   { module: job, action: show, sf_format: html }
  requirements: { sf_method: get }
```

 Some routes generated by **sfDoctrineRouteCollection** have the same URL. The routing is still able to use them because they all have different HTTP method requirements.

The **job_delete** and **job_update** routes requires HTTP methods that are not supported by browsers (**DELETE** and **PUT** respectively). This works because symfony simulates them. Open the **_form.php** template to see an example:

Listing
5-33

```php
// apps/frontend/modules/job/templates/_form.php
<form action="..." ...>
<?php if (!$form->getObject()->isNew()): ?>
  <input type="hidden" name="sf_method" value="PUT" />
<?php endif; ?>

<?php echo link_to(
  'Delete',
  'job/delete?id='.$form->getObject()->getId(),
  array('method' => 'delete', 'confirm' => 'Are you sure?')
) ?>
```

All the symfony helpers can be told to simulate whatever HTTP method you want by passing the special **sf_method** parameter.

symfony has other special parameters like **sf_method**, all starting with the **sf_** prefix. In the generated routes above, you can see another one: **sf_format**, which will be explained in a coming day.

Route Debugging

When you use collection routes, it is sometimes useful to list the generated routes. The **app:routes** task outputs all the routes for a given application:

Listing 5-34
```
$ php symfony app:routes frontend
```

You can also have a lot of debugging information for a route by passing its name as an additional argument:

Listing 5-35
```
$ php symfony app:routes frontend job_edit
```

Default Routes

It is a good practice to define routes for all your URLs. As the **job** route defines all the routes needed to describe the Jobeet application, go ahead and remove or comment the default routes from the **routing.yml** configuration file:

Listing 5-36
```
# apps/frontend/config/routing.yml
#default_index:
#  url:   /:module
#  param: { action: index }
#
#default:
#  url:   /:module/:action/*
```

The Jobeet application must still work as before.

See you Tomorrow

Today was packed with a lot of new information. You have learned how to use the routing framework of symfony and how to decouple your URLs from the technical implementation.

Tomorrow, we won't introduce any new concepts, but rather spend time going deeper into what we've covered so far.

Day 6

More with the Model

Yesterday was a great day. You learned how to create pretty URLs and how to use the symfony framework to automate a lot of things for you.

Today, we will enhance the Jobeet website by tweaking the code here and there. In the process, you will learn more about all the features we have introduced during the first five days of this tutorial.

The Doctrine Query Object

From day 2 requirements:

"When a user comes to the Jobeet website, she sees a list of active jobs."

But as of now, all jobs are displayed, whether they are active or not:

Listing
6-1

```php
// apps/frontend/modules/job/actions/actions.class.php
class jobActions extends sfActions
{
  public function executeIndex(sfWebRequest $request)
  {
    $this->jobeet_job_list = Doctrine::getTable('JobeetJob')
      ->createQuery('a')
      ->execute();
  }

  // ...
}
```

An active job is one that was posted less than 30 days ago. The `Doctrine_Query::execute()` method will make a request to the database. In the code above, we are not specifying any where condition which means that all the records are retrieved from the database.

Let's change it to only select active jobs:

Listing
6-2

```
public function executeIndex(sfWebRequest $request)
{
  $q = Doctrine_Query::create()
    ->from('JobeetJob j')
    ->where('j.created_at > ?',
      ➥ date('Y-m-d H:i:s', time() - 86400 * 30));

  $this->jobeet_job_list = $q->execute();
}
```

Debugging Doctrine generated SQL

As you don't write the SQL statements by hand, Doctrine will take care of the differences between database engines and will generate SQL statements optimized for the database engine you choose during day 3. But sometimes, it is of great help to see the SQL generated by Doctrine; for instance, to debug a query that does not work as expected. In the **dev** environment, symfony logs these queries (along with much more) in the **log/** directory. There is one log file for every combination of an application and an environment. The file we are looking for is named **frontend_dev.log**:

Listing
6-3

```
# log/frontend_dev.log
Dec 04 13:58:33 symfony [info] {sfDoctrineLogger} executeQuery :
SELECT
j.id AS j__id, j.category_id AS j__category_id, j.type AS j__type,
j.company AS j__company, j.logo AS j__logo, j.url AS j__url,
j.position AS j__position, j.location AS j__location,
j.description AS j__description, j.how_to_apply AS j__how_to_apply,
j.token AS j__token, j.is_public AS j__is_public,
j.is_activated AS j__is_activated, j.email AS j__email,
j.expires_at AS j__expires_at, j.created_at AS j__created_at,
j.updated_at AS j__updated_at FROM jobeet_job j
WHERE j.created_at > ? (2008-11-08 01:13:35)
```

You can see for yourself that Doctrine has a where clause for the **created_at** column (WHERE **j.created_at > ?**).

The **?** string in the query indicates that Doctrine generates prepared statements. The actual value of **?** ('2008-11-08 01:13:35' in the example above) is passed during the execution of the query and properly escaped by the database engine. The use of prepared statements dramatically reduces your exposure to SQL injection[39] attacks.

This is good, but it's a bit annoying to have to switch between the browser, the IDE, and the log file every time you need to test a change. Thanks to the symfony web debug toolbar, all the information you need is also available within the comfort of your browser:

Object Serialization

Even if the above code works, it is far from perfect as it does not take into account some requirements from day 2:

"A user can come back to re-activate or extend the validity of the job ad for an extra 30 days..."

But as the above code only relies on the **created_at** value, and because this column stores the creation date, we cannot satisfy the above requirement.

But if you remember the database schema we have described during day 3, we also have defined an **expires_at** column. Currently this value is always empty as it is not set in the fixture data. But when a job is created, it can be automatically set to 30 days after the current date.

When you need to do something automatically before a Doctrine object is serialized to the database, you can override the **save()** method of the model class:

```php
// lib/model/doctrine/JobeetJob.class.php
class JobeetJob extends BaseJobeetJob
{
  public function save(Doctrine_Connection $conn = null)
  {
    if ($this->isNew() && !$this->getExpiresAt())
    {
      $now = $this->getCreatedAt() ?
$this->getDateTimeObject('created_at')->format('U') : time();
      $this->setExpiresAt(date('Y-m-d H:i:s', $now + 86400 * 30));
```

Listing 6-4

---

39. http://en.wikipedia.org/wiki/Sql_injection

```
        }

        return parent::save($conn);
    }

    // ...
}
```

The **isNew()** method returns **true** when the object has not been serialized yet in the database, and **false** otherwise.

Now, let's change the action to use the **expires_at** column instead of the **created_at** one to select the active jobs:

Listing 6-5
```
public function executeIndex(sfWebRequest $request)
{
    $q = Doctrine_Query::create()
      ->from('JobeetJob j')
      ->where('j.expires_at > ?', date('Y-m-d H:i:s', time()));

    $this->jobeet_job_list = $q->execute();
}
```

We restrict the query to only select jobs with the **expires_at** date in the future.

More with Fixtures

Refreshing the Jobeet homepage in your browser won't change anything as the jobs in the database have been posted just a few days ago. Let's change the fixtures to add a job that is already expired:

Listing 6-6
```
# data/fixtures/jobs.yml
JobeetJob:
  # other jobs

  expired_job:
    JobeetCategory:  programming
    company:         Sensio Labs
    position:        Web Developer
    location:        Paris, France
    description:     Lorem ipsum dolor sit amet, consectetur
adipisicing elit.
    how_to_apply:    Send your resume to lorem.ipsum [at] dolor.sit
    is_public:       true
```

```
is_activated:      true
created_at:        '2005-12-01 00:00:00'
token:             job_expired
email:             job@example.com
```

 Be careful when you copy and paste code in a fixture file to not break the indentation. The **expired_job** must only have two spaces before it.

As you can see in the job we have added in the fixture file, the **created_at** column value can be defined even if it is automatically filled by Doctrine. The defined value will override the default one. Reload the fixtures and refresh your browser to ensure that the old job does not show up:

```
$ php symfony doctrine:data-load
```

Listing 6-7

You can also execute the following query to make sure that the **expires_at** column is automatically filled by the **save()** method, based on the **created_at** value:

```
SELECT `position`, `created_at`, `expires_at` FROM `jobeet_job`;
```

Listing 6-8

Custom Configuration

In the **JobeetJob::save()** method, we have hardcoded the number of days for the job to expire. It would have been better to make the 30 days configurable. The symfony framework provides a built-in configuration file for application specific settings, the **app.yml** file. This YAML file can contain any setting you want:

```
# apps/frontend/config/app.yml
all:
  active_days: 30
```

Listing 6-9

In the application, these settings are available through the global **sfConfig** class:

```
sfConfig::get('app_active_days')
```

Listing 6-10

The setting has been prefixed by **app_** because the **sfConfig** class also provides access to symfony settings as we will see later on.

Let's update the code to take this new setting into account:

Listing 6-11

```
public function save(Doctrine_Connection $conn = null)
{
  if ($this->isNew() && !$this->getExpiresAt())
  {
    $now = $this->getCreatedAt() ?
$this->getDateTimeObject('created_at')->format('U') : time();
    $this->setExpiresAt(date('Y-m-d H:i:s', $now + 86400 *
sfConfig::get('app_active_days')));
  }

  return parent::save($conn);
}
```

The **app.yml** configuration file is a great way to centralize ~global settings|Global Settings~ for your application.

Last, if you need project-wide settings, just create a new **app.yml** file in the **config** folder at the root of your symfony project.

Refactoring

Although the code we have written works fine, it's not quite right yet. Can you spot the problem?

The **Doctrine_Query** code does not belong to the action (the Controller layer), it belongs to the Model layer. In the MVC model, the Model defines all the business logic, and the Controller only calls the Model to retrieve data from it. As the code returns a collection of jobs, let's move the code to the **JobeetJobTable** class and create a **getActiveJobs()** method:

Listing 6-12
```
// lib/model/doctrine/JobeetJobTable.class.php
class JobeetJobTable extends Doctrine_Table
{
  public function getActiveJobs()
  {
    $q = $this->createQuery('j')
      ->where('j.expires_at > ?', date('Y-m-d H:i:s', time()));

    return $q->execute();
  }
}
```

Now the action code can use this new method to retrieve the active jobs.

```
public function executeIndex(sfWebRequest $request)
{
  $this->jobeet_job_list =
    ➥ Doctrine::getTable('JobeetJob')->getActiveJobs();
}
```

Listing
6-13

This refactoring has several benefits over the previous code:

- The logic to get the active jobs is now in the Model, where it belongs
- The code in the controller is much more readable
- The `getActiveJobs()` method is re-usable (for instance in another action)
- The model code is now unit testable

Let's sort the jobs by the `expires_at` column:

```
public function getActiveJobs()
{
  $q = $this->createQuery('j')
    ->where('j.expires_at > ?', date('Y-m-d H:i:s', time()))
    ->orderBy('j.expires_at DESC');

  return $q->execute();
}
```

Listing
6-14

The `orderBy` methods sets the `ORDER  BY` clause to the generated SQL (`addOrderBy()` also exists).

Categories on the Homepage

From day 2 requirements:

"The jobs are sorted by category and then by publication date (newer jobs first)."

Until now, we have not taken the job category into account. From the requirements, the homepage must display jobs by category. First, we need to get all categories with at least one active job.

Open the `JobeetCategoryTable` class and add a `getWithJobs()` method:

```
// lib/model/doctrine/JobeetCategoryTable.class.php
class JobeetCategoryTable extends Doctrine_Table
{
  public function getWithJobs()
  {
```

Listing
6-15

```
        $q = $this->createQuery('c')
          ->leftJoin('c.JobeetJobs j')
          ->where('j.expires_at > ?', date('Y-m-d H:i:s', time())));

        return $q->execute();
    }
}
```

Change the **index** action accordingly:

Listing
6-16
```
// apps/frontend/modules/job/actions/actions.class.php
public function executeIndex(sfWebRequest $request)
{
  $this->categories =
    ➥ Doctrine::getTable('JobeetCategory')->getWithJobs();
}
```

In the template, we need to iterate through all categories and display the active jobs:

Listing
6-17
```
// apps/frontend/modules/job/templates/indexSuccess.php
<?php use_stylesheet('jobs.css') ?>

<div id="jobs">
  <?php foreach ($categories as $category): ?>
    <div class="category_<?php echo
Jobeet::slugify($category->getName()) ?>">
      <div class="category">
        <div class="feed">
          <a href="">Feed</a>
        </div>
        <h1><?php echo $category ?></h1>
      </div>

      <table class="jobs">
        <?php foreach ($category->getActiveJobs() as $i => $job): ?>
          <tr class="<?php echo fmod($i, 2) ? 'even' : 'odd' ?>">
            <td class="location">
              <?php echo $job->getLocation() ?>
            </td>
            <td class="position">
              <?php echo link_to($job->getPosition(), 'job_show_user',
$job) ?>
            </td>
            <td class="company">
```

```
        <?php echo $job->getCompany() ?>
      </td>
    </tr>
    <?php endforeach; ?>
  </table>
</div>
<?php endforeach; ?>
</div>
```

 To display the category name in the template, we have used echo $category. Does this sound weird? $category is an object, how can echo magically display the category name? The answer was given during day 3 when we have defined the magic __toString() method for all the model classes.

For this to work, we need to add the getActiveJobs() method to the JobeetCategory class:

Listing 6-18

```
// lib/model/doctrine/JobeetCategory.class.php
public function getActiveJobs()
{
  $q = Doctrine_Query::create()
    ->from('JobeetJob j')
    ->where('j.category_id = ?', $this->getId());

  return Doctrine::getTable('JobeetJob')->getActiveJobs($q);
}
```

The JobeetCategory::getActiveJobs() method uses the Doctrine::getTable('JobeetJob')->getActiveJobs() method to retrieve the active jobs for the given category.

When calling the Doctrine::getTable('JobeetJob')->getActiveJobs(), we want to restrict the condition even more by providing a category. Instead of passing the category object, we have decided to pass a Doctrine_Query object as this is the best way to encapsulate a generic condition.

The getActiveJobs() needs to merge this Doctrine_Query object with its own query. As the Doctrine_Query is an object, this is quite simple:

Listing 6-19

```
// lib/model/doctrine/JobeetJobTable.class.php
public function getActiveJobs(Doctrine_Query $q = null)
{
  if (is_null($q))
  {
    $q = Doctrine_Query::create()
```

```
      ->from('JobeetJob j');
}

$q->andWhere('j.expires_at > ?', date('Y-m-d H:i:s', time()))
  ->addOrderBy('j.expires_at DESC');

return $q->execute();
}
```

Limit the Results

There is still one requirement to implement for the homepage job list:

"For each category, the list only shows the first 10 jobs and a link allows to list all the jobs for a given category."

That's simple enough to add to the **getActiveJobs()** method:

Listing
6-20

```
// lib/model/doctrine/JobeetCategory.class.php
public function getActiveJobs($max = 10)
{
  $q = Doctrine_Query::create()
    ->from('JobeetJob j')
    ->where('j.category_id = ?', $this->getId())
    ->limit($max);

  return Doctrine::getTable('JobeetJob')->getActiveJobs($q);
}
```

The appropriate **LIMIT** clause is now hard-coded into the Model, but it is better for this value to be configurable. Change the template to pass a maximum number of jobs set in **app.yml**:

Listing
6-21

```
<!-- apps/frontend/modules/job/templates/indexSuccess.php -->
<?php foreach
($category->getActiveJobs(sfConfig::get('app_max_jobs_on_homepage'))
as $i => $job): ?>
```

and add a new setting in **app.yml**:

Listing
6-22

```
all:
  active_days:          30
  max_jobs_on_homepage: 10
```

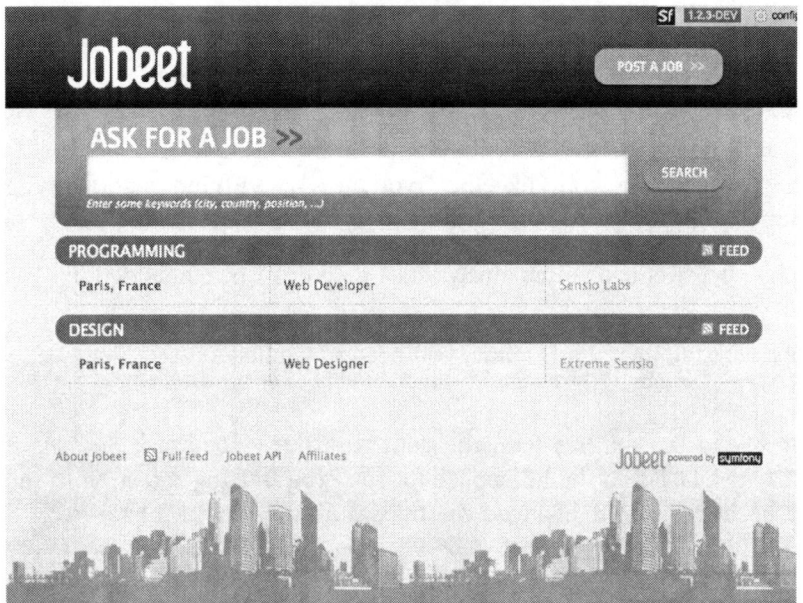

Dynamic Fixtures

Unless you lower the `max_jobs_on_homepage` setting to one, you won't see any difference. We need to add a bunch of jobs to the fixture. So, you can copy and paste an existing job ten or twenty times by hand... but there's a better way. Duplication is bad, even in fixture files.

symfony to the rescue! YAML files in symfony can contain PHP code that will be evaluated just before the parsing of the file. Edit the `jobs.yml` fixtures file and add the following code at the end:

Listing
6-23

```
# Starts at the beginning of the line (no whitespace before)
<?php for ($i = 100; $i <= 130; $i++): ?>
  job_<?php echo $i ?>:
    JobeetCategory: programming
    company:      Company <?php echo $i."\n" ?>
    position:     Web Developer
    location:     Paris, France
    description:  Lorem ipsum dolor sit amet, consectetur adipisicing
elit.
    how_to_apply: |
      Send your resume to lorem.ipsum [at] company_<?php echo $i ?>.sit
    is_public:    true
    is_activated: true
```

```
    token:        job_<?php echo $i."\n" ?>
    email:        job@example.com

<?php endfor; ?>
```

Be careful, the YAML parser won't like you if you mess up with Indentation. Keep in mind the following simple tips when adding PHP code to a YAML file:

- The `<?php ?>` statements must always start the line or be embedded in a value.

- If a `<?php ?>` statement ends a line, you need to explicly output a new line ("\n").

You can now reload the fixtures with the **doctrine:data-load** task and see if only **10** jobs are displayed on the homepage for the **Programming** category. In the following screenshot, we have changed the maximum number of jobs to five to make the image smaller:

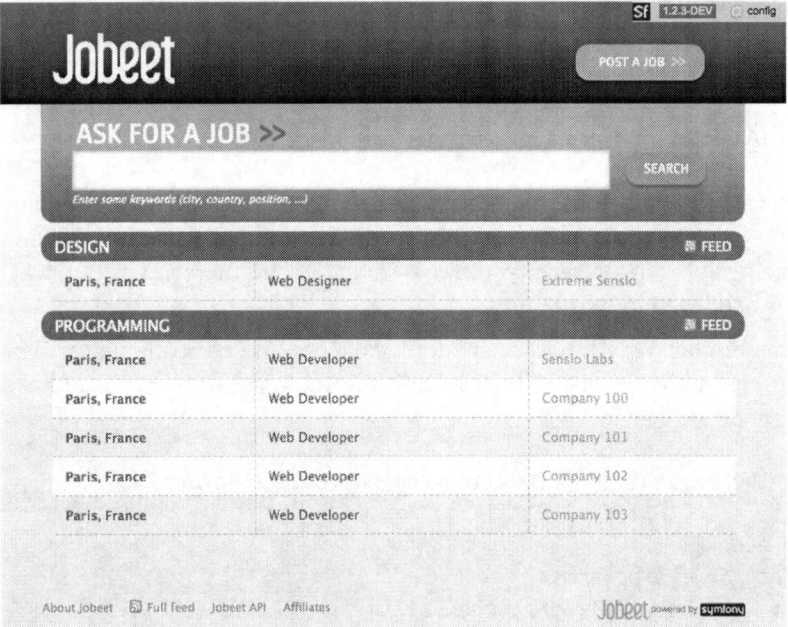

Secure the Job Page

When a job expires, even if you know the URL, it must not be possible to access it anymore. Try the URL for the expired job (replace the **id** with the actual **id** in your database - `SELECT id, token FROM jobeet_job WHERE expires_at < NOW()`):

```
/frontend_dev.php/job/sensio-labs/paris-france/ID/web-developer-expired
```
Listing
6-24

Instead of displaying the job, we need to forward the user to a 404 page. But how can we do this as the job is retrieved automatically by the route?

Listing
6-25

```
# apps/frontend/config/routing.yml
job_show_user:
  url:      /job/:company_slug/:location_slug/:id/:position_slug
  class:    sfDoctrineRoute
  options:
    model: JobeetJob
    type:  object
    method_for_query: retrieveActiveJob
  param:    { module: job, action: show }
  requirements:
    id: \d+
    sf_method: [GET]
```

The **retrieveActiveJob** method will receive the **Doctrine_Query** object built by the route:

Listing
6-26

```
// lib/model/doctrine/JobeetJobTable.class.php
class JobeetJobTable extends Doctrine_Table
{
  public function retrieveActiveJob(Doctrine_Query $q)
  {
    $q->andWhere('a.expires_at > ?', date('Y-m-d H:i:s', time()));

    return $q->fetchOne();
  }

  // ...
}
```

Now, if you try to get an expired job, you will be forwarded to a 404 page.

```
404 | Not Found | sfError404Exception

Unable to find the JobeetJobPeer object with the following parameters "array {
'company_slug' => 'sensio-labs', 'location_slug' => 'paris-france', 'id' => '8',
'position_slug' => 'web-developer-expired',)}".

stack trace

1.  at ()
    in SF_ROOT_DIR/lib/vendor/symfony/lib/routing/sfObjectRoute.class.php line 111 ...
       108.        // check the related object
       109.        if (!($this->object = $this->getObjectForParameters($this->parameters)) && (!isset($this->o
       110.        {
       111.            throw new sfError404Exception(sprintf('Unable to find the %s object with the following pa
       112.        }
       113.
       114.        return $this->object;

2.  at sfObjectRoute->getObject()
    in SF_ROOT_DIR/apps/frontend/modules/job/actions/actions.class.php line 20 ...

3.  at jobActions->executeShow(object('sfWebRequest'))
    in SF_ROOT_DIR/lib/vendor/symfony/lib/action/sfActions.class.php line 53 ...

4.  at sfActions->execute(object('sfWebRequest'))
    in SF_ROOT_DIR/lib/vendor/symfony/lib/filter/sfExecutionFilter.class.php line 90 ...

5.  at sfExecutionFilter->executeAction(object('jobActions'))
    in SF_ROOT_DIR/lib/vendor/symfony/lib/filter/sfExecutionFilter.class.php line 76 ...

6.  at sfExecutionFilter->handleAction(object('sfFilterChain'), object('jobActions'))
    in SF_ROOT_DIR/lib/vendor/symfony/lib/filter/sfExecutionFilter.class.php line 42 ...

7.  at sfExecutionFilter->execute(object('sfFilterChain'))
    in SF_ROOT_DIR/lib/vendor/symfony/lib/filter/sfFilterChain.class.php line 53 ...

8.  at sfFilterChain->execute()
    in SF_ROOT_DIR/lib/vendor/symfony/lib/filter/sfCommonFilter.class.php line 29 ...

9.  at sfCommonFilter->execute(object('sfFilterChain'))
    in SF_ROOT_DIR/lib/vendor/symfony/lib/filter/sfFilterChain.class.php line 53 ...

10. at sfFilterChain->execute()
    in SF_ROOT_DIR/lib/vendor/symfony/lib/filter/sfRenderingFilter.class.php line 33 ...

11. at sfRenderingFilter->execute(object('sfFilterChain'))
```

Link to the Category Page

Now, let's add a link to the category page on the homepage and create the category page.

But, wait a minute. the hour is not yet over and we haven't worked that much. So, you have plenty of free time and enough knowledge to implement this all by yourself! Let's make an exercise of it. Check back tomorrow for our implementation.

See you Tomorrow

Do work on an implementation on your local Jobeet project. Please, abuse the online API documentation[40] and all the free documentation[41] available on the symfony website to help you out. We'll see you again tomorrow with our take on this implementation.

Good luck!

---

40. http://www.symfony-project.org/api/1_4/
41. http://www.symfony-project.org/doc/1_4/

Day 7

Playing with the Category Page

Yesterday you expanded your knowledge of symfony in a lot of different areas: querying with Doctrine, fixtures, routing, debugging, and custom configuration. And we finished with a little challenge for today.

I hope you worked on the Jobeet category page as today's tutorial will then be much more valuable for you.

Ready? Let's talk about a possible implementation.

The Category Route

First, we need to add a route to define a pretty URL for the category page. Add it at the beginning of the routing file:

Listing 7-1

```
# apps/frontend/config/routing.yml
category:
  url:      /category/:slug
  class:    sfDoctrineRoute
  param:    { module: category, action: show }
  options:  { model: JobeetCategory, type: object }
```

 Whenever you start implementing a new feature, it is a good practice to first think about the URL and create the associated route. And it is mandatory if you removed the default routing rules.

A route can use any column from its related object as a parameter. It can also use any other value if there is a related accessor defined in the object class. Because the **slug** parameter has no corresponding column in the **category** table, we need to add a virtual accessor in **JobeetCategory** to make the route works:

Listing
7-2
```
// lib/model/doctrine/JobeetCategory.class.php
public function getSlug()
{
  return Jobeet::slugify($this->getName());
}
```

The Category Link

Now, edit the **indexSuccess.php** template of the **job** module to add the link to the category page:

Listing
7·3
```
<!-- some HTML code -->

      <h1>
        <?php echo link_to($category, 'category', $category) ?>
      </h1>

<!-- some HTML code -->

    </table>

    <?php if (($count = $category->countActiveJobs() -
        ➥ sfConfig::get('app_max_jobs_on_homepage')) > 0): ?>
      <div class="more_jobs">
        and <?php echo link_to($count, 'category', $category) ?>
        more...
      </div>
    <?php endif; ?>
  </div>
  <?php endforeach; ?>
</div>
```

We only add the link if there are more than 10 jobs to display for the current category. The link contains the number of jobs not displayed. For this template to work, we need to add the **countActiveJobs()** method to **JobeetCategory**:

Listing
7.4
```
// lib/model/doctrine/JobeetCategory.class.php
public function countActiveJobs()
{
  $q = Doctrine_Query::create()
    ->from('JobeetJob j')
    ->where('j.category_id = ?', $this->getId());
```

```
  return Doctrine::getTable('JobeetJob')->countActiveJobs($q);
}
```

The countActiveJobs() method uses a countActiveJobs() method that does not exist yet in JobeetJobTable. Replace the content of the JobeetJobTable.php file with the following code:

Listing 7-5

```php
// lib/model/doctrine/JobeetJobTable.class.php
class JobeetJobTable extends Doctrine_Table
{
  public function retrieveActiveJob(Doctrine_Query $q)
  {
    return $this->addActiveJobsQuery($q)->fetchOne();
  }

  public function getActiveJobs(Doctrine_Query $q = null)
  {
    return $this->addActiveJobsQuery($q)->execute();
  }

  public function countActiveJobs(Doctrine_Query $q = null)
  {
    return $this->addActiveJobsQuery($q)->count();
  }

  public function addActiveJobsQuery(Doctrine_Query $q = null)
  {
    if (is_null($q))
    {
      $q = Doctrine_Query::create()
        ->from('JobeetJob j');
    }

    $alias = $q->getRootAlias();

    $q->andWhere($alias . '.expires_at > ?', date('Y-m-d H:i:s',
time()))
      ->addOrderBy($alias . '.created_at DESC');

    return $q;
  }
}
```

As you can see for yourself, we have refactored the whole code of `JobeetJobTable` to introduce a new shared `addActiveJobsQuery()` method to make the code more DRY (Don't Repeat Yourself)[42].

 The first time a piece of code is re-used, copying the code may be sufficient. But if you find another use for it, you need to refactor all uses to a shared function or a method, as we have done here.

In the `countActiveJobs()` method, instead of using `execute()` and then count the number of results, we have used the much faster `count()` method.

We have changed a lot of files, just for this simple feature. But each time we have added some code, we have tried to put it in the right layer of the application and we have also tried to make the code reusable. In the process, we have also refactored some existing code. That's a typical workflow when working on a symfony project. In the following screenshot we are showing 5 jobs to keep it short, you should see 10 (the `max_jobs_on_homepage` setting):

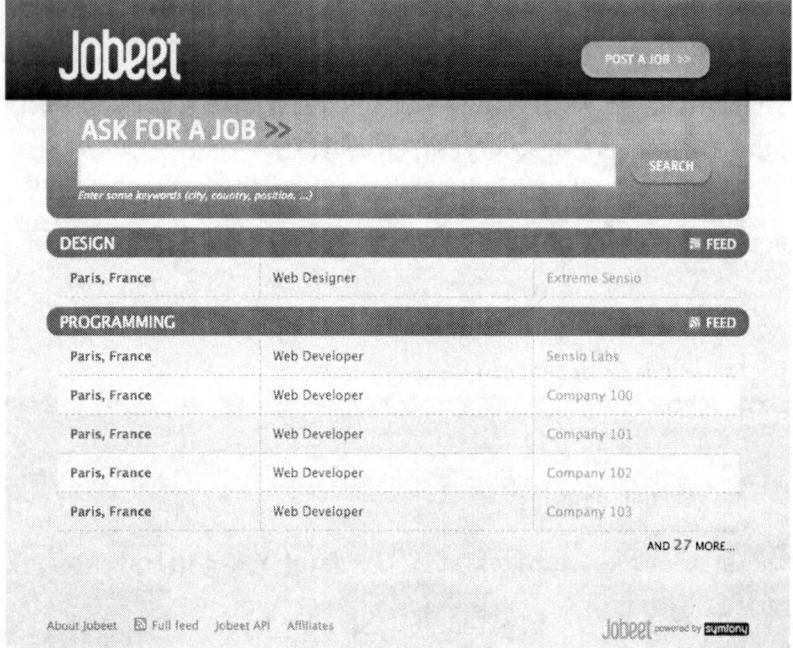

---

42. `http://en.wikipedia.org/wiki/Don%27t_repeat_yourself`

Job Category Module Creation

It's time to create the **category** module:

```
$ php symfony generate:module frontend category
```
Listing
7-6

If you have created a module, you have probably used the **doctrine:generate-module**. That's fine but as we won't need 90% of the generated code, I have used the **generate:module** which creates an empty module.

 Why not add a **category** action to the **job** module? We could, but as the main subject of the category page is a category, it feels more natural to create a dedicated **category** module.

When accessing the category page, the **category** route will have to find the category associated with the request **slug** variable. But as the slug is not stored in the database, and because we cannot deduce the category name from the slug, there is no way to find the category associated with the slug.

Update the Database

We need to add a **slug** column for the **category** table:

This **slug** column can be taken care of by a Doctrine behavior named **Sluggable**. We simply need to enable the behavior on our **JobeetCategory** model and it will take care of everything for you.

```
# config/doctrine/schema.yml
JobeetCategory:
  actAs:
    Timestampable: ~
    Sluggable:
      fields: [name]
  columns:
    name:
      type: string(255)
      notnull:  true
```
Listing
7-7

Now that **slug** is a real column, you need to remove the **getSlug()** method from **JobeetCategory**.

The setting of the slug column is taken care of automatically when you save a record. The slug is built using the value of the **name** field and set to the object.

Use the **doctrine:build-all-reload** task to update the database tables, and repopulate the database with our fixtures:

Listing
7-8

```
$ php symfony doctrine:build-all-reload --no-confirmation
```

We have now everything in place to create the **executeShow()** method. Replace the content of the **category** actions file with the following code:

Listing
7-9

```php
// apps/frontend/modules/category/actions/actions.class.php
class categoryActions extends sfActions
{
  public function executeShow(sfWebRequest $request)
  {
    $this->category = $this->getRoute()->getObject();
  }
}
```

 Because we have removed the generated **executeIndex()** method, you can also remove the automatically generated **indexSuccess.php** template (apps/frontend/modules/category/templates/indexSuccess.php).

The last step is to create the **showSuccess.php** template:

Listing
7-10

```php
// apps/frontend/modules/category/templates/showSuccess.php
<?php use_stylesheet('jobs.css') ?>

<?php slot('title', sprintf('Jobs in the %s category',
$category->getName())) ?>

<div class="category">
  <div class="feed">
    <a href="">Feed</a>
  </div>
  <h1><?php echo $category ?></h1>
</div>

<table class="jobs">
  <?php foreach ($category->getActiveJobs() as $i => $job): ?>
    <tr class="<?php echo fmod($i, 2) ? 'even' : 'odd' ?>">
      <td class="location">
```

```
      <?php echo $job->getLocation() ?>
    </td>
    <td class="position">
      <?php echo link_to($job->getPosition(), 'job_show_user', $job)
?>
    </td>
    <td class="company">
      <?php echo $job->getCompany() ?>
    </td>
  </tr>
  <?php endforeach; ?>
</table>
```

Partials

Notice that we have copied and pasted the `<table>` tag that create a list of jobs from the job **indexSuccess.php** template. That's bad. Time to learn a new trick. When you need to reuse some portion of a template, you need to create a **partial**. A partial is a snippet of template code that can be shared among several templates. A partial is just another template that starts with an underscore (_).

Create the _**list.php** file:

```
// apps/frontend/modules/job/templates/_list.php
<table class="jobs">
  <?php foreach ($jobs as $i => $job): ?>
    <tr class="<?php echo fmod($i, 2) ? 'even' : 'odd' ?>">
      <td class="location">
        <?php echo $job->getLocation() ?>
      </td>
      <td class="position">
        <?php echo link_to($job->getPosition(), 'job_show_user', $job)
?>
      </td>
      <td class="company">
        <?php echo $job->getCompany() ?>
      </td>
    </tr>
  <?php endforeach; ?>
</table>
```

Listing 7-11

You can include a partial by using the **include_partial()** helper:

```
<?php include_partial('job/list', array('jobs' => $jobs)) ?>
```

Listing 7-12

The first argument of **include_partial()** is the partial name (made of the module name, a /, and the partial name without the leading _). The second argument is an array of variables to pass to the partial.

 Why not use the PHP built-in **include()** method instead of the **include_partial()** helper? The main difference between the two is the built-in cache support of the **include_partial()** helper.

Replace the **<table>** HTML code from both templates with the call to include_partial():

Listing 7-13
```php
// in apps/frontend/modules/job/templates/indexSuccess.php
<?php include_partial('job/list', array('jobs' =>
$category->getActiveJobs(sfConfig::get('app_max_jobs_on_homepage'))))
?>

// in apps/frontend/modules/category/templates/showSuccess.php
<?php include_partial('job/list', array('jobs' =>
$category->getActiveJobs())) ?>
```

List Pagination

From day 2 requirements:

"The list is paginated with 20 jobs per page."

To paginate a list of Doctrine objects, symfony provides a dedicated class: **sfDoctrinePager**[43]. In the **category** action, instead of passing the job objects to the **showSuccess** template, we pass a pager:

Listing 7-14
```php
// apps/frontend/modules/category/actions/actions.class.php
public function executeShow(sfWebRequest $request)
{
  $this->category = $this->getRoute()->getObject();

  $this->pager = new sfDoctrinePager(
    'JobeetJob',
    sfConfig::get('app_max_jobs_on_category')
  );
  $this->pager->setQuery($this->category->getActiveJobsQuery());
  $this->pager->setPage($request->getParameter('page', 1));
```

---

43. http://www.symfony-project.org/api/1_4/sfDoctrinePager

```
  $this->pager->init();
}
```

 The sfRequest::getParameter() method takes a default value as a second argument. In the action above, if the page request parameter does not exist, then getParameter() will return 1.

The sfDoctrinePager constructor takes a model class and the maximum number of items to return per page. Add the latter value to your configuration file:

```
# apps/frontend/config/app.yml
all:
  active_days:          30
  max_jobs_on_homepage: 10
  max_jobs_on_category: 20
```

Listing 7-15

The sfDoctrinePager::setQuery() method takes a Doctrine_Query object to use when selecting the items from the database.

Add the getActiveJobsQuery() method:

```
// lib/model/doctrine/JobeetCategory.class.php
public function getActiveJobsQuery()
{
  $q = Doctrine_Query::create()
    ->from('JobeetJob j')
    ->where('j.category_id = ?', $this->getId());

  return Doctrine::getTable('JobeetJob')->addActiveJobsQuery($q);
}
```

Listing 7-16

Now that we have defined the getActiveJobsQuery() method, we can refactor other JobeetCategory methods to use it:

```
// lib/model/doctrine/JobeetCategory.class.php
public function getActiveJobs($max = 10)
{
  $q = $this->getActiveJobsQuery()
    ->limit($max);

  return $q->execute();
}

public function countActiveJobs()
{
```

Listing 7-17

```php
  return $this->getActiveJobsQuery()->count();
}
```

Finally, let's update the template:

```php
<!-- apps/frontend/modules/category/templates/showSuccess.php -->
<?php use_stylesheet('jobs.css') ?>

<?php slot('title', sprintf('Jobs in the %s category',
$category->getName())) ?>

<div class="category">
  <div class="feed">
    <a href="">Feed</a>
  </div>
  <h1><?php echo $category ?></h1>
</div>

<?php include_partial('job/list', array('jobs' =>
$pager->getResults())) ?>

<?php if ($pager->haveToPaginate()): ?>
  <div class="pagination">
    <a href="<?php echo url_for('category', $category) ?>?page=1">
      <img src="http://www.symfony-project.org/images/first.png"
alt="First page" />
    </a>

    <a href="<?php echo url_for('category', $category) ?>?page=<?php
echo $pager->getPreviousPage() ?>">
      <img src="http://www.symfony-project.org/images/previous.png"
alt="Previous page" title="Previous page" />
    </a>

    <?php foreach ($pager->getLinks() as $page): ?>
      <?php if ($page == $pager->getPage()): ?>
        <?php echo $page ?>
      <?php else: ?>
        <a href="<?php echo url_for('category', $category)
?>?page=<?php echo $page ?>"><?php echo $page ?></a>
      <?php endif; ?>
    <?php endforeach; ?>

    <a href="<?php echo url_for('category', $category) ?>?page=<?php
echo $pager->getNextPage() ?>">
```

```
      <img src="http://www.symfony-project.org/images/next.png"
alt="Next page" title="Next page" />
    </a>

    <a href="<?php echo url_for('category', $category) ?>?page=<?php
echo $pager->getLastPage() ?>">
      <img src="http://www.symfony-project.org/images/last.png"
alt="Last page" title="Last page" />
    </a>
  </div>
<?php endif; ?>

<div class="pagination_desc">
  <strong><?php echo count($pager) ?></strong> jobs in this category

  <?php if ($pager->haveToPaginate()): ?>
    - page <strong><?php echo $pager->getPage() ?>/<?php echo
$pager->getLastPage() ?></strong>
  <?php endif; ?>
</div>
```

Most of this code deals with the links to other pages. Here are the list of
sfDoctrinePager methods used in this template:

- getResults(): Returns an array of Doctrine objects for the current page
- getNbResults(): Returns the total number of results
- haveToPaginate(): Returns **true** if there is more than one page
- getLinks(): Returns a list of page links to display
- getPage(): Returns the current page number
- getPreviousPage(): Returns the previous page number
- getNextPage(): Returns the next page number
- getLastPage(): Returns the last page number

As **sfDoctrinePager** also implements the **Iterator** and **Countable** interfaces,
you can use **count()** function to get the number of results instead of the
getNbResults() method.

See you Tomorrow

If you worked on your own implementation yesterday and feel that you didn't learn much today, it means that you are getting used to the symfony philosophy. The process to add a new feature to a symfony website is always the same: think about the URLs, create some actions, update the model, and write some templates. And, if you can apply some good development practices to the mix, you will become a symfony master very fast.

Tomorrow will be the start of a new week for Jobeet. To celebrate, we will talk about a brand new topic: tests.

Day 8

The Unit Tests

During the last two days, we reviewed all the features learned during the first five days of the advent calendar to customize Jobeet features and add new ones. In the process, we have also touched on other more advanced symfony features.

Today, we will start talking about something completely different: automated **tests**. As the topic is quite large, it will take us two full days to cover everything.

Tests in symfony

There are two different kinds of automated tests in symfony: **unit tests** and **functional tests**.

Unit tests verify that each method and function is working properly. Each test must be as independent as possible from the others.

On the other hand, functional tests verify that the resulting application behaves correctly as a whole.

All tests in symfony are located under the **test/** directory of the project. It contains two sub-directories, one for unit tests (**test/unit/**) and one for functional tests (**test/functional/**).

Unit tests will be covered in today's tutorial, whereas tomorrow's will be dedicated to functional tests.

Unit Tests

Writing unit tests is perhaps one of the hardest web development best practices to put into action. As web developers are not really used to test their work, a lot of questions arise: Do I have to write tests before implementing a feature? What do I need to test? Do my tests need to cover every single edge case? How can I be sure that everything is well tested? But usually, the first question is much more basic: Where to start?

Even if we strongly advocate testing, the symfony approach is pragmatic: it's always better to have some tests than no test at all. Do you already have a lot of code without any test? No problem. You don't need to have a full test suite to benefit from the advantages of having tests. Start by adding tests whenever you find a bug in your code. Over time, your code will become better, the code coverage will rise, and you will become more confident about it. By starting with a pragmatic approach, you will feel more comfortable with tests over time. The next step is to write tests for new features. In no time, you will become test addict.

The problem with most testing libraries is their steep learning curve. That's why symfony provides a very simple testing library, **lime**, to make writing test insanely easy.

 Even if this tutorial describes the lime built-in library extensively, you can use any testing library, like the excellent PHPUnit[44] library.

The `lime` Testing Framework

All unit tests written with the lime framework start with the same code:

Listing 8-1
```
require_once dirname(__FILE__).'/../bootstrap/unit.php';

$t = new lime_test(1);
```

First, the **unit.php** bootstrap file is included to initialize a few things. Then, a new **lime_test** object is created and the number of tests planned to be launched is passed as an argument.

 The plan allows lime to output an error message in case too few tests are run (for instance when a test generates a PHP fatal error).

Testing works by calling a method or a function with a set of predefined inputs and then comparing the results with the expected output. This comparison determines whether a test passes or fails.

To ease the comparison, the **lime_test** object provides several methods:

44. http://www.phpunit.de/

Method	Description
ok($test)	Tests a condition and passes if it is true
is($value1, $value2)	Compares two values and passes if they are equal (==)
isnt($value1, $value2)	Compares two values and passes if they are not equal
like($string, $regexp)	Tests a string against a regular expression
unlike($string, $regexp)	Checks that a string doesn't match a regular expression
is_deeply($array1, $array2)	Checks that two arrays have the same values

 You may wonder why lime defines so many test methods, as all tests can be written just by using the ok() method. The benefit of alternative methods lies in much more explicit error messages in case of a failed test and in improved readability of the tests.

The lime_test object also provides other convenient test methods:

Method	Description
fail()	Always fails—useful for testing exceptions
pass()	Always passes—useful for testing exceptions
skip($msg, $nb_tests)	Counts as $nb_tests tests—useful for conditional tests
todo()	Counts as a test—useful for tests yet to be written

Finally, the comment($msg) method outputs a comment but runs no test.

Running Unit Tests

All unit tests are stored under the **test/unit/** directory. By convention, tests are named after the class they test and suffixed by **Test**. Although you can organize the files under the **test/unit/** directory anyway you like, we recommend you replicate the directory structure of the **lib/** directory.

To illustrate unit testing, we will test the **Jobeet** class.

Create a **test/unit/JobeetTest.php** file and copy the following code inside:

Listing
8-2

```
// test/unit/JobeetTest.php
require_once dirname(__FILE__).'/../bootstrap/unit.php';

$t = new lime_test(1);
$t->pass('This test always passes.');
```

To launch the tests, you can execute the file directly:

Listing
8-3

```
$ php test/unit/JobeetTest.php
```

Or use the **test:unit** task:

Listing
8-4

```
$ php symfony test:unit Jobeet
```

```
~/work/jobeet $ php symfony test:unit Jobeet
1..1
ok 1 - This test always passes.
Looks like everything went fine.
~/work/jobeet $
```

 Windows command line unfortunately cannot highlight test results in red or green color. But if you use Cygwin, you can force symfony to use colors by passing the **--color** option to the task.

Testing slugify

Let's start our trip to the wonderful world of unit testing by writing tests for the **Jobeet::slugify()** method.

We created the **slugify()** method during day 5 to clean up a string so that it can be safely included in a URL. The conversion consists in some basic transformations like converting all non-ASCII characters to a dash (-) or converting the string to lowercase:

Input	Output
Sensio Labs	sensio-labs
Paris, France	paris-france

Replace the content of the test file with the following code:

```
// test/unit/JobeetTest.php
require_once dirname(__FILE__).'/../bootstrap/unit.php';

$t = new lime_test(6);

$t->is(Jobeet::slugify('Sensio'), 'sensio');
$t->is(Jobeet::slugify('sensio labs'), 'sensio-labs');
$t->is(Jobeet::slugify('sensio    labs'), 'sensio-labs');
$t->is(Jobeet::slugify('paris,france'), 'paris-france');
$t->is(Jobeet::slugify('  sensio'), 'sensio');
$t->is(Jobeet::slugify('sensio  '), 'sensio');
```
Listing
8-5

If you take a closer look at the tests we have written, you will notice that each line only tests one thing. That's something you need to keep in mind when writing unit tests. Test one thing at a time.

You can now execute the test file. If all tests pass, as we expect them to, you will enjoy the "*green bar*". If not, the infamous "*red bar*" will alert you that some tests do not pass and that you need to fix them.

```
~/work/jobeet $ php symfony test:unit Jobeet
1..6
ok 1
ok 2
ok 3
ok 4
ok 5
ok 6
Looks like everything went fine.
~/work/jobeet $
```

If a test fails, the output will give you some information about why it failed; but if you have hundreds of tests in a file, it can be difficult to quickly identify the behavior that fails.

All lime test methods take a string as their last argument that serves as the description for the test. It's very convenient as it forces you to describe what your are really testing. It can also serve as a form of documentation for a method's expected behavior. Let's add some messages to the **slugify** test file:

```
require_once dirname(__FILE__).'/../bootstrap/unit.php';

$t = new lime_test(6);

$t->comment('::slugify()');
$t->is(Jobeet::slugify('Sensio'), 'sensio',
  ➥ '::slugify() converts all characters to lower case');
$t->is(Jobeet::slugify('sensio labs'), 'sensio-labs',
  ➥ '::slugify() replaces a white space by a -');
```
Listing
8-6

```
$t->is(Jobeet::slugify('sensio   labs'), 'sensio-labs',
  ➥ '::slugify() replaces several white spaces by a single -');
$t->is(Jobeet::slugify('  sensio'), 'sensio',
  ➥ '::slugify() removes - at the beginning of a string');
$t->is(Jobeet::slugify('sensio  '), 'sensio',
  ➥ '::slugify() removes - at the end of a string');
$t->is(Jobeet::slugify('paris,france'), 'paris-france',
  ➥ '::slugify() replaces non-ASCII characters by a -');
```

```
~/work/jobeet $ php symfony test:unit Jobeet
1..6
# ::slugify()
ok 1 - ::slugify() converts all characters to lower case
ok 2 - ::slugify() replaces a white space by a -
ok 3 - ::slugify() replaces several white spaces by a single -
ok 4 - ::slugify() replaces non-ASCII characters by a -
ok 5 - ::slugify() removes - at the beginning of a string
ok 6 - ::slugify() removes - at the end of a string
Looks like everything went fine.
~/work/jobeet $
```

The test description string is also an valuable tool when trying to figure out what
to test. You can see a pattern in the test strings: they are sentences describing how
the method must behave and they always start with the method name to test.

Code Coverage

When you write tests, it is easy to forget a portion of the code.

To help you check that all your code is well tested, symfony provides the
test:coverage task. Pass this task a test file or directory and a lib file or
directory as arguments and it will tell you the code coverage of your code:

Listing
8-7
```
$ php symfony test:coverage test/unit/JobeetTest.php lib/
Jobeet.class.php
```

If you want to know which lines are not covered by your tests, pass the --
detailed option:

Listing
8-8
```
$ php symfony test:coverage --detailed test/unit/JobeetTest.php lib/
Jobeet.class.php
```

Keep in mind that when the task indicates that your code is fully unit tested,
it just means that each line has been executed, not that all the edge cases have
been tested.

As the **test:coverage** relies on **XDebug** to collect its information, you need to
install it and enable it first.

Adding Tests for new Features

The slug for an empty string is an empty string. You can test it, it will work. But an empty string in a URL is not that a great idea. Let's change the `slugify()` method so that it returns the "n-a" string in case of an empty string.

You can write the test first, then update the method, or the other way around. It is really a matter of taste but writing the test first gives you the confidence that your code actually implements what you planned:

```
$t->is(Jobeet::slugify(''), 'n-a',
  ➥ '::slugify() converts the empty string to n-a');
```

Listing
8.9

This development methodology, where you first write tests then implement features, is known as Test Driven Development (TDD)[45].

If you launch the tests now, you must have a red bar. If not, it means that the feature is already implemented or that your test does not test what it is supposed to test.

Now, edit the **Jobeet** class and add the following condition at the beginning:

```
// lib/Jobeet.class.php
static public function slugify($text)
{
  if (empty($text))
  {
    return 'n-a';
  }

  // ...
}
```

Listing
8.10

The test must now pass as expected, and you can enjoy the green bar, but only if you have remembered to update the test plan. If not, you will have a message that says you planned six tests and ran one extra. Having the planned test count up to date is important, as it you will keep you informed if the test script dies early on.

---

45. http://en.wikipedia.org/wiki/Test_Driven_Development

Adding Tests because of a Bug

Let's say that time has passed and one of your users reports a weird bug: some job links point to a 404 error page. After some investigation, you find that for some reason, these jobs have an empty company, position, or location slug.

How is it possible?

You look through the records in the database and the columns are definitely not empty. You think about it for a while, and bingo, you find the cause. When a string only contains non-ASCII characters, the slugify() method converts it to an empty string. So happy to have found the cause, you open the Jobeet class and fix the problem right away. That's a bad idea. First, let's add a test:

Listing 8-11

```
$t->is(Jobeet::slugify(' - '), 'n-a',
  ➡ '::slugify() converts a string that only contains non-ASCII
characters to n-a');
```

```
~/work/jobeet $ php symfony test:unit Jobeet
1..8
# ::slugify()
ok 1 - ::slugify() converts all characters to lower case
ok 2 - ::slugify() replaces a white space by a -
ok 3 - ::slugify() replaces several white spaces by a single -
ok 4 - ::slugify() replaces non-ASCII characters by a -
ok 5 - ::slugify() removes - at the beginning of a string
ok 6 - ::slugify() removes - at the end of a string
ok 7 - ::slugify() replaces the empty string by n-a
not ok 8 - ::slugify() replaces a string that only contains non-ASCII ch
#     Failed test (/Users/fabien/work/symfony/dev/1.2/lib/vendor/lime/li
#           got: ''
#      expected: 'n-a'
Looks like you failed 1 tests of 8.
~/work/jobeet $ 
```

After checking that the test does not pass, edit the Jobeet class and move the empty string check to the end of the method:

Listing 8-12

```
static public function slugify($text)
{
  // ...

  if (empty($text))
  {
    return 'n-a';
  }

  return $text;
}
```

The new test now passes, as do all the other ones. The `slugify()` had a bug despite our 100% coverage.

You cannot think about all edge cases when writing tests, and that's fine. But when you discover one, you need to write a test for it before fixing your code. It also means that your code will get better over time, which is always a good thing.

You probably know that symfony has been created by French people, so let's add a test with a French word that contains an "accent":

Listing 8-13

```
$t->is(Jobeet::slugify('Développeur Web'), 'developpeur-web',
'::slugify() removes accents');
```

The test must fail. Instead of replacing é by e, the **slugify()** method has replaced it by a dash (-). That's a tough problem, called transliteration. Hopefully, if you have "iconv" installed, it will do the job for us. Replace the code of the **slugify** method with the following:

Listing 8-14

```
// code derived from http://php.vrana.cz/
vytvoreni-pratelskeho-url.php
static public function slugify($text)
{
  // replace non letter or digits by -
  $text = preg_replace('~[^\\pL\d]+~u', '-', $text);

  // trim
  $text = trim($text, '-');

  // transliterate
  if (function_exists('iconv'))
  {
    $text = iconv('utf-8', 'us-ascii//TRANSLIT', $text);
  }

  // lowercase
  $text = strtolower($text);

  // remove unwanted characters
  $text = preg_replace('~[^-\w]+~', '', $text);

  if (empty($text))
  {
    return 'n-a';
  }

  return $text;
}
```

Remember to save all your PHP files with the UTF-8 encoding, as this is the default symfony encoding, and the one used by "iconv" to do the transliteration.

Also change the test file to run the test only if "iconv" is available:

Listing
8-15

```php
if (function_exists('iconv'))
{
  $t->is(Jobeet::slugify('Développeur Web'), 'developpeur-web',
'::slugify() removes accents');
}
else
{
  $t->skip('::slugify() removes accents - iconv not installed');
}
```

Doctrine Unit Tests

Database Configuration

Unit testing a Doctrine model class is a bit more complex as it requires a database connection. You already have the one you use for your development, but it is a good habit to create a dedicated database for tests.

During day 1, we introduced the environments as a way to vary an application's settings. By default, all symfony tests are run in the **test** environment, so let's configure a different database for the **test** environment:

Listing
8-16

```
$ php symfony configure:database --name=doctrine
  ➥ --class=sfDoctrineDatabase --env=test
  ➥ "mysql:host=localhost;dbname=jobeet_test" root mYsEcret
```

The **env** option tells the task that the database configuration is only for the **test** environment. When we used this task during day 3, we did not pass any **env** option, so the configuration was applied to all environments.

 If you are curious, open the **config/databases.yml** configuration file to see how symfony makes it easy to change the configuration depending on the environment.

Now that we have configured the database, we can bootstrap it by using the `doctrine:insert-sql` task:

Listing 8-17

```
$ mysqladmin -uroot -pmYsEcret create jobeet_test
$ php symfony doctrine:insert-sql --env=test
```

Configuration Principles in symfony

During day 4, we saw that settings coming from configuration files can be defined at different levels.

These settings can also be environment dependent. This is true for most configuration files we have used until now: **databases.yml**, **app.yml**, **view.yml**, and **settings.yml**. In all those files, the main key is the environment, the **all** key indicating its settings are for all environments:

Listing 8-18

```
# config/databases.yml
dev:
  doctrine:
    class: sfDoctrineDatabase

test:
  doctrine:
    class: sfDoctrineDatabase
    param:
      dsn: 'mysql:host=localhost;dbname=jobeet_test'

all:
  doctrine:
    class: sfDoctrineDatabase
    param:
      dsn: 'mysql:host=localhost;dbname=jobeet'
      username: root
      password: null
```

Test Data

Now that we have a dedicated database for our tests, we need a way to load some test data. During day 3, you learned to use the `doctrine:data-load` task, but for tests, we need to reload the data each time we run them to put the database in a known state.

The `doctrine:data-load` task internally uses the `Doctrine::loadData()` method to load the data:

```
Doctrine::loadData(sfConfig::get('sf_test_dir').'/fixtures');
```

Listing 8-19

 The **sfConfig** object can be used to get the full path of a project sub-directory. Using it allows for the default directory structure to be customized.

The **loadData()** method takes a directory or a file as its first argument. It can also take an array of directories and/or files.

We have already created some initial data in the **data/fixtures/** directory. For tests, we will put the fixtures into the **test/fixtures/** directory. These fixtures will be used for Doctrine unit and functional tests.

For now, copy the files from **data/fixtures/** to the **test/fixtures/** directory.

Testing JobeetJob

Let's create some unit tests for the **JobeetJob** model class.

As all our Doctrine unit tests will begin with the same code, create a **Doctrine.php** file in the **bootstrap/** test directory with the following code:

Listing 8-20

```
// test/bootstrap/Doctrine.php
include(dirname(__FILE__).'/unit.php');

$configuration =
  ➥ ProjectConfiguration::getApplicationConfiguration(
  ➥ 'frontend', 'test', true);

new sfDatabaseManager($configuration);

Doctrine::loadData(sfConfig::get('sf_test_dir').'/fixtures');
```

The script is pretty self-explanatory:

- As for the front controllers, we initialize a configuration object for the **test** environment:

  Listing 8-21

  ```
  $configuration =
    ➥ ProjectConfiguration::getApplicationConfiguration(
    ➥ 'frontend', 'test', true);
  ```

- We create a database manager. It initializes the Doctrine connection by loading the **databases.yml** configuration file.

  Listing 8-22

  ```
  new sfDatabaseManager($configuration);
  ```

- We load our test data by using `Doctrine::loadData()`:

Listing 8-23
```
Doctrine::loadData(sfConfig::get('sf_test_dir').'/fixtures');
```

 Doctrine connects to the database only if it has some SQL statements to execute.

Now that everything is in place, we can start testing the `JobeetJob` class.

First, we need to create the `JobeetJobTest.php` file in **test/unit/model**:

Listing 8-24
```
// test/unit/model/JobeetJobTest.php
include(dirname(__FILE__).'/../../bootstrap/Doctrine.php');

$t = new lime_test(1);
```

Then, let's start by adding a test for the `getCompanySlug()` method:

Listing 8-25
```
$t->comment('->getCompanySlug()');
$job = Doctrine::getTable('JobeetJob')->createQuery()->fetchOne();
$t->is($job->getCompanySlug(), Jobeet::slugify($job->getCompany()),
'->getCompanySlug() return the slug for the company');
```

Notice that we only test the `getCompanySlug()` method and not if the slug is correct or not, as we are already testing this elsewhere.

Writing tests for the **save()** method is slightly more complex:

Listing 8-26
```
$t->comment('->save()');
$job = create_job();
$job->save();
$expiresAt = date('Y-m-d', time() + 86400
    ➥ * sfConfig::get('app_active_days'));
$t->is($job->getDateTimeObject('expires_at')->format('Y-m-d'),
$expiresAt, '->save() updates expires_at if not set');

$job = create_job(array('expires_at' => '2008-08-08'));
$job->save();
$t->is($job->getDateTimeObject('expires_at')->format('Y-m-d'),
'2008-08-08', '->save() does not update expires_at if set');

function create_job($defaults = array())
{
  static $category = null;
```

```
if (is_null($category))
{
  $category = Doctrine::getTable('JobeetCategory')
    ->createQuery()
    ->limit(1)
    ->fetchOne();
}

$job = new JobeetJob();
$job->fromArray(array_merge(array(
  'category_id'  => $category->getId(),
  'company'      => 'Sensio Labs',
  'position'     => 'Senior Tester',
  'location'     => 'Paris, France',
  'description'  => 'Testing is fun',
  'how_to_apply' => 'Send e-Mail',
  'email'        => 'job@example.com',
  'token'        => rand(1111, 9999),
  'is_activated' => true,
), $defaults));

  return $job;
}
```

 Each time you add tests, don't forget to update the number of expected tests (the plan) in the lime_test constructor method. For the JobeetJobTest file, you need to change it from 1 to 3.

Test other Doctrine Classes

You can now add tests for all other Doctrine classes. As you are now getting used to the process of writing unit tests, it should be quite easy.

Unit Tests Harness

The test:unit task can also be used to launch all unit tests for a project:

```
$ php symfony test:unit
```

Listing 8-27

The task outputs whether each test file passes or fails:

```
~/work/jobeet $ ./symfony test:unit
JobeetTest.............................................................ok
model/JobeetJobTest....................................................ok
All tests successful.
Files=2, Tests=12
~/work/jobeet $ █
```

 If the `test:unit` task returns a "dubious status" for a file, it indicates that the script died before end. Running the test file alone will give you the exact error message.

See you Tomorrow

Even if testing an application is quite important, I know that some of you might have been tempted to just skip today's tutorial. I'm glad you have not.

Sure, embracing symfony is about learning all the great features the framework provides, but it's also about its philosophy of development and the best practices it advocates. And testing is one of them. Sooner or later, unit tests will save the day for you. They give you a solid confidence about your code and the freedom to refactor it without fear. Unit tests are a safe guard that will alert you if you break something. The symfony framework itself has more than 9000 tests.

Tomorrow we will write some functional tests for the **job** and **category** modules. Until then, take some time to write more unit tests for the Jobeet model classes.

Day 9

The Functional Tests

Yesterday, we saw how to unit test our Jobeet classes using the lime testing library packaged with symfony.

Today, we will write functional tests for the features we have already implemented in the **job** and **category** modules.

Functional Tests

Functional tests are a great tool to test your application from end to end: from the request made by a browser to the response sent by the server. They test all the layers of an application: the routing, the model, the actions, and the templates. They are very similar to what you probably already do manually: each time you add or modify an action, you need to go to the browser and check that everything works as expected by clicking on links and checking elements on the rendered page. In other words, you run a scenario corresponding to the use case you have just implemented.

As the process is manual, it is tedious and error prone. Each time you change something in your code, you must step through all the scenarios to ensure that you did not break something. That's insane. Functional tests in symfony provide a way to easily describe scenarios. Each scenario can then be played automatically over and over again by simulating the experience a user has in a browser. Like unit tests, they give you the confidence to code in peace.

 The functional test framework does not replace tools like "Selenium[46]". Selenium runs directly in the browser to automate testing across many platforms and browsers and as such, it is able to test your application's JavaScript.

The sfBrowser class

In symfony, functional tests are run through a special browser, implemented by the sfBrowser[47] class. It acts as a browser tailored for your application and directly connected to it, without the need for a web server. It gives you access to all symfony objects before and after each request, giving you the opportunity to introspect them and do the checks you want programatically.

sfBrowser provides methods that simulates navigation done in a classic browser:

Method	Description
get()	Gets a URL
post()	Posts to a URL
call()	Calls a URL (used for PUT and DELETE methods)
back()	Goes back one page in the history
forward()	Goes forward one page in the history
reload()	Reloads the current page
click()	Clicks on a link or a button
select()	selects a radiobutton or checkbox
deselect()	deselects a radiobutton or checkbox
restart()	Restarts the browser

Here are some usage examples of the sfBrowser methods:

Listing 9-1
```
$browser = new sfBrowser();

$browser->
  get('/')->
  click('Design')->
  get('/category/programming?page=2')->
  get('/category/programming', array('page' => 2))->
  post('search', array('keywords' => 'php'))
;
```

sfBrowser contains additional methods to configure the browser behavior:

---

46. http://selenium.seleniumhq.org/
47. http://www.symfony-project.org/api/1_4/sfBrowser

Method	Description
setHttpHeader()	Sets an HTTP header
setAuth()	Sets the basic authentication credentials
setCookie()	Set a cookie
removeCookie()	Removes a cookie
clearCookies()	Clears all current cookies
followRedirect()	Follows a redirect

The sfTestFunctional class

We have a browser, but we need a way to introspect the symfony objects to do the actual testing. It can be done with lime and some **sfBrowser** methods like getResponse() and getRequest() but symfony provides a better way.

The test methods are provided by another class, **sfTestFunctional**[48] that takes a **sfBrowser** instance in its constructor. The **sfTestFunctional** class delegates the tests to **tester** objects. Several testers are bundled with symfony, and you can also create your own.

As we saw yesterday, functional tests are stored under the test/functional/ directory. For Jobeet, tests are to be found in the test/functional/frontend/ sub-directory as each application has its own subdirectory. This directory already contains two files: **categoryActionsTest.php**, and **jobActionsTest.php** as all tasks that generate a module automatically create a basic functional test file:

```
// test/functional/frontend/categoryActionsTest.php
include(dirname(__FILE__).'/../../bootstrap/functional.php');

$browser = new sfTestFunctional(new sfBrowser());

$browser->
  get('/category/index')->

  with('request')->begin()->
    isParameter('module', 'category')->
    isParameter('action', 'index')->
  end()->

  with('response')->begin()->
```

Listing 9.2

---

48. http://www.symfony-project.org/api/1_4/sfTestFunctional

```
    isStatusCode(200)->
    checkElement('body', '!/This is a temporary page/')->
  end()
;
```

At first, the script above may look a bit strange to you. That's because methods of **sfBrowser** and **sfTestFunctional** implement a fluent interface[49] by always returning **$this**. It allows you to chain the method calls for better readability. The above snippet is equivalent to:

Listing 9-3

```
// test/functional/frontend/categoryActionsTest.php
include(dirname(__FILE__).'/../../bootstrap/functional.php');

$browser = new sfTestFunctional(new sfBrowser());

$browser->get('/category/index');
$browser->with('request')->begin();
$browser->isParameter('module', 'category');
$browser->isParameter('action', 'index');
$browser->end();

$browser->with('response')->begin();
$browser->isStatusCode(200);
$browser->checkElement('body', '!/This is a temporary page/');
$browser->end();
```

Tests are run within a tester block context. A tester block context begins with **with('TESTER NAME')->begin()** and ends with **end()**:

Listing 9-4

```
$browser->
  with('request')->begin()->
    isParameter('module', 'category')->
    isParameter('action', 'index')->
  end()
;
```

The code tests that the request parameter **module** equals **category** and **action** equals **index**.

 When you only need to call one test method on a tester, you don't need to create a block: **with('request')->isParameter('module', 'category')**.

---

49. http://en.wikipedia.org/wiki/Fluent_interface

The Request Tester

The **request tester** provides tester methods to introspect and test the sfWebRequest object:

Method	Description
isParameter()	Checks a request parameter value
isFormat()	Checks the format of a request
isMethod()	Checks the method
hasCookie()	Checks whether the request has a cookie with the given name
isCookie()	Checks the value of a cookie

The Response Tester

There is also a **response tester** class that provides tester methods against the sfWebResponse object:

Method	Description
checkElement()	Checks if a response CSS selector match some criteria
isHeader()	Checks the value of a header
isStatusCode()	Checks the response status code
isRedirected()	Checks if the current response is a redirect
isValid()	Checks if a response is well-formed XML (you also validate the response again its document type be passing **true** as an argument)

 We will describe more testers[50] classes in the coming days (for forms, user, cache, ...).

Running Functional Tests

As for unit tests, launching functional tests can be done by executing the test file directly:

---

50. http://www.symfony-project.org/api/1_4/test

Listing
9-5
```
$ php test/functional/frontend/categoryActionsTest.php
```

Or by using the **test:functional** task:

Listing
9-6
```
$ php symfony test:functional frontend categoryActions
```

```
~/work/jobeet $ ./symfony test:functional frontend categoryActions
# get /category/index
ok 1 - request parameter module is category
not ok 2 - request parameter action is index
#     Failed test (/Users/fabien/work/symfony/dev/1.2/lib/test/sfTesterRequest.class.php at line 48)
#           got: 'show'
#      expected: 'index'
not ok 3 - status code is 200
#     Failed test (/Users/fabien/work/symfony/dev/1.2/lib/test/sfTesterResponse.class.php at line 257)
#           got: 404
#      expected: 200
ok 4 - response selector body does not match regex /This is a temporary page/
1..4
Looks like you failed 2 tests of 4.
~/work/jobeet $
```

Test Data

As for Doctrine unit tests, we need to load test data each time we launch a functional test. We can reuse the code we have written yesterday:

Listing
9-7
```
include(dirname(__FILE__).'/../../bootstrap/functional.php');

$browser = new sfTestFunctional(new sfBrowser());
Doctrine::loadData(sfConfig::get('sf_test_dir').'/fixtures');
```

Loading data in a functional test is a bit easier than in unit tests as the database has already been initialized by the bootstrapping script.

As for unit tests, we won't copy and paste this snippet of code in each test file, but we will rather create our own functional class that inherits from **sfTestFunctional**:

Listing
9-8
```
// lib/test/JobeetTestFunctional.class.php
class JobeetTestFunctional extends sfTestFunctional
{
  public function loadData()
  {
    Doctrine::loadData(sfConfig::get('sf_test_dir').'/fixtures');

    return $this;
  }
}
```

Writing Functional Tests

Writing functional tests is like playing a scenario in a browser. We already have written all the scenarios we need to test as part of the day 2 stories.

First, let's test the Jobeet homepage by editing the **jobActionsTest.php** test file. Replace the code with the following one:

Expired jobs are not listed

Listing
9.0

```php
// test/functional/frontend/jobActionsTest.php
include(dirname(__FILE__).'/../../bootstrap/functional.php');

$browser = new JobeetTestFunctional(new sfBrowser());
$browser->loadData();

$browser->info('1 - The homepage')->
  get('/')->
  with('request')->begin()->
    isParameter('module', 'job')->
    isParameter('action', 'index')->
  end()->
  with('response')->begin()->
    info('  1.1 - Expired jobs are not listed')->
    checkElement('.jobs td.position:contains("expired")', false)->
  end()
;
```

As with **lime**, an informational message can be inserted by calling the **info()** method to make the output more readable. To verify the exclusion of expired jobs from the homepage, we check that the CSS selector **.jobs td.position:contains("expired")** does not match anywhere in the response HTML content (remember that in the fixture files, the only expired job we have contains "expired" in the position). When the second argument of the **checkElement()** method is a Boolean, the method tests the existence of nodes that match the CSS selector.

 The **checkElement()** method is able to interpret most valid CSS3 selectors.

Only n jobs are listed for a category

Add the following code at the end of the test file:

Listing
9.10

```
// test/functional/frontend/jobActionsTest.php
$max = sfConfig::get('app_max_jobs_on_homepage');

$browser->info('1 - The homepage')->
  get('/')->
  info(sprintf('  1.2 - Only %s jobs are listed for a category',
$max))->
  with('response')->
    checkElement('.category_programming tr', $max)
;
```

The `checkElement()` method can also check that a CSS selector matches 'n' nodes in the document by passing an integer as its second argument.

A category has a link to the category page only if too many jobs

Listing
9.11

```
// test/functional/frontend/jobActionsTest.php
$browser->info('1 - The homepage')->
  get('/')->
  info('  1.3 - A category has a link to the category page only if too
many jobs')->
  with('response')->begin()->
    checkElement('.category_design .more_jobs', false)->
    checkElement('.category_programming .more_jobs')->
  end()
;
```

In these tests, we check that there is no "more jobs" link for the design category (`.category_design .more_jobs` does not exist), and that there is a "more jobs" link for the programming category (`.category_programming .more_jobs` does exist).

Jobs are sorted by date

Listing
9.12

```
$q = Doctrine_Query::create()
  ->select('j.*')
  ->from('JobeetJob j')
  ->leftJoin('j.JobeetCategory c')
  ->where('c.slug = ?', 'programming')
  ->andWhere('j.expires_at > ?', date('Y-m-d', time()))
```

```
    ->orderBy('j.created_at DESC');

$job = $q->fetchOne();

$browser->info('1 - The homepage')->
  get('/')->
  info('  1.4 - Jobs are sorted by date')->
  with('response')->begin()->
    checkElement(sprintf('.category_programming tr:first a[href*="/%d/
"]', $job->getId()))->
  end()
;
```

To test if jobs are actually sorted by date, we need to check that the first job listed on the homepage is the one we expect. This can be done by checking that the URL contains the expected primary key. As the primary key can change between runs, we need to get the Doctrine object from the database first.

Even if the test works as is, we need to refactor the code a bit, as getting the first job of the programming category can be reused elsewhere in our tests. We won't move the code to the Model layer as the code is test specific. Instead, we will move the code to the **JobeetTestFunctional** class we have created earlier. This class acts as a Domain Specific ~functional tester class|Testers~ for Jobeet:

Listing
9-13

```php
// lib/test/JobeetTestFunctional.class.php
class JobeetTestFunctional extends sfTestFunctional
{
  public function getMostRecentProgrammingJob()
  {
    $q = Doctrine_Query::create()
      ->select('j.*')
      ->from('JobeetJob j')
      ->leftJoin('j.JobeetCategory c')
      ->where('c.slug = ?', 'programming');
    $q = Doctrine::getTable('JobeetJob')->addActiveJobsQuery($q);

    return $q->fetchOne();
  }

  // ...
}
```

You can now replace the previous test code by the following one:

Listing
9-14

```php
// test/functional/frontend/jobActionsTest.php
$browser->info('1 - The homepage')->
```

```
get('/')->
info('  1.4 - Jobs are sorted by date')->
with('response')->begin()->
  checkElement(sprintf('.category_programming tr:first a[href*="/%d/
"]',
      $browser->getMostRecentProgrammingJob()->getId()))->
end()
;
```

Each job on the homepage is clickable

Listing
9-15
```
$browser->info('2 - The job page')->
  get('/')->

  info('  2.1 - Each job on the homepage is clickable and give
detailed information')->
  click('Web Developer', array(), array('position' => 1))->
  with('request')->begin()->
    isParameter('module', 'job')->
    isParameter('action', 'show')->
    isParameter('company_slug', 'sensio-labs')->
    isParameter('location_slug', 'paris-france')->
    isParameter('position_slug', 'web-developer')->
    isParameter('id',
$browser->getMostRecentProgrammingJob()->getId())->
  end()
;
```

To test the job link on the homepage, we simulate a click on the "Web Developer" text. As there are many of them on the page, we have explicitly to asked the browser to click on the first one (**array('position' => 1)**).

Each request parameter is then tested to ensure that the routing has done its job correctly.

Learn by the Example

In this section, we have provided all the code needed to test the job and category pages. Read the code carefully as you may learn some new neat tricks:

Listing
9-16
```
// lib/test/JobeetTestFunctional.class.php
class JobeetTestFunctional extends sfTestFunctional
{
```

```php
  public function loadData()
  {
    Doctrine::loadData(sfConfig::get('sf_test_dir').'/fixtures');

    return $this;
  }

  public function getMostRecentProgrammingJob()
  {
    $q = Doctrine_Query::create()
      ->select('j.*')
      ->from('JobeetJob j')
      ->leftJoin('j.JobeetCategory c')
      ->where('c.slug = ?', 'programming');
    $q = Doctrine::getTable('JobeetJob')->addActiveJobsQuery($q);

    return $q->fetchOne();
  }

  public function getExpiredJob()
  {
    $q = Doctrine_Query::create()
      ->from('JobeetJob j')
      ->where('j.expires_at < ?', date('Y-m-d', time()));

    return $q->fetchOne();
  }
}

// test/functional/frontend/jobActionsTest.php
include(dirname(__FILE__).'/../../bootstrap/functional.php');

$browser = new JobeetTestFunctional(new sfBrowser());
$browser->loadData();

$browser->info('1 - The homepage')->
  get('/')->
  with('request')->begin()->
    isParameter('module', 'job')->
    isParameter('action', 'index')->
  end()->
  with('response')->begin()->
    info('  1.1 - Expired jobs are not listed')->
    checkElement('.jobs td.position:contains("expired")', false)->
  end()
```

```
;

$max = sfConfig::get('app_max_jobs_on_homepage');

$browser->info('1 - The homepage')->
  info(sprintf('  1.2 - Only %s jobs are listed for a category',
$max))->
  with('response')->
    checkElement('.category_programming tr', $max)
;

$browser->info('1 - The homepage')->
  get('/')->
  info('  1.3 - A category has a link to the category page only if too
many jobs')->
  with('response')->begin()->
    checkElement('.category_design .more_jobs', false)->
    checkElement('.category_programming .more_jobs')->
  end()
;

$browser->info('1 - The homepage')->
  info('  1.4 - Jobs are sorted by date')->
  with('response')->begin()->
    checkElement(sprintf('.category_programming tr:first a[href*="/%d/
"]', $browser->getMostRecentProgrammingJob()->getId()))->
  end()
;

$browser->info('2 - The job page')->
  info('  2.1 - Each job on the homepage is clickable and give
detailed information')->
  click('Web Developer', array(), array('position' => 1))->
  with('request')->begin()->
    isParameter('module', 'job')->
    isParameter('action', 'show')->
    isParameter('company_slug', 'sensio-labs')->
    isParameter('location_slug', 'paris-france')->
    isParameter('position_slug', 'web-developer')->
    isParameter('id',
$browser->getMostRecentProgrammingJob()->getId())->
  end()->

  info('  2.2 - A non-existent job forwards the user to a 404')->
  get('/job/foo-inc/milano-italy/0/painter')->
```

```
  with('response')->isStatusCode(404)->

  info('  2.3 - An expired job page forwards the user to a 404')->
  get(sprintf('/job/sensio-labs/paris-france/%d/web-developer',
$browser->getExpiredJob()->getId()))->
  with('response')->isStatusCode(404)
;

// test/functional/frontend/categoryActionsTest.php
include(dirname(__FILE__).'/../../bootstrap/functional.php');

$browser = new JobeetTestFunctional(new sfBrowser());
$browser->loadData();

$browser->info('1 - The category page')->
  info('  1.1 - Categories on homepage are clickable')->
  get('/')->
  click('Programming')->
  with('request')->begin()->
    isParameter('module', 'category')->
    isParameter('action', 'show')->
    isParameter('slug', 'programming')->
  end()->

  info(sprintf('  1.2 - Categories with more than %s jobs also have a
"more" link', sfConfig::get('app_max_jobs_on_homepage')))->
  get('/')->
  click('27')->
  with('request')->begin()->
    isParameter('module', 'category')->
    isParameter('action', 'show')->
    isParameter('slug', 'programming')->
  end()->

  info(sprintf('  1.3 - Only %s jobs are listed',
sfConfig::get('app_max_jobs_on_category')))->
  with('response')->checkElement('.jobs tr',
sfConfig::get('app_max_jobs_on_category'))->

  info('  1.4 - The job listed is paginated')->
  with('response')->begin()->
    checkElement('.pagination_desc', '/32 jobs/')->
    checkElement('.pagination_desc', '#page 1/2#')->
  end()->
```

```
click('2')->
with('request')->begin()->
  isParameter('page', 2)->
end()->
with('response')->checkElement('.pagination_desc', '#page 2/2#')
;
```

Debugging Functional Tests

Sometimes a functional test fails. As symfony simulates a browser without any graphical interface, it can be hard to diagnose the problem. Thankfully, symfony provides the **debug()** method to output the response header and content:

Listing 9-17

```
$browser->with('response')->debug();
```

The **debug()** method can be inserted anywhere in a **response** tester block and will halt the script execution.

Functional Tests Harness

The **test:functional** task can also be used to launch all functional tests for an application:

Listing 9-18

```
$ php symfony test:functional frontend
```

The task outputs a single line for each test file:

```
~/work/jobeet $ ./symfony test:functional frontend
categoryActionsTest...............................................ok
jobActionsTest....................................................ok
All tests successful.
Files=2, Tests=27
~/work/jobeet $
```

Tests Harness

As you may expect, there is also a task to launch all tests for a project (unit and functional):

Listing 9-19

```
$ php symfony test:all
```

```
~/work/jobeet $ ./symfony test:all
functional/frontend/categoryActionsTest.............................ok
functional/frontend/jobActionsTest..................................ok
unit/JobeetTest.....................................................ok
unit/model/JobeetJobTest............................................ok
All tests successful.
Files=4, Tests=39
~/work/jobeet $
```

When you have a large suite of tests, it can be very time consuming to launch all tests every time you make a change, especially if some tests fail. That's because each time you fix a test, you should run the whole test suite again to ensure that you have not break something else. But as long as the failed tests are not fixed, there is no point in re-executing all other tests. The **test:all** tasks have a **--only-failed** option that forces the task to only re-execute tests that failed during the previous run:

```
$ php symfony test:all --only-failed
```

Listing
9-20

The first time you run the task, all tests are run as usual. But for subsequent test runs, only tests that failed last time are executed. As you fix your code, some tests will pass, and will be removed from subsequent runs. When all tests pass again, the full test suite is run... you can then rinse and repeat.

 If you want to integrate your test suite in a continuous integration process, use the **--xml** option to force the **test:all** task to generate a JUnit compatible XML output.

```
$ php symfony test:all --xml=log.xml
```

Listing
9-21

See you Tomorrow

That wraps up our tour of the symfony test tools. You have no excuse anymore to not test your applications! With the lime framework and the functional test framework, symfony provides powerful tools to help you write tests with little effort.

We have just scratched the surface of functional tests. From now on, each time we implement a feature, we will also write tests to learn more features of the test framework.

Tomorrow, we will talk about yet another great feature of symfony: the form framework.

Day 10

The Forms

The second week of Jobeet got off to a flying start with the introduction of the symfony test framework. We will continue today with the form framework.

The Form Framework

Any website has forms; from the simple contact form to the complex ones with lots of fields. Writing forms is also one of the most complex and tedious task for a web developer: you need to write the HTML form, implement validation rules for each field, process the values to store them in a database, display error messages, repopulate fields in case of errors, and much more...

Of course, instead of reinventing the wheel over and over again, symfony provides a framework to ease form management. The form framework is made of three parts:

- **validation**: The validation sub-framework provides classes to validate inputs (integer, string, email address, ...)
- **widgets**: The widget sub-framework provides classes to output HTML fields (input, textarea, select, ...)
- **forms**: The form classes represent forms made of widgets and validators and provide methods to help manage the form. Each form field has its own validator and widget.

Forms

A symfony form is a class made of fields. Each field has a name, a validator, and a widget. A simple `ContactForm` can be defined with the following class:

Listing
10-1
```
class ContactForm extends sfForm
{
  public function configure()
  {
    $this->setWidgets(array(
      'email'   => new sfWidgetFormInputText(),
      'message' => new sfWidgetFormTextarea(),
    ));

    $this->setValidators(array(
      'email'   => new sfValidatorEmail(),
      'message' => new sfValidatorString(array('max_length' => 255)),
    ));
  }
}
```

Form fields are configured in the **configure()** method, by using the **setValidators()** and **setWidgets()** methods.

The form framework comes bundled with a lot of widgets[51] and validators[52]. The API describes them quite extensively with all the options, errors, and default error messages.

The widget and validator class names are quite explicit: the **email** field will be rendered as an HTML **<input>** tag (**sfWidgetFormInputText**) and validated as an email address (**sfValidatorEmail**). The **message** field will be rendered as a **<textarea>** tag (**sfWidgetFormTextarea**), and must be a string of no more than 255 characters (**sfValidatorString**).

By default all fields are required, as the default value for the **required** option is **true**. So, the validation definition for **email** is equivalent to **new sfValidatorEmail(array('required' => true))**.

You can merge a form in another one by using the **mergeForm()** method, or embed one by using the **embedForm()** method:

Listing
10-2
```
$this->mergeForm(new AnotherForm());
$this->embedForm('name', new AnotherForm());
```

---

51. http://www.symfony-project.org/api/1_4/widget
52. http://www.symfony-project.org/api/1_4/validator

Doctrine Forms

Most of the time, a form has to be serialized to the database. As symfony already knows everything about your database model, it can automatically generate forms based on this information. In fact, when you launched the **doctrine:build-all** task during day 3, symfony automatically called the **doctrine:build-forms** task:

```
$ php symfony doctrine:build-forms
```

*Listing
10-3*

The **doctrine:build-forms** task generates form classes in the **lib/form/** directory. The organization of these generated files is similar to that of **lib/model/**. Each model class has a related form class (for instance **JobeetJob** has **JobeetJobForm**), which is empty by default as it inherits from a base class:

```php
// lib/form/doctrine/JobeetJobForm.class.php
class JobeetJobForm extends BaseJobeetJobForm
{
  public function configure()
  {
  }
}
```

*Listing
10-4*

 By browsing the generated files under the **lib/form/doctrine/base/** sub-directory, you will see a lot of great usage examples of symfony built-in widgets and validators.

 You can disable form generation on certain models by passing parameters to the **symfony** Propel behavior:

```yml
[yml]
SomeModel:
  options:
    symfony:
      form: false
      filter: false
```

*Listing
10-5*

Customizing the Job Form

The job form is a perfect example to learn ~form customization|Forms (Customization)~. Let's see how to customize it, step by step.

First, change the "Post a Job" link in the layout to be able to check changes directly in your browser:

Listing
10-6
```php
<!-- apps/frontend/templates/layout.php -->
<a href="<?php echo url_for('@job_new') ?>">Post a Job</a>
```

By default, a Doctrine form displays fields for all the table columns. But for the job form, some of them must not be editable by the end user. Removing fields from a form is as simple as unsetting them:

Listing
10-7
```php
// lib/form/doctrine/JobeetJobForm.class.php
class JobeetJobForm extends BaseJobeetJobForm
{
  public function configure()
  {
    unset(
      $this['created_at'], $this['updated_at'],
      $this['expires_at'], $this['is_activated']
    );
  }
}
```

Unsetting a field means that both the field widget and validator are removed.

Instead of unsetting the fields you don't want to display, you can also explicitly list the fields you want by using the **useFields()** method:

Listing
10-8
```php
// lib/form/doctrine/JobeetJobForm.class.php
class JobeetJobForm extends BaseJobeetJobForm
{
  public function configure()
  {
    $this->useFields(array('category_id', 'type', 'company', 'logo',
      ➥ 'url', 'position', 'location', 'description', 'how_to_apply',
      ➥ 'token', 'is_public', 'email'));
  }
}
```

The **useFields()** method does two things automatically for you: it adds the hidden fields and the array of fields is used to change the fields order.

Explicitly listing the form fields you want to display means that when adding new fields to a base form, they won't automagically appear in your form (think of a model form where you add a new column to the related table).

The form configuration must sometimes be more precise than what can be introspected from the database schema. For example, the **email** column is a **varchar** in the schema, but we need this column to be validated as an email. Let's change the default **sfValidatorString** to a **sfValidatorEmail**:

Listing 10-9

```php
// lib/form/doctrine/JobeetJobForm.class.php
public function configure()
{
  // ...

  $this->validatorSchema['email'] = new sfValidatorEmail();
}
```

Replacing the default validator is not always the best solution, as the default validation rules introspected from the database schema are lost (**new sfValidatorString(array('max_length' => 255))**). It is almost always better to add the new validator to the existing ones by using the special **sfValidatorAnd** validator:

Listing 10-10

```php
// lib/form/doctrine/JobeetJobForm.class.php
public function configure()
{
  // ...

  $this->validatorSchema['email'] = new sfValidatorAnd(array(
    $this->validatorSchema['email'],
    new sfValidatorEmail(),
  ));
}
```

The **sfValidatorAnd** validator takes an array of validators that must pass for the value to be valid. The trick here is to reference the current validator ($this->validatorSchema['email']), and to add the new one.

 You can also use the **sfValidatorOr** validator to force a value to pass at least one validator. And of course, you can mix and match **sfValidatorAnd** and **sfValidatorOr** validators to create complex boolean based validators.

Even if the **type** column is also a **varchar** in the schema, we want its value to be restricted to a list of choices: full time, part time, or freelance.

First, let's define the possible values in **JobeetJobTable**:

Listing
10-11
```php
// lib/model/doctrine/JobeetJobTable.class.php
class JobeetJobTable extends Doctrine_Table
{
  static public $types = array(
    'full-time' => 'Full time',
    'part-time' => 'Part time',
    'freelance' => 'Freelance',
  );

  public function getTypes()
  {
    return self::$types;
  }

  // ...
}
```

Then, use **sfWidgetFormChoice** for the **type** widget:

Listing
10-12
```php
$this->widgetSchema['type'] = new sfWidgetFormChoice(array(
  'choices'  => Doctrine::getTable('JobeetJob')->getTypes(),
  'expanded' => true,
));
```

sfWidgetFormChoice represents a choice widget which can be rendered by a different widget according to some configuration options (**expanded** and **multiple**):

- Dropdown list (**<select>**): **array('multiple' => false, 'expanded' => false)**
- Dropdown box (**<select multiple="multiple">**): **array('multiple' => true, 'expanded' => false)**
- List of radio buttons: **array('multiple' => false, 'expanded' => true)**
- List of checkboxes: **array('multiple' => true, 'expanded' => true)**

 If you want one of the radio button to be selected by default (**full-time** for instance), you can change the default value in the database schema.

Even if you think nobody can submit a non-valid value, a hacker can easily bypass the widget choices by using tools like curl[53] or the Firefox Web Developer Toolbar[54]. Let's change the validator to restrict the possible choices:

Listing
10-13

```
$this->validatorSchema['type'] = new sfValidatorChoice(array(
  'choices' => array_keys(Doctrine::getTable('JobeetJob')->getTypes()),
));
```

As the logo column will store the filename of the logo associated with the job, we need to change the widget to a file input tag:

Listing
10-14

```
$this->widgetSchema['logo'] = new sfWidgetFormInputFile(array(
  'label' => 'Company logo',
));
```

For each field, symfony automatically generates a label (which will be used in the rendered <label> tag). This can be changed with the label option.

You can also change labels in a batch with the setLabels() method of the widget array:

Listing
10-15

```
$this->widgetSchema->setLabels(array(
  'category_id'    => 'Category',
  'is_public'      => 'Public?',
  'how_to_apply'   => 'How to apply?',
));
```

We also need to change the default validator:

Listing
10-16

```
$this->validatorSchema['logo'] = new sfValidatorFile(array(
  'required'    => false,
  'path'        => sfConfig::get('sf_upload_dir').'/jobs',
  'mime_types' => 'web_images',
));
```

sfValidatorFile is quite interesting as it does a number of things:

- Validates that the uploaded file is an image in a web format (mime_types)
- Renames the file to something unique
- Stores the file in the given path
- Updates the logo column with the generated name

---

53. http://curl.haxx.se/
54. http://chrispederick.com/work/web-developer/

You need to create the logo directory (web/uploads/jobs/) and check that it is writable by the web server.

As the validator will save the relative path in the database, change the path used in the showSuccess template:

Listing 10-17
```
// apps/frontend/modules/job/templates/showSuccess.php
<img src="http://www.symfony-project.org/uploads/jobs/<?php echo
$job->getLogo() ?>" alt="<?php echo $job->getCompany() ?> logo" />
```

 If a generateLogoFilename() method exists in the model, it will be called by the validator and the result will override the default generated logo filename. The method is given the sfValidatedFile object as an argument.

Just as you can override the generated label of any field, you can also define a help message. Let's add one for the is_public column to better explain its significance:

Listing 10-18
```
$this->widgetSchema->setHelp('is_public', 'Whether the job can also be
published on affiliate websites or not.');
```

The final JobeetJobForm class reads as follows:

Listing 10-19
```
// lib/form/doctrine/JobeetJobForm.class.php
class JobeetJobForm extends BaseJobeetJobForm
{
  public function configure()
  {
    unset(
      $this['created_at'], $this['updated_at'],
      $this['expires_at'], $this['is_activated']
    );

    $this->validatorSchema['email'] = new sfValidatorAnd(array(
      $this->validatorSchema['email'],
      new sfValidatorEmail(),
    ));

    $this->widgetSchema['type'] = new sfWidgetFormChoice(array(
      'choices'  => Doctrine::getTable('JobeetJob')->getTypes(),
      'expanded' => true,
    ));
    $this->validatorSchema['type'] = new sfValidatorChoice(array(
      'choices' =>
```

```
array_keys(Doctrine::getTable('JobeetJob')->getTypes()),
    ));

    $this->widgetSchema['logo'] = new sfWidgetFormInputFile(array(
      'label' => 'Company logo',
    ));

    $this->widgetSchema->setLabels(array(
      'category_id'    => 'Category',
      'is_public'      => 'Public?',
      'how_to_apply'   => 'How to apply?',
    ));

    $this->validatorSchema['logo'] = new sfValidatorFile(array(
      'required'    => false,
      'path'        => sfConfig::get('sf_upload_dir').'/jobs',
      'mime_types'  => 'web_images',
    ));

    $this->widgetSchema->setHelp('is_public', 'Whether the job can
also be published on affiliate websites or not.');
  }
}
```

The Form Template

Now that the form class has been customized, we need to display it. The template for the form is the same whether you want to create a new job or edit an existing one. In fact, both **newSuccess.php** and **editSuccess.php** templates are quite similar:

Listing
10-20

```
<!-- apps/frontend/modules/job/templates/newSuccess.php -->
<?php use_stylesheet('job.css') ?>

<h1>Post a Job</h1>

<?php include_partial('form', array('form' => $form)) ?>
```

 If you have not added the **job** stylesheet yet, it is time to do so in both templates (`<?php use_stylesheet('job.css') ?>`).

The form itself is rendered in the **_form** partial. Replace the content of the generated **_form** partial with the following code:

Listing
10-21

```
<!-- apps/frontend/modules/job/templates/_form.php -->
<?php include_stylesheets_for_form($form) ?>
<?php include_javascripts_for_form($form) ?>

<?php echo form_tag_for($form, '@job') ?>
  <table id="job_form">
    <tfoot>
      <tr>
        <td colspan="2">
          <input type="submit" value="Preview your job" />
        </td>
      </tr>
    </tfoot>
    <tbody>
      <?php echo $form ?>
    </tbody>
  </table>
</form>
```

The `include_javascripts_for_form()` and `include_stylesheets_for_form()` helpers include JavaScript and stylesheet dependencies needed for the form widgets.

 Even if the job form does not need any JavaScript or stylesheet file, it is a good habit to keep these helper calls "just in case". It can save your day later if you decide to change a widget that needs some JavaScript or a specific stylesheet.

The `form_tag_for()` helper generates a `<form>` tag for the given form and route and changes the HTTP methods to **POST** or **PUT** depending on whether the object is new or not. It also takes care of the `~multipart|Forms (Multipart)~` attribute if the form has any file input tags.

Eventually, the `<?php echo $form ?>` renders the form widgets.

By default, the `<?php echo $form ?>` renders the form widgets as table rows.

Most of the time, you will need to customize the layout of your forms. The form object provides many useful methods for this customization:

Method	Description
render()	Renders the form (equivalent to the output of echo $form)
renderHiddenFields()	Renders the hidden fields
hasErrors()	Returns **true** if the form has some errors
hasGlobalErrors()	Returns **true** if the form has global errors
getGlobalErrors()	Returns an array of global errors
renderGlobalErrors()	Renders the global errors

The form also behaves like an array of fields. You can access the **company** field with `$form['company']`. The returned object provides methods to render each element of the field:

Method	Description
renderRow()	Renders the field row
render()	Renders the field widget
renderLabel()	Renders the field label
renderError()	Renders the field error messages if any
renderHelp()	Renders the field help message

The `echo $form` statement is equivalent to:

```php
<?php foreach ($form as $widget): ?>
  <?php echo $widget->renderRow() ?>
<?php endforeach; ?>
```

Listing 10-22

The Form Action

We now have a form class and a template that renders it. Now, it's time to actually make it work with some actions.

The job form is managed by five methods in the **job** module:

- **new**: Displays a blank form to create a new job
- **edit**: Displays a form to edit an existing job
- **create**: Creates a new job with the user submitted values
- **update**: Updates an existing job with the user submitted values
- **processForm**: Called by **create** and **update**, it processes the form (validation, form repopulation, and serialization to the database)

All forms have the following life-cycle:

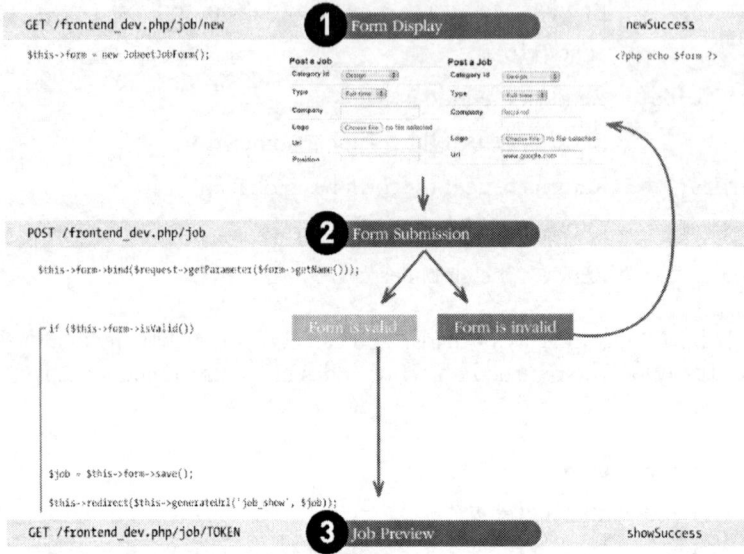

As we have created a Doctrine route collection 5 days ago for the **job** module, we can simplify the code for the form management methods:

Listing 10-23

```php
// apps/frontend/modules/job/actions/actions.class.php
public function executeNew(sfWebRequest $request)
{
  $this->form = new JobeetJobForm();
}

public function executeCreate(sfWebRequest $request)
{
  $this->form = new JobeetJobForm();
  $this->processForm($request, $this->form);
  $this->setTemplate('new');
}

public function executeEdit(sfWebRequest $request)
```

```
{
  $this->form = new JobeetJobForm($this->getRoute()->getObject());
}

public function executeUpdate(sfWebRequest $request)
{
  $this->form = new JobeetJobForm($this->getRoute()->getObject());
  $this->processForm($request, $this->form);
  $this->setTemplate('edit');
}

public function executeDelete(sfWebRequest $request)
{
  $request->checkCSRFProtection();

  $job = $this->getRoute()->getObject();
  $job->delete();

  $this->redirect('job/index');
}

protected function processForm(sfWebRequest $request, sfForm $form)
{
  $form->bind(
    $request->getParameter($form->getName()),
    $request->getFiles($form->getName())
  );

  if ($form->isValid())
  {
    $job = $form->save();

    $this->redirect('job_show', $job);
  }
}
```

When you browse to the /**job/new** page, a new form instance is created and passed to the template (**new** action).

When the user submits the form (**create** action), the form is bound (**bind()** method) with the user submitted values and the validation is triggered.

Once the form is bound, it is possible to check its validity using the **isValid()** method: If the form is valid (returns **true**), the job is saved to the database (**$form->save()**), and the user is redirected to the job preview page; if not, the newSuccess.php template is displayed again with the user submitted values and the associated error messages.

 The setTemplate() method changes the template used for a given action. If the submitted form is not valid, the create and update methods use the same template as the new and edit action respectively to re-display the form with error messages.

The modification of an existing job is quite similar. The only difference between the new and the edit action is that the job object to be modified is passed as the first argument of the form constructor. This object will be used for default widget values in the template (default values are an object for Doctrine forms, but a plain array for simple forms).

You can also define default values for the creation form. One way is to declare the values in the database schema. Another one is to pass a pre-modified Job object to the form constructor.

Change the executeNew() method to define full-time as the default value for the type column:

Listing
10-24

```
// apps/frontend/modules/job/actions/actions.class.php
public function executeNew(sfWebRequest $request)
{
  $job = new JobeetJob();
  $job->setType('full-time');

  $this->form = new JobeetJobForm($job);
}
```

 When the form is bound, the default values are replaced with the user submitted ones. The user submitted values will be used for form repopulation when the form is redisplayed in case of validation errors.

Protecting the Job Form with a Token

Everything must work fine by now. As of now, the user must enter the token for the job. But the job token must be generated automatically when a new job is created, as we don't want to rely on the user to provide a unique token.

Update the save() method of JobeetJob to add the logic that generates the token before a new job is saved:

Listing
10-25

```php
// lib/model/doctrine/JobeetJob.class.php
public function save(Doctrine_Connection $con = null)
{
  // ...

  if (!$this->getToken())
  {
    $this->setToken(sha1($this->getEmail().rand(11111, 99999)));
  }

  return parent::save($conn);
}
```

You can now remove the **token** field from the form:

Listing
10-26

```php
// lib/form/doctrine/JobeetJobForm.class.php
class JobeetJobForm extends BaseJobeetJobForm
{
  public function configure()
  {
    unset(
      $this['created_at'], $this['updated_at'],
      $this['expires_at'], $this['is_activated'],
      $this['token']
    );

    // ...
  }

  // ...
}
```

If you remember the user stories from day 2, a job can be edited only if the user knows the associated token. Right now, it is pretty easy to edit or delete any job, just by guessing the URL. That's because the edit URL is like **/job/ID/edit**, where **ID** is the primary key of the job.

By default, a **sfDoctrineRouteCollection** route generates URLs with the primary key, but it can be changed to any unique column by passing the **column** option:

Listing
10-27

```yaml
# apps/frontend/config/routing.yml
job:
  class:        sfDoctrineRouteCollection
  options:      { model: JobeetJob, column: token }
  requirements: { token: \w+ }
```

Notice that we have also changed the **token** parameter requirement to match any string as the symfony default requirements is **\d+** for the unique key.

Now, all routes related to the jobs, except the **job_show_user** one, embed the token. For instance, the route to edit a job is now of the following pattern:

Listing 10-28
```
http://jobeet.localhost/job/TOKEN/edit
```

You will also need to change the "Edit" link in the **showSuccess** template:

Listing 10-29
```php
<!-- apps/frontend/modules/job/templates/showSuccess.php -->
<a href="<?php echo url_for('job_edit', $job) ?>">Edit</a>
```

The Preview Page

The preview page is the same as the job page display. Thanks to the routing, if the user comes with the right token, it will be accessible in the **token** request parameter.

If the user comes in with the tokenized URL, we will add an admin bar at the top. At the beginning of the **showSuccess** template, add a partial to host the admin bar and remove the **edit** link at the bottom:

Listing 10-30
```php
<!-- apps/frontend/modules/job/templates/showSuccess.php -->
<?php if ($sf_request->getParameter('token') == $job->getToken()): ?>
  <?php include_partial('job/admin', array('job' => $job)) ?>
<?php endif; ?>
```

Then, create the **_admin** partial:

Listing 10-31
```php
<!-- apps/frontend/modules/job/templates/_admin.php -->
<div id="job_actions">
  <h3>Admin</h3>
  <ul>
    <?php if (!$job->getIsActivated()): ?>
      <li><?php echo link_to('Edit', 'job_edit', $job) ?></li>
      <li><?php echo link_to('Publish', 'job_edit', $job) ?></li>
    <?php endif; ?>
    <li><?php echo link_to('Delete', 'job_delete', $job,
array('method' => 'delete', 'confirm' => 'Are you sure?')) ?></li>
    <?php if ($job->getIsActivated()): ?>
      <li<?php $job->expiresSoon() and print ' class="expires_soon"'
?>>
        <?php if ($job->isExpired()): ?>
```

```
      Expired
    <?php else: ?>
      Expires in <strong><?php echo $job->getDaysBeforeExpires()
?></strong> days
    <?php endif; ?>

    <?php if ($job->expiresSoon()): ?>
      - <a href="">Extend</a> for another <?php echo
sfConfig::get('app_active_days') ?> days
    <?php endif; ?>
  </li>
  <?php else: ?>
    <li>
      [Bookmark this <?php echo link_to('URL', 'job_show', $job,
true) ?> to manage this job in the future.]
    </li>
  <?php endif; ?>
  </ul>
</div>
```

There is a lot of code, but most of the code is simple to understand.

To make the template more readable, we have added a bunch of shortcut methods in the JobeetJob class:

Listing 10.32

```
// lib/model/doctrine/JobeetJob.class.php
public function getTypeName()
{
  $types = Doctrine::getTable('JobeetJob')->getTypes();
  return $this->getType() ? $types[$this->getType()] : '';
}

public function isExpired()
{
  return $this->getDaysBeforeExpires() < 0;
}

public function expiresSoon()
{
  return $this->getDaysBeforeExpires() < 5;
}

public function getDaysBeforeExpires()
{
  return floor($this->getDateTimeObject('expires_at')->format('U') /
```

```
86400);
}
```

The admin bar displays the different actions depending on the job status:

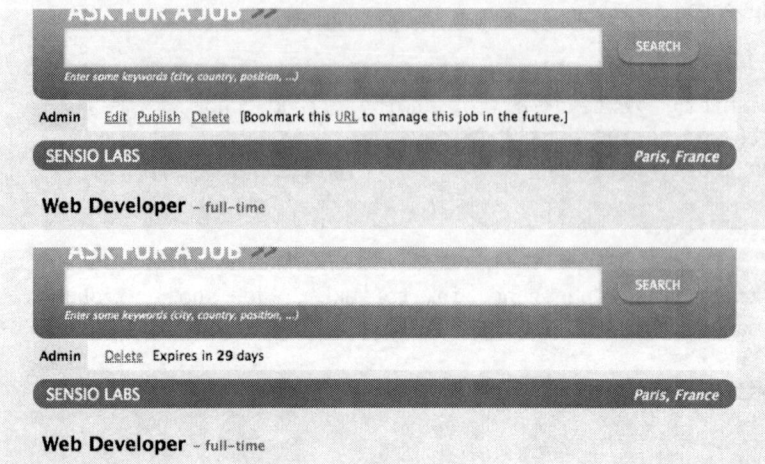

 You will be able to see the "activated" bar after the next section.

Job Activation and Publication

In the previous section, there is a link to publish the job. The link needs to be changed to point to a new **publish** action. Instead of creating a new route, we can just configure the existing **job** route:

Listing 10-33
```
# apps/frontend/config/routing.yml
job:
  class:    sfDoctrineRouteCollection
  options:
    model:          JobeetJob
    column:         token
    object_actions: { publish: put }
  requirements:
    token: \w+
```

The **object_actions** takes an array of additional actions for the given object. We can now change the link of the "Publish" link:

```
<!-- apps/frontend/modules/job/templates/_admin.php -->
<li>
  <?php echo link_to('Publish', 'job_publish', $job, array('method' =>
'put')) ?>
</li>
```

Listing
10-34

The last step is to create the **publish** action:

```
// apps/frontend/modules/job/actions/actions.class.php
public function executePublish(sfWebRequest $request)
{
  $request->checkCSRFProtection();

  $job = $this->getRoute()->getObject();
  $job->publish();

  $this->getUser()->setFlash('notice', sprintf('Your job is now online
for %s days.', sfConfig::get('app_active_days')));

  $this->redirect('job_show_user', $job);
}
```

Listing
10-35

The astute reader will have noticed that the "Publish" link is submitted with the HTTP put method. To simulate the put method, the link is automatically converted to a form when you click on it.

And because we have enabled the CSRF protection, the **link_to()** helper embeds a CSRF token in the link and the **checkCSRFProtection()** method of the request object checks the validity of it on submission.

The **executePublish()** method uses a new **publish()** method that can be defined as follows:

```
// lib/model/doctrine/JobeetJob.class.php
public function publish()
{
  $this->setIsActivated(true);
  $this->save();
}
```

Listing
10-36

You can now test the new publish feature in your browser.

But we still have something to fix. The non-activated jobs must not be accessible, which means that they must not show up on the Jobeet homepage, and must not be accessible by their URL. As we have created an **addActiveJobsQuery()** method to restrict a `Doctrine_Query` to active jobs, we can just edit it and add the new requirements at the end:

Listing 10-37

```php
// lib/model/doctrine/JobeetJobTable.class.php
public function addActiveJobsQuery(Doctrine_Query $q = null)
{
  // ...

  $q->andWhere($alias . '.is_activated = ?', 1);

  return $q;
}
```

That's all. You can test it now in your browser. All non-activated jobs have disappeared from the homepage; even if you know their URLs, they are not accessible anymore. They are, however, accessible if one knows the job's token URL. In that case, the job preview will show up with the admin bar.

That's one of the great advantages of the MVC pattern and the refactorization we have done along the way. Only a single change in one method was needed to add the new requirement.

 When we created the `getWithJobs()` method, we forgot to use the `addActiveJobsQuery()` method. So, we need to edit it and add the new requirement:

Listing 10-38

```php
class JobeetCategoryTable extends Doctrine_Table
{
  public function getWithJobs()
  {
    // ...

    $q->andWhere('j.is_activated = ?', 1);

    return $q->execute();
  }
}
```

See you Tomorrow

Today's tutorial was packed with a lot of new information, but hopefully you now have a better understanding of symfony's form framework.

I know that some of you noticed that we forgot something today... We have not implemented any test for the new features. Because writing tests is an important part of developing an application, this is the first thing we will do tomorrow.

Day 11

Testing your Forms

Yesterday we created our first form with symfony. People are now able to post a new job on Jobeet but we ran out of time before we could add some tests.

That's what we will do today. Along the way, we will also learn more about the form framework.

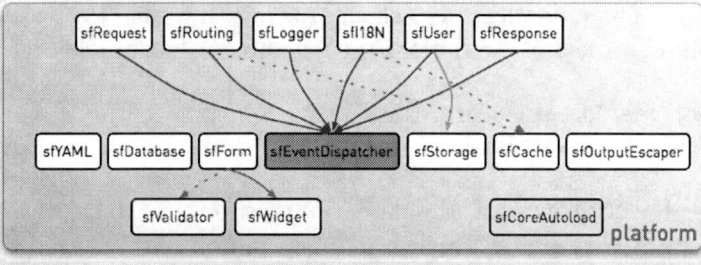

Submitting a Form

Let's open the jobActionsTest file to add functional tests for the job creation and validation process.

At the end of the file, add the following code to get the job creation page:

Listing
11-1

```
// test/functional/frontend/jobActionsTest.php
$browser->info('3 - Post a Job page')->
  info('  3.1 - Submit a Job')->

  get('/job/new')->
  with('request')->begin()->
    isParameter('module', 'job')->
    isParameter('action', 'new')->
  end()
;
```

We have already used the **click()** method to simulate clicks on links. The same **click()** method can be used to submit a form. For a form, you can pass the values to submit for each field as a second argument of the method. Like a real browser, the browser object will merge the default values of the form with the submitted values.

But to pass the field values, we need to know their names. If you open the source code or use the Firefox Web Developer Toolbar "Forms > Display Form Details" feature, you will see that the name for the **company** field is **jobeet_job[company]**.

 When PHP encounters an input field with a name like **jobeet_job[company]**, it automatically converts it to an array of name **jobeet_job**.

To make things look a bit more clean, let's change the format to **job[%s]** by adding the following code at the end of the **configure()** method of **JobeetJobForm**:

Listing
11-2

```
// lib/form/doctrine/JobeetJobForm.class.php
$this->widgetSchema->setNameFormat('job[%s]');
```

After this change, the **company** name should be **job[company]** in your browser. It is now time to actually click on the "Preview your job" button and pass valid values to the form:

Listing
11-3

```
// test/functional/frontend/jobActionsTest.php
$browser->info('3 - Post a Job page')->
    info('  3.1 - Submit a Job')->
```

```
  get('/job/new')->
  with('request')->begin()->
    isParameter('module', 'job')->
    isParameter('action', 'new')->
  end()->

  click('Preview your job', array('job' => array(
    'company'      => 'Sensio Labs',
    'url'          => 'http://www.sensio.com/',
    'logo'         => sfConfig::get('sf_upload_dir').'/jobs/
sensio-labs.gif',
    'position'     => 'Developer',
    'location'     => 'Atlanta, USA',
    'description'  => 'You will work with symfony to develop websites
for our customers.',
    'how_to_apply' => 'Send me an email',
    'email'        => 'for.a.job@example.com',
    'is_public'    => false,
  )))->

  with('request')->begin()->
    isParameter('module', 'job')->
    isParameter('action', 'create')->
  end()
;
```

The browser also simulates file uploads if you pass the absolute path to the file to upload.

After submitting the form, we checked that the executed action is **create**.

The Form Tester

The form we have submitted should be valid. You can test this by using the **form tester**:

```
with('form')->begin()->
  hasErrors(false)->
end()->
```

Listing 11-4

The form tester has several methods to test the current form status, like the errors.

If you make a mistake in the test, and the test does not pass, you can use the `with('response')->debug()` statement we have seen during day 9. But you will have to dig into the generated HTML to check for error messages. That's not really convenient. The form tester also provides a debug() method that outputs the form status and all error messages associated with it:

Listing
11-5
```
with('form')->debug()
```

Redirection Test

As the form is valid, the job should have been created and the user redirected to the show page:

Listing
11-6
```
isRedirected()->
followRedirect()->

with('request')->begin()->
  isParameter('module', 'job')->
  isParameter('action', 'show')->
end()->
```

The isRedirected() tests if the page has been redirected and the followRedirect() method follows the redirect.

 The browser class does not follow redirects automatically as you might want to introspect objects before the redirection.

The Doctrine Tester

Eventually, we want to test that the job has been created in the database and check that the is_activated column is set to false as the user has not published it yet.

This can be done quite easily by using yet another tester, the **Doctrine tester**. As the Doctrine tester is not registered by default, let's add it now:

Listing
11-7
```
$browser->setTester('doctrine', 'sfTesterDoctrine');
```

The Doctrine tester provides the check() method to check that one or more objects in the database matches the criteria passed as an argument.

Listing
11-8
```
with('doctrine')->begin()->
  check('JobeetJob', array(
    'location'     => 'Atlanta, USA',
```

```
    'is_activated' => false,
    'is_public'    => false,
  ))->
end()
```

The criteria can be an array of values like above, or a **Doctrine_Query** instance
for more complex queries. You can test the existence of objects matching the
criteria with a Boolean as the third argument (the default is **true**), or the number
of matching objects by passing an integer.

Testing for Errors

The job form creation works as expected when we submit valid values. Let's add a
test to check the behavior when we submit non-valid data:

Listing
11-9

```
$browser->
  info(' 3.2 - Submit a Job with invalid values')->

  get('/job/new')->
  click('Preview your job', array('job' => array(
    'company'      => 'Sensio Labs',
    'position'     => 'Developer',
    'location'     => 'Atlanta, USA',
    'email'        => 'not.an.email',
  )))->

  with('form')->begin()->
    hasErrors(3)->
    isError('description', 'required')->
    isError('how_to_apply', 'required')->
    isError('email', 'invalid')->
  end()
;
```

The **hasErrors()** method can test the number of errors if passed an integer. The
isError() method tests the error code for a given field.

 In the tests we have written for the non-valid data submission, we have not
re-tested the entire form all over again. We have only added tests for specific
things.

You can also test the generated HTML to check that it contains the error messages,
but it is not necessary in our case as we have not customized the form layout.

Now, we need to test the admin bar found on the job preview page. When a job has not been activated yet, you can edit, delete, or publish the job. To test those three links, we will need to first create a job. But that's a lot of copy and paste. As I don't like to waste e-trees, let's add a job creator method in the JobeetTestFunctional class:

Listing
11-10

```
// lib/test/JobeetTestFunctional.class.php
class JobeetTestFunctional extends sfTestFunctional
{
  public function createJob($values = array())
  {
    return $this->
      get('/job/new')->
      click('Preview your job', array('job' => array_merge(array(
        'company'      => 'Sensio Labs',
        'url'          => 'http://www.sensio.com/',
        'position'     => 'Developer',
        'location'     => 'Atlanta, USA',
        'description'  => 'You will work with symfony to develop
websites for our customers.',
        'how_to_apply' => 'Send me an email',
        'email'        => 'for.a.job@example.com',
        'is_public'    => false,
      ), $values)))->
      followRedirect()
    ;
  }

  // ...
}
```

The createJob() method creates a job, follows the redirect and returns the browser to not break the fluent interface. You can also pass an array of values that will be merged with some default values.

Forcing the HTTP Method of a link

Testing the "Publish" link is now more simple:

Listing
11-11

```
$browser->info('  3.3 - On the preview page, you can publish the
job')->
  createJob(array('position' => 'FOO1'))->
  click('Publish', array(), array('method' => 'put', '_with_csrf' =>
```

```
true))->

  with('doctrine')->begin()->
    check('JobeetJob', array(
      'position'     => 'F001',
      'is_activated' => true,
    ))->
  end()
;
```

If you remember from day 10, the "Publish" link has been configured to be called with the HTTP **PUT** method. As browsers don't understand **PUT** requests, the **link_to()** helper converts the link to a form with some JavaScript. As the test browser does not execute JavaScript, we need to force the method to **PUT** by passing it as a third option of the **click()** method. Moreover, the **link_to()** helper also embeds a CSRF token as we have enabled CSRF protection during day 1; the **_with_csrf** option simulates this token.

Testing the "Delete" link is quite similar:

Listing
11-12

```
$browser->info(' 3.4 - On the preview page, you can delete the job')->
  createJob(array('position' => 'F002'))->
  click('Delete', array(), array('method' => 'delete', '_with_csrf' =>
true))->

  with('doctrine')->begin()->
    check('JobeetJob', array(
      'position' => 'F002',
    ), false)->
  end()
;
```

Tests as a SafeGuard

When a job is published, you cannot edit it anymore. Even if the "Edit" link is not displayed anymore on the preview page, let's add some tests for this requirement.

First, add another argument to the **createJob()** method to allow automatic publication of the job, and create a **getJobByPosition()** method that returns a job given its position value:

Listing
11-13

```
// lib/test/JobeetTestFunctional.class.php
class JobeetTestFunctional extends sfTestFunctional
{
```

```php
  public function createJob($values = array(), $publish = false)
  {
    $this->
      get('/job/new')->
      click('Preview your job', array('job' => array_merge(array(
        'company'     => 'Sensio Labs',
        'url'         => 'http://www.sensio.com/',
        'position'    => 'Developer',
        'location'    => 'Atlanta, USA',
        'description' => 'You will work with symfony to develop
websites for our customers.',
        'how_to_apply' => 'Send me an email',
        'email'       => 'for.a.job@example.com',
        'is_public'   => false,
      ), $values)))->
      followRedirect()
    ;

    if ($publish)
    {
      $this->
        click('Publish', array(), array('method' => 'put',
'_with_csrf' => true))->
        followRedirect()
      ;
    }

    return $this;
  }

  public function getJobByPosition($position)
  {
    $q = Doctrine_Query::create()
      ->from('JobeetJob j')
      ->where('j.position = ?', $position);

    return $q->fetchOne();
  }

  // ...
}
```

If a job is published, the edit page must return a 404 status code:

Listing
11-14

```
$browser->info('  3.5 - When a job is published, it cannot be edited
anymore')->
  createJob(array('position' => 'FOO3'), true)->
  get(sprintf('/job/%s/edit',
$browser->getJobByPosition('FOO3')->getToken()))->

  with('response')->begin()->
    isStatusCode(404)->
  end()
;
```

But if you run the tests, you won't have the expected result as we forgot to
implement this security measure yesterday. Writing tests is also a great way to
discover bugs, as you need to think about all ~edge cases|Edge Cases~.

Fixing the bug is quite simple as we just need to forward to a 404 page if the job is
activated:

*Listing
11-15*

```php
// apps/frontend/modules/job/actions/actions.class.php
public function executeEdit(sfWebRequest $request)
{
  $job = $this->getRoute()->getObject();
  $this->forward404If($job->getIsActivated());

  $this->form = new JobeetJobForm($job);
}
```

The fix is trivial, but are you sure that everything else still works as expected? You
can open your browser and start testing all possible combinations to access the
edit page. But there is a simpler way: run your test suite; if you have introduced a
regression, symfony will tell you right away.

Back to the Future in a Test

When a job is expiring in less than five days, or if it is already expired, the user can
extend the job validation for another 30 days from the current date.

Testing this requirement in a browser is not easy as the expiration date is
automatically set when the job is created to 30 days in the future. So, when getting
the job page, the link to extend the job is not present. Sure, you can hack the
expiration date in the database, or tweak the template to always display the link,
but that's tedious and error prone. As you have already guessed, writing some tests
will help us one more time.

As always, we need to add a new route for the **extend** method first:

Listing
11-16
```
# apps/frontend/config/routing.yml
job:
  class:    sfDoctrineRouteCollection
  options:
    model:            JobeetJob
    column:           token
    object_actions: { publish: PUT, extend: PUT }
  requirements:
    token: \w+
```

Then, update the "Extend" link code in the _admin partial:

Listing
11-17
```
<!-- apps/frontend/modules/job/templates/_admin.php -->
<?php if ($job->expiresSoon()): ?>
  - <?php echo link_to('Extend', 'job_extend', $job, array('method' =>
'put')) ?> for another <?php echo sfConfig::get('app_active_days') ?>
days
<?php endif; ?>
```

Then, create the **extend** action:

Listing
11-18
```
// apps/frontend/modules/job/actions/actions.class.php
public function executeExtend(sfWebRequest $request)
{
  $request->checkCSRFProtection();

  $job = $this->getRoute()->getObject();
  $this->forward404Unless($job->extend());

  $this->getUser()->setFlash('notice', sprintf('Your job validity has
been extended until %s.',
$job->getDateTimeObject('expires_at')->format('m/d/Y')));

  $this->redirect('job_show_user', $job);
}
```

As expected by the action, the **extend()** method of JobeetJob returns **true** if the
job has been extended or **false** otherwise:

Listing
11-19
```
// lib/model/doctrine/JobeetJob.class.php
class JobeetJob extends BaseJobeetJob
{
  public function extend()
  {
    if (!$this->expiresSoon())
```

```
  {
    return false;
  }

    $this->setExpiresAt(date('Y-m-d', time() + 86400 *
sfConfig::get('app_active_days')));

    $this->save();

    return true;
  }

  // ...
}
```

Eventually, add a test scenario:

Listing
11-20

```
$browser->info(' 3.6 - A job validity cannot be extended before the
job expires soon')->
  createJob(array('position' => 'F004'), true)->
  call(sprintf('/job/%s/extend',
$browser->getJobByPosition('F004')->getToken()), 'put',
array('_with_csrf' => true))->
  with('response')->begin()->
    isStatusCode(404)->
  end()
;

$browser->info(' 3.7 - A job validity can be extended when the job
expires soon')->
  createJob(array('position' => 'F005'), true)
;

$job = $browser->getJobByPosition('F005');
$job->setExpiresAt(date('Y-m-d'));
$job->save();

$browser->
  call(sprintf('/job/%s/extend', $job->getToken()), 'put',
array('_with_csrf' => true))->
  with('response')->isRedirected()
;

$job->refresh();
$browser->test()->is(
```

```
$job->getDateTimeObject('expires_at')->format('y/m/d'),
  date('y/m/d', time() + 86400 * sfConfig::get('app_active_days'))
);
```

This test scenario introduces a few new things:

- The call() method retrieves a URL with a method different from GET or POST
- After the job has been updated by the action, we need to reload the local object with $job->refresh()
- At the end, we use the embedded lime object directly to test the new expiration date.

Forms Security

Form Serialization Magic!

Doctrine forms are very easy to use as they automate a lot of work. For instance, serializing a form to the database is as simple as a call to $form->save().

But how does it work? Basically, the save() method follows the following steps:

- Begin a transaction (because nested Doctrine forms are all saved in one fell swoop)
- Process the submitted values (by calling updateCOLUMNColumn() methods if they exist)
- Call Doctrine object fromArray() method to update the column values
- Save the object to the database
- Commit the transaction

Built-in Security Features

The fromArray() method takes an array of values and updates the corresponding column values. Does this represent a security issue? What if someone tries to submit a value for a column for which he does not have authorization? For instance, can I force the token column?

Let's write a test to simulate a job submission with a token field:

Listing 11-21
```
// test/functional/frontend/jobActionsTest.php
$browser->
  get('/job/new')->
  click('Preview your job', array('job' => array(
```

```
      'token' => 'fake_token',
  )))->

  with('form')->begin()->
    hasErrors(7)->
    hasGlobalError('extra_fields')->
  end()
;
```

When submitting the form, you must have an **extra_fields** global error. That's because by default forms do not allow extra fields to be present in the submitted values. That's also why all form fields must have an associated validator.

 You can also submit additional fields from the comfort of your browser using tools like the Firefox Web Developer Toolbar.

You can bypass this security measure by setting the **allow_extra_fields** option to **true**:

```
class MyForm extends sfForm
{
  public function configure()
  {
    // ...

    $this->validatorSchema->setOption('allow_extra_fields', true);
  }
}
```

Listing
11-22

The test must now pass but the **token** value has been filtered out of the values. So, you are still not able to bypass the security measure. But if you really want the value, set the **filter_extra_fields** option to **false**:

```
$this->validatorSchema->setOption('filter_extra_fields', false);
```

Listing
11-23

 The tests written in this section are only for demonstration purpose. You can now remove them from the Jobeet project as tests do not need to validate symfony features.

XSS and CSRF Protection

During day 1, you learned the the **generate:app** task created a secured application by default.

First, it enabled the protection against XSS. It means that all variables used in templates are escaped by default. If you try to submit a job description with some HTML tags inside, you will notice that when symfony renders the job page, the HTML tags from the description are not interpreted, but rendered as plain text.

Then, it enabled the CSRF protection. When a CSRF token is set, all forms embed a **_csrf_token** hidden field.

 The escaping strategy and the CSRF secret can be changed at any time by editing the **apps/frontend/config/settings.yml** configuration file. As for the **databases.yml** file, the settings are configurable by environment:

Listing 11-24
```
all:
  .settings:
    # Form security secret (CSRF protection)
    csrf_secret: Unique$ecret

    # Output escaping settings
    escaping_strategy: true
    escaping_method:   ESC_SPECIALCHARS
```

Maintenance Tasks

Even if symfony is a web framework, it comes with a ~command line|Command Line~ tool. You have already used it to create the default directory structure of the project and the application, but also to generate various files for the model. Adding a new task is quite easy as the tools used by the symfony command line are packaged in a framework.

When a user creates a job, he must activate it to put it online. But if not, the database will grow with stale jobs. Let's create a task that remove stale jobs from the database. This task will have to be run regularly in a cron job.

Listing 11-25
```
// lib/task/JobeetCleanupTask.class.php
class JobeetCleanupTask extends sfBaseTask
{
  protected function configure()
  {
```

```
    $this->addOptions(array(
        new sfCommandOption('application', null,
sfCommandOption::PARAMETER_REQUIRED, 'The application', 'frontend'),
        new sfCommandOption('env', null,
sfCommandOption::PARAMETER_REQUIRED, 'The environement', 'prod'),
        new sfCommandOption('days', null,
sfCommandOption::PARAMETER_REQUIRED, '', 90),
    ));

    $this->namespace = 'jobeet';
    $this->name = 'cleanup';
    $this->briefDescription = 'Cleanup Jobeet database';

    $this->detailedDescription = <<<EOF
The [jobeet:cleanup|INFO] task cleans up the Jobeet database:

  [./symfony jobeet:cleanup --env=prod --days=90|INFO]
EOF;
  }

  protected function execute($arguments = array(), $options = array())
  {
    $databaseManager = new sfDatabaseManager($this->configuration);

    $nb = Doctrine::getTable('JobeetJob')->cleanup($options['days']);
    $this->logSection('doctrine', sprintf('Removed %d stale jobs',
$nb));
  }
}
```

The task configuration is done in the **configure()** method. Each task must have a unique name (**namespace:name**), and can have arguments and options.

 Browse the built-in symfony tasks (**lib/task/**) for more examples of usage.

The **jobeet:cleanup** task defines two options: **--env** and **--days** with some sensible defaults.

Running the task is similar to running any other symfony built-in task:

```
$ php symfony jobeet:cleanup --days=10 --env=dev
```
Listing
11-26

As always, the database cleanup code has been factored out in the **JobeetJobTable** class:

Listing
11-27
```php
// lib/model/doctrine/JobeetJobTable.class.php
public function cleanup($days)
{
  $q = $this->createQuery('a')
    ->delete()
    ->andWhere('a.is_activated = ?', 0)
    ->andWhere('a.created_at < ?', date('Y-m-d', time() - 86400 *
$days));

  return $q->execute();
}
```

 The symfony tasks behave nicely with their environment as they return a value according to the success of the task. You can force a return value by returning an integer explicitly at the end of the task.

See you Tomorrow

Testing is at the heart of the symfony philosophy and tools. Today, we have learned again how to leverage symfony tools to make the development process easier, faster, and more important, safer.

The symfony form framework provides much more than just widgets and validators: it gives you a simple way to test your forms and ensure that your forms are secure by default.

Our tour of great symfony features do not end today. Tomorrow, we will create the backend application for Jobeet. Creating a backend interface is a must for most web projects, and Jobeet is no different. But how will we be able to develop such an interface in just one hour? Simple, we will use the symfony admin generator framework. Until then, take care.

Day 12

The Admin Generator

With the addition we made yesterday on Jobeet, the frontend application is now fully useable by job seekers and job posters. It's time to talk a bit about the backend application.

Today, thanks to the admin generator functionality of symfony, we will develop a complete backend interface for Jobeet in just one hour.

Backend Creation

The very first step is to create the backend application. If your memory serves you well, you should remember how to do it with the **generate:app** task:

```
$ php symfony generate:app backend
```

Listing 12-1

The backend application is now available at **http://jobeet.localhost/ backend.php/** for the **prod** environment, and at **http://jobeet.localhost/ backend_dev.php/** for the **dev** environment.

 When you created the frontend application, the production front controller was named **index.php**. As you can only have one **index.php** file per directory, symfony creates an **index.php** file for the very first production front controller and names the others after the application name.

If you try to reload the data fixtures with the **doctrine:data-load** task, it won't work anymore. That's because the **JobeetJob::save()** method needs access to the **app.yml** configuration file from the **frontend** application. As we have now two applications, symfony uses the first it finds, which is now the **backend** one.

But as seen during day 8, the settings can be configured at different levels. By moving the content of the apps/frontend/config/app.yml file to config/app.yml, the settings will be shared among all applications and the problem will be fixed. Do the change now as we will use the model classes quite extensively in the admin generator, and so we will need the variables defined in app.yml in the backend application.

 The doctrine:data-load task also takes a --application option. So, if you need some specific settings from one application or another, this is the way to go:

Listing 12-2
```
$ php symfony doctrine:data-load --application=frontend
```

Backend Modules

For the frontend application, the doctrine:generate-module task has been used to bootstrap a basic CRUD module based on a model class. For the backend, the doctrine:generate-admin task will be used as it generates a full working backend interface for a model class:

Listing 12-3
```
$ php symfony doctrine:generate-admin backend JobeetJob --module=job
$ php symfony doctrine:generate-admin backend JobeetCategory
    ➥ --module=category
```

These two commands create a job and a category module for the JobeetJob and the JobeetCategory model classes respectively.

The optional --module option overrides the module name generated by default by the task (which would have been otherwise jobeet_job for the JobeetJob class).

Behind the scenes, the task has also created a custom route for each module:

Listing 12-4
```
# apps/backend/config/routing.yml
jobeet_job:
  class: sfDoctrineRouteCollection
  options:
    model:                JobeetJob
    module:               job
    prefix_path:          job
    column:               id
    with_wildcard_routes: true
```

It should come as no surprise that the route class used by the ~admin generator|Admin Generator~ is sfDoctrineRouteCollection, as the main goal of an admin interface is the management of the life-cycle of model objects.

The route definition also defines some options we have not seen before:

- **prefix_path**: Defines the prefix path for the generated route (for instance, the edit page will be something like **/job/1/edit**).
- **column**: Defines the table column to use in the URL for links that references an object.
- **with_wildcard_routes**: As the admin interface will have more than the classic CRUD operations, this option allows to define more object and collection actions without editing the route.

 As always, it is a good idea to read the help before using a new task.

```
$ php symfony help doctrine:generate-admin
```
Listing 12-5

It will give you all the task arguments and options as well as some classic usage examples.

Backend Look and Feel

Right off the bat, you can use the generated modules:

```
http://jobeet.localhost/backend_dev.php/job
http://jobeet.localhost/backend_dev.php/category
```
Listing 12-6

The admin modules have many more features than the simple modules we have generated in previous days. Without writing a single line of PHP, each module provides these great features:

- The list of objects is **paginated**
- The list is **sortable**
- The list can be **filtered**
- Objects can be **created**, **edited**, and **deleted**
- Selected objects can be deleted in a **batch**
- The form **validation** is enabled
- **Flash messages** give immediate feedback to the user
- ... and much much more

The admin generator provides all the features you need to create a backend interface in a simple to configure package.

To make the user experience a bit better, we need to customize the default backend. We will also add a simple menu to make it easy to navigate between the different modules.

Replace the default **layout.php** file content with the code below:

Listing 12-7

```
// apps/backend/templates/layout.php
<!DOCTYPE html PUBLIC "-//W3C//DTD XHTML 1.0 Transitional//EN"
  "http://www.w3.org/TR/xhtml1/DTD/xhtml1-transitional.dtd">
<html xmlns="http://www.w3.org/1999/xhtml" xml:lang="en" lang="en">
  <head>
    <title>Jobeet Admin Interface</title>
    <link rel="shortcut icon" href="/favicon.ico" />
    <?php use_stylesheet('admin.css') ?>
    <?php include_javascripts() ?>
    <?php include_stylesheets() ?>
  </head>
  <body>
    <div id="container">
      <div id="header">
        <h1>
          <a href="<?php echo url_for('@homepage') ?>">
            <img src="http://www.symfony-project.org/images/logo.jpg"
alt="Jobeet Job Board" />
          </a>
        </h1>
      </div>

      <div id="menu">
        <ul>
          <li>
            <?php echo link_to('Jobs', '@jobeet_job_job') ?>
          </li>
          <li>
            <?php echo link_to('Categories',
'@jobeet_category_category') ?>
          </li>
        </ul>
      </div>

      <div id="content">
        <?php echo $sf_content ?>
      </div>

      <div id="footer">
        <img src="http://www.symfony-project.org/images/
```

```
jobeet-mini.png" />
        powered by <a href="http://www.symfony-project.org/">
        <img src="http://www.symfony-project.org/images/symfony.gif"
alt="symfony framework" /></a>
      </div>
    </div>
  </body>
</html>
```

This layout uses an **admin.css** stylesheet. This file must already be present in **web/css/** as it was installed with the other stylesheets during day 4.

Eventually, change the default symfony homepage in **routing.yml**:

Listing
12-8

```
# apps/backend/config/routing.yml
homepage:
  url:    /
  param: { module: job, action: index }
```

The symfony Cache

If you are curious enough, you have probably already opened the files generated by the task under the **apps/backend/modules/** directory. If not, please open them now. Surprise! The templates directories are empty, and the **actions.class.php** files are quite empty as well:

Listing
12-9

```
// apps/backend/modules/job/actions/actions.class.php
require_once dirname(__FILE__).'/../lib/
jobGeneratorConfiguration.class.php';
require_once dirname(__FILE__).'/../lib/jobGeneratorHelper.class.php';
```

```
class jobActions extends autoJobActions
{
}
```

How can it possibly work? If you have a closer look, you will notice that the **jobActions** class extends **autoJobActions**. The **autoJobActions** class is automatically generated by symfony if it does not exist. It is to be found in the **cache/backend/dev/modules/autoJob/** directory, which contains the "real" module:

Listing 12-10

```
// cache/backend/dev/modules/autoJob/actions/actions.class.php
class autoJobActions extends sfActions
{
  public function preExecute()
  {
    $this->configuration = new jobGeneratorConfiguration();

    if (!$this->getUser()->hasCredential(
      $this->configuration->getCredentials($this->getActionName())
    ))
    {

// ...
```

The way the admin generator works should remind you of some known behavior. In fact, it is quite similar to what we have already learned about the model and form classes. Based on the model schema definition, symfony generates the model and form classes. For the admin generator, the generated module can be configured by editing the **config/generator.yml** file found in the module:

Listing 12-11

```
# apps/backend/modules/job/config/generator.yml
generator:
  class: sfDoctrineGenerator
  param:
    model_class:           JobeetJob
    theme:                 admin
    non_verbose_templates: true
    with_show:             false
    singular:              ~
    plural:                ~
    route_prefix:          jobeet_job
    with_doctrine_route:   1

    config:
```

```
actions:  ~
fields:   ~
list:     ~
filter:   ~
form:     ~
edit:     ~
new:      ~
```

Each time you update the `generator.yml` file, symfony regenerates the cache. As we will see today, customizing the admin generated modules is easy, fast, and fun.

 The automatic re-generation of cache files only occurs in the development environment. In the production one, you will need to clear the cache manually with the `cache:clear` task.

Backend Configuration

An admin module can be customized by editing the `config` key of the `generator.yml` file. The configuration is organized in seven sections:

- **actions**: Default configuration for the actions found on the list and on the forms
- **fields**: Default configuration for the fields
- **list**: Configuration for the list
- **filter**: Configuration for the filters
- **form**: Configuration for the new/edit form
- **edit**: Specific configuration for the edit page
- **new**: Specific configuration for the new page

Let's start the customization.

Title Configuration

The `list`, `edit`, and `new` section titles of `category` module can be customized by defining a `title` option:

```
# apps/backend/modules/category/config/generator.yml
config:
  actions: ~
  fields:  ~
  list:
```

Listing
12-12

```
    title: Category Management
  filter: ~
  form:    ~
  edit:
    title: Editing Category "%%name%%"
  new:
    title: New Category
```

The **title** for the **edit** section contains dynamic values: all strings enclosed between **%%** are replaced by their corresponding object column values.

The configuration for the **job** module is quite similar:

Listing
12-13
```
# apps/backend/modules/job/config/generator.yml
config:
  actions: ~
  fields:  ~
  list:
    title: Job Management
  filter: ~
  form:    ~
  edit:
    title: Editing Job "%%company%% is looking for a %%position%%"
  new:
    title: Job Creation
```

Fields Configuration

The different views (**list**, **new**, and **edit**) are composed of fields. A field can be a column of the model class, or a virtual column as we will see later on.

The default fields configuration can be customized with the **fields** section:

Listing
12-14
```
# apps/backend/modules/job/config/generator.yml
config:
  fields:
    is_activated: { label: Activated?, help: Whether the user has
```

```
activated the job, or not }
    is_public:    { label: Public?, help: Whether the job can also be
published on affiliate websites, or not }
```

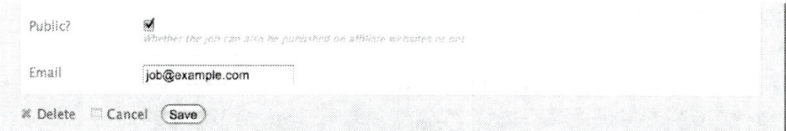

The **fields** section overrides the fields configuration for all views, which means that the **label** for the **is_activated** field will be changed for the **list**, **edit**, and **new** views.

The admin generator configuration is based on a configuration cascade principle. For instance, if you want to change a label for the **list** view only, define a **fields** option under the **list** section:

Listing 12-15

```
# apps/backend/modules/job/config/generator.yml
config:
  list:
    fields:
      is_public:    { label: "Public? (label for the list)" }
```

Any configuration that is set under the main **fields** section can be overridden by view-specific configuration. The overriding rules are the following:

- **new** and **edit** inherit from **form** which inherits from **fields**
- **list** inherits from **fields**
- **filter** inherits from **fields**

 For form sections (**form**, **edit**, and **new**), the **label** and **help** options override the ones defined in the form classes.

List View Configuration

display

By default, the columns of the list view are all the columns of the model, in the order of the schema file. The **display** option overrides the default by defining the ordered columns to be displayed:

Listing 12-16

```
# apps/backend/modules/category/config/generator.yml
config:
  list:
    title:   Category Management
    display: [=name, slug]
```

The = sign before the name column is a convention to convert the string to a link.

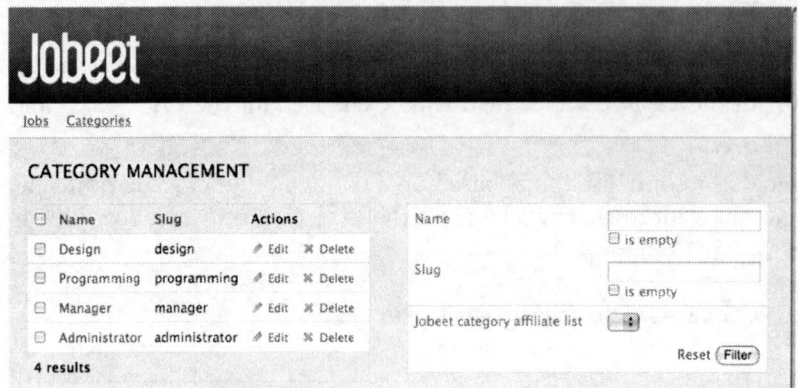

Let's do the same for the **job** module to make it more readable:

Listing
12-17
```
# apps/backend/modules/job/config/generator.yml
config:
  list:
    title:   Job Management
    display: [company, position, location, url, is_activated, email]
```

layout

The list can be displayed with different layouts. By default, the layout is **tabular**, which means that each column value is in its own table column. But for the **job** module, it would be better to use the **stacked** layout, which is the other built-in layout:

Listing
12-18
```
# apps/backend/modules/job/config/generator.yml
config:
  list:
    title:   Job Management
    layout:  stacked
    display: [company, position, location, url, is_activated, email]
    params:  |
      %%is_activated%% <small>%%category_id%%</small> - %%company%%
      (<em>%%email%%</em>) is looking for a %%=position%%
(%%location%%)
```

In a **stacked** layout, each object is represented by a single string, which is defined by the **params** option.

 The **display** option is still needed as it defines the columns that will be sortable by the user.

"Virtual" columns

With this configuration, the **%%category_id%%** segment will be replaced by the category primary key. But it would be more meaningful to display the name of the category.

Whenever you use the **%%** notation, the variable does not need to correspond to an actual column in the database schema. The admin generator only need to find a related getter in the model class.

To display the category name, we can define a **getCategoryName()** method in the **JobeetJob** model class and replace **%%category_id%%** by **%%category_name%%**.

But the **JobeetJob** class already has a **getJobeetCategory()** method that returns the related category object. And if you use **%%jobeet_category%%**, it works as the **JobeetCategory** class has a magic **__toString()** method that converts the object to a string.

```
# apps/backend/modules/job/config/generator.yml
%%is_activated%% <small>%%jobeet_category%%</small> - %%company%%
  (<em>%%email%%</em>) is looking for a %%=position%% (%%location%%)
```

Listing
12-19

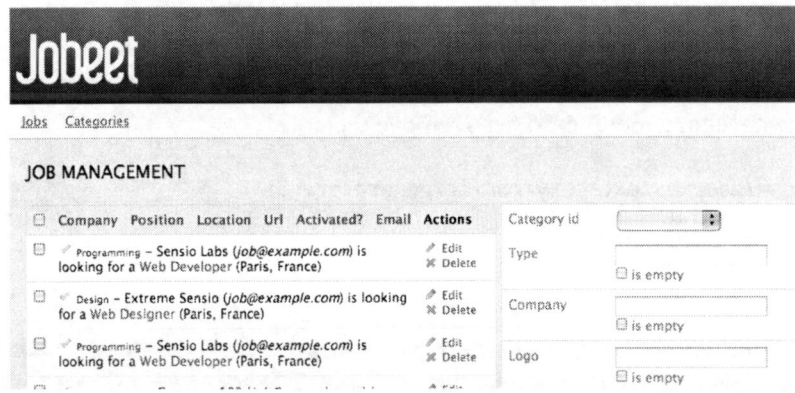

sort

As an administrator, you will be probably more interested in seeing the latest posted jobs. You can configure the default sort column by adding a **sort** option:

Listing
12-20
```
# apps/backend/modules/job/config/generator.yml
config:
  list:
    sort: [expires_at, desc]
```

max_per_page

By default, the list is paginated and each page contains 20 items. This can be changed with the **max_per_page** option:

Listing
12-21
```
# apps/backend/modules/job/config/generator.yml
config:
  list:
    max_per_page: 10
```

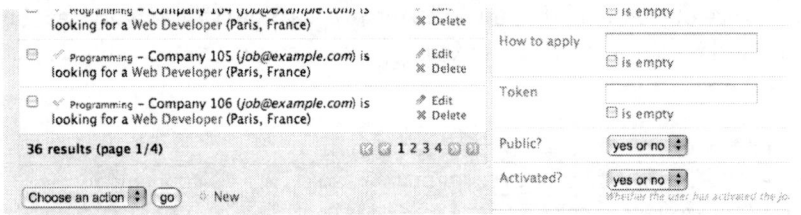

batch_actions

On a list, an action can be run on several objects. These batch actions are not needed for the **category** module, so, let's remove them:

Listing
12-22
```
# apps/backend/modules/category/config/generator.yml
config:
  list:
    batch_actions: {}
```

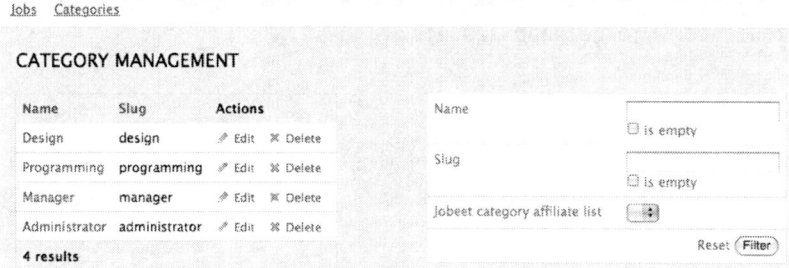

The **batch_actions** option defines the list of batch actions. The empty array allows the removal of the feature.

By default, each module has a **delete** batch action defined by the framework, but for the **job** module, let's pretend we need a way to extend the validity of some selected jobs for another 30 days:

Listing
12-23

```
# apps/backend/modules/job/config/generator.yml
config:
  list:
    batch_actions:
      _delete:   ~
      extend:    ~
```

All actions beginning with a _ are built-in actions provided by the framework. If you refresh your browser and select the extend batch actions, symfony will throw an exception telling you to create a **executeBatchExtend()** method:

Listing
12-24

```php
// apps/backend/modules/job/actions/actions.class.php
class jobActions extends autoJobActions
{
  public function executeBatchExtend(sfWebRequest $request)
  {
    $ids = $request->getParameter('ids');

    $q = Doctrine_Query::create()
      ->from('JobeetJob j')
      ->whereIn('j.id', $ids);

    foreach ($q->execute() as $job)
    {
      $job->extend(true);
    }
```

```
    $this->getUser()->setFlash('notice', 'The selected jobs have been
extended successfully.');

    $this->redirect('@jobeet_job_job');
  }
}
```

The selected primary keys are stored in the **ids** request parameter. For each selected job, the **JobeetJob::extend()** method is called with an extra argument to bypass the expiration check.

Update the **extend()** method to take this new argument into account:

Listing 12-25
```
// lib/model/doctrine/JobeetJob.class.php
class JobeetJob extends BaseJobeetJob
{
  public function extend($force = false)
  {
    if (!$force && !$this->expiresSoon())
    {
      return false;
    }

    $this->setExpiresAt(date('Y-m-d', time() + 86400 *
sfConfig::get('app_active_days')));
    $this->save();

    return true;
  }

  // ...
}
```

After all jobs have been extended, the user is redirected to the **job** module homepage.

object_actions

In the list, there is an additional column for actions you can run on a single object. For the **category** module, let's remove them as we have a link on the category name to edit it, and we don't really need to be able to delete one directly from the list:

Listing
12-26

```
# apps/backend/modules/category/config/generator.yml
config:
  list:
    object_actions: {}
```

For the **job** module, let's keep the existing actions and add a new **extend** action similar to the one we have added as a batch action:

Listing
12-27

```
# apps/backend/modules/job/config/generator.yml
config:
  list:
    object_actions:
      extend:     ~
      _edit:      ~
      _delete:    ~
```

As for batch actions, the **_delete** and **_edit** actions are the ones defined by the framework. We need to define the **listExtend()** action to make the **extend** link work:

Listing
12-28

```php
// apps/backend/modules/job/actions/actions.class.php
class jobActions extends autoJobActions
{
  public function executeListExtend(sfWebRequest $request)
  {
    $job = $this->getRoute()->getObject();
    $job->extend(true);

    $this->getUser()->setFlash('notice', 'The selected jobs have been
extended successfully.');

    $this->redirect('@jobeet_job_job');
  }

  // ...
}
```

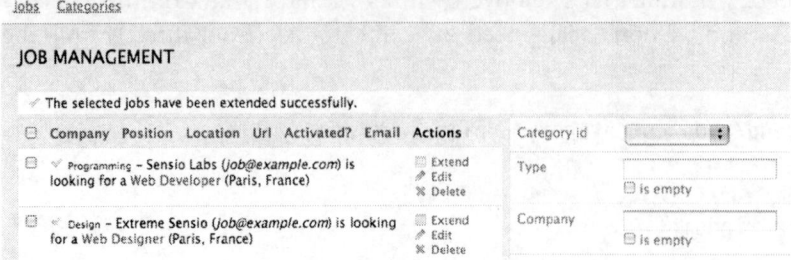

actions

We have already seen how to link an action to a list of objects or a single object. The **actions** option defines actions that take no object at all, like the creation of a new object. Let's remove the default **new** action and add a new action that deletes all jobs that have not been activated by the poster for more than 60 days:

Listing 12-29

```
# apps/backend/modules/job/config/generator.yml
config:
  list:
    actions:
      deleteNeverActivated: { label: Delete never activated jobs }
```

Until now, all actions we have defined had ~, which means that symfony configures the action automatically. Each action can be customized by defining an array of parameters. The **label** option overrides the default label generated by symfony.

By default, the action executed when you click on the link is the name of the action prefixed with **list**.

Create the **listDeleteNeverActivated** action in the **job** module:

Listing 12-30

```
// apps/backend/modules/job/actions/actions.class.php
class jobActions extends autoJobActions
{
  public function executeListDeleteNeverActivated(sfWebRequest
$request)
  {
    $nb = Doctrine::getTable('JobeetJob')->cleanup(60);

    if ($nb)
    {
      $this->getUser()->setFlash('notice', sprintf('%d never activated
```

```
jobs have been deleted successfully.', $nb));
    }
    else
    {
      $this->getUser()->setFlash('notice', 'No job to delete.');
    }

    $this->redirect('@jobeet_job_job');
  }

  // ...
}
```

We have reused the `JobeetJobTable::cleanup()` method defined yesterday. That's another great example of the reusability provided by the MVC pattern.

You can also change the action to execute by passing an **action** parameter:

```
deleteNeverActivated: { label: Delete never activated jobs, action:
foo }
```

Listing
12-31

table_method

The number of database requests needed to display the job list page is 14, as shown by the web debug toolbar.

If you click on that number, you will see that most requests are to retrieve the category name for each job:

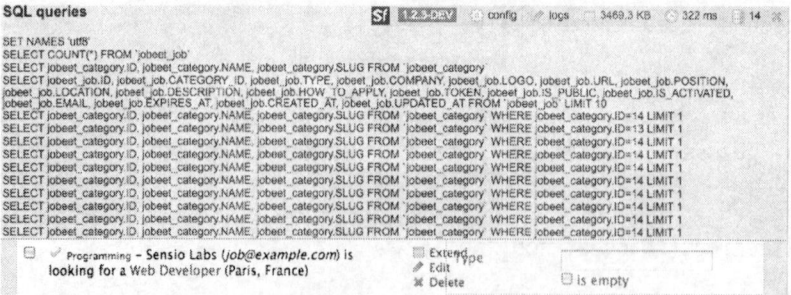

To reduce the number of requests, we can change the default method used to get the jobs by using the `table_method` option:

Listing 12-32

```yaml
# apps/backend/modules/job/config/generator.yml
config:
  list:
    table_method: retrieveBackendJobList
```

Now you must create the `retrieveBackendJobList` method in `JobeetJobTable` located in `lib/model/doctrine/JobeetJobTable.class.php`.

Listing 12-33

```php
// lib/model/doctrine/JobeetJobTable.class.php
class JobeetJobTable extends Doctrine_Table
{
  public function retrieveBackendJobList(Doctrine_Query $q)
  {
    $rootAlias = $q->getRootAlias();
    $q->leftJoin($rootAlias . '.JobeetCategory c');
    return $q;
  }

  // ...
```

The `retrieveBackendJobList()` method adds a join between the `job` and the `category` tables and automatically creates the category object related to each job.

The number of requests is now down to four:

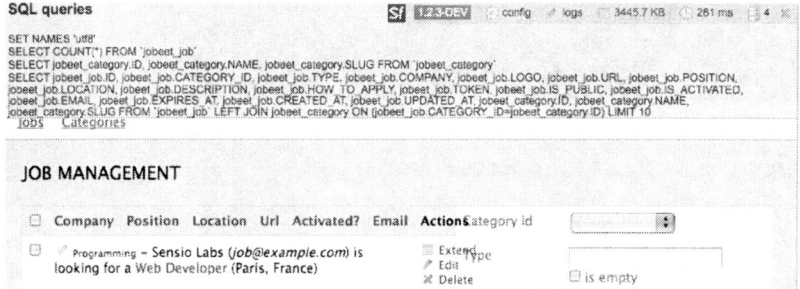

Form Views Configuration

The form views configuration is done in three sections: **form**, **edit**, and **new**. They all have the same configuration capabilities and the **form** section only exists as a fallback for the **edit** and **new** sections.

display

As for the list, you can change the order of the displayed fields with the **display** option. But as the displayed form is defined by a class, don't try to remove a field as it could lead to unexpected validation errors.

The **display** option for form views can also be used to arrange fields into groups:

```
# apps/backend/modules/job/config/generator.yml
config:
  form:
    display:
      Content: [category_id, type, company, logo, url, position,
        ➞ location, description, how_to_apply, is_public, email]
      Admin:   [_generated_token, is_activated, expires_at]
```

Listing 12-14

The above configuration defines two groups (**Content** and **Admin**), each containing a subset of the form fields.

The columns in the **Admin** group do not show up in the browser yet because they have been unset in the job form definition. They will appear in a few sections when we define a custom job form class for the admin application.

The admin generator has built-in support for many to many relationship. On the category form, you have an input for the name, one for the slug, and a drop-down box for the related affiliates. As it does not make sense to edit this relation on this page, let's remove it:

Listing 12-35

```
// lib/form/doctrine/JobeetCategoryForm.class.php
class JobeetCategoryForm extends BaseJobeetCategoryForm
{
  public function configure()
  {
    unset($this['created_at'], $this['updated_at'],
$this['jobeet_affiliates_list']);
  }
}
```

"Virtual" columns

In the `display` options for the job form, the `_generated_token` field starts with an underscore (_). This means that the rendering for this field will be handled by a custom partial named `_generated_token.php`

Create this partial with the following content:

Listing 12-36

```
// apps/backend/modules/job/templates/_generated_token.php
<div class="sf_admin_form_row">
  <label>Token</label>
```

```php
<?php echo $form->getObject()->getToken() ?>
</div>
```

In the partial, you have access to the current form (**$form**) and the related object is accessible via the **getObject()** method.

 You can also delegate the rendering to a component by prefixing the field name by a tilde (**~**).

---

class

As the form will be used by administrators, we have displayed more information than for the user job form. But for now, some of them do not appear on the form as they have been removed in the **JobeetJobForm** class.

To have different forms for the frontend and the backend, we need to create two form classes. Let's create a **BackendJobeetJobForm** class that extends the **JobeetJobForm** class. As we won't have the same hidden fields, we also need to refactor the **JobeetJobForm** class a bit to move the **unset()** statement in a method that will be overridden in **BackendJobeetJobForm**:

```php
// lib/form/doctrine/JobeetJobForm.class.php
class JobeetJobForm extends BaseJobeetJobForm
{
  public function configure()
  {
    $this->removeFields();

    $this->validatorSchema['email'] = new sfValidatorAnd(array(
      $this->validatorSchema['email'],
      new sfValidatorEmail(),
    ));

    // ...
  }

  protected function removeFields()
  {
    unset(
      $this['created_at'], $this['updated_at'],
      $this['expires_at'], $this['is_activated'],
      $this['token']
    );
  }
}
```

Listing
12-37

```
    }

    // lib/form/doctrine/BackendJobeetJobForm.class.php
    class BackendJobeetJobForm extends JobeetJobForm
    {
      public function configure()
      {
        parent::configure();
      }

      protected function removeFields()
      {
        unset(
          $this['created_at'], $this['updated_at'],
          $this['token']
        );
      }
    }
```

The default form class used by the admin generator can be overridden by setting the **class** option:

Listing 12-38

```
# apps/backend/modules/job/config/generator.yml
config:
  form:
    class: BackendJobeetJobForm
```

 As we have added a new class, don't forget to clear the cache.

The **edit** form still has a small annoyance. The current ~uploaded|File Upload~ logo does not show up anywhere and you cannot remove the current one. The **sfWidgetFormInputFileEditable** widget adds editing capabilities to a simple input file widget:

Listing 12-39

```
// lib/form/doctrine/BackendJobeetJobForm.class.php
class BackendJobeetJobForm extends JobeetJobForm
{
  public function configure()
  {
    parent::configure();

    $this->widgetSchema['logo'] = new
sfWidgetFormInputFileEditable(array(
```

```
       'label'    => 'Company logo',
       'file_src' => '/uploads/jobs/'.$this->getObject()->getLogo(),
       'is_image' => true,
       'edit_mode' => !$this->isNew(),
       'template' => '<div>%file%<br />%input%<br />%delete%
%delete_label%</div>',
    ));

    $this->validatorSchema['logo_delete'] = new sfValidatorPass();
  }

  // ...
}
```

The sfWidgetFormInputFileEditable widget takes several options to tweak its features and rendering:

- file_src: The web path to the current uploaded file
- is_image: If true, the file will be rendered as an image
- edit_mode: Whether the form is in edit mode or not
- with_delete: Whether to display the delete checkbox
- template: The template to use to render the widget

 The look of the admin generator can be tweaked very easily as the generated templates define a lot of **class** and **id** attributes. For instance, the logo field can be customized by using the sf_admin_form_field_logo class. Each field also has a class depending on the field type like sf_admin_text or sf_admin_boolean.

The edit_mode option uses the sfDoctrineRecord::isNew() method.

It returns **true** if the model object of the form is new, and **false** otherwise. This is of great help when you need to have different widgets or validators depending on the status of the embedded object.

Filters Configuration

Configuring filters is quite the same as configuring the form views. As a matter of fact, filters are just forms. And as for the forms, the classes have been generated by the **doctrine:build-all** task. You can also re-generate them with the **doctrine:build-filters** task.

The form filter classes are located under the **lib/filter/** directory and each model class has an associated filter form class (**JobeetJobFormFilter** for **JobeetJobForm**).

Let's remove them completely for the **category** module:

Listing
12-40
```
# apps/backend/modules/category/config/generator.yml
config:
  filter:
    class: false
```

For the **job** module, let's remove some of them:

Listing
12-41
```
# apps/backend/modules/job/config/generator.yml
filter:
  display: [category_id, company, position, description, is_activated,
    ➡ is_public, email, expires_at]
```

As filters are always optional, there is no need to override the filter form class to configure the fields to be displayed.

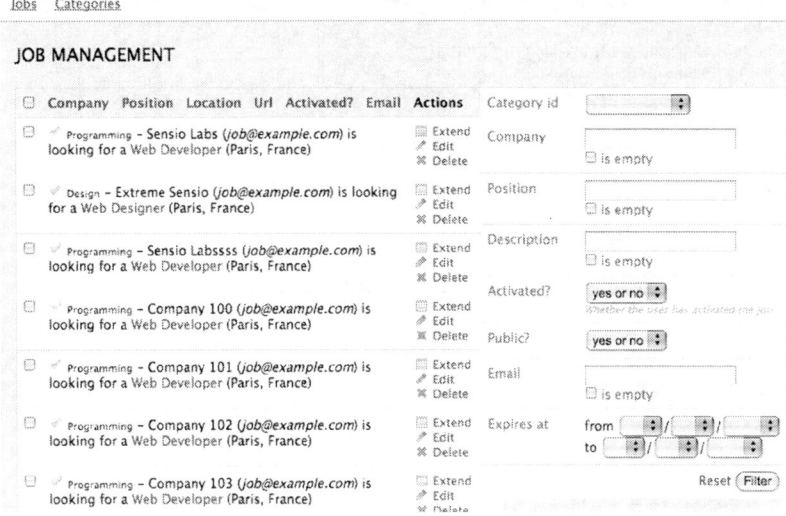

Actions Customization

When configuration is not sufficient, you can add new methods to the action class as we have seen with the extend feature, but you can also override the generated action methods:

Method	Description
executeIndex()	list view action
executeFilter()	Updates the filters
executeNew()	new view action
executeCreate()	Creates a new Job
executeEdit()	edit view action
executeUpdate()	Updates a Job
executeDelete()	Deletes a Job
executeBatch()	Executes a batch action
executeBatchDelete()	Executes the _delete batch action
processForm()	Processes the Job form
getFilters()	Returns the current filters

Method	Description
setFilters()	Sets the filters
getPager()	Returns the list pager
getPage()	Gets the pager page
setPage()	Sets the pager page
buildCriteria()	Builds the **Criteria** for the list
addSortCriteria()	Adds the sort **Criteria** for the list
getSort()	Returns the current sort column
setSort()	Sets the current sort column

As each generated method does only one thing, it is easy to change a behavior without having to copy and paste too much code.

Templates Customization

We have seen how to customize the generated templates thanks to the **class** and **id** attributes added by the admin generator in the HTML code.

As for the classes, you can also override the original templates. As templates are plain PHP files and not PHP classes, a template can be overridden by creating a template of the same name in the module (for instance in the **apps/backend/ modules/job/templates/** directory for the **job** admin module):

Template	Description
_assets.php	Renders the CSS and JS to use for templates
_filters.php	Renders the filters box
_filters_field.php	Renders a single filter field
_flashes.php	Renders the flash messages
_form.php	Displays the form
_form_actions.php	Displays the form actions
_form_field.php	Displays a singe form field
_form_fieldset.php	Displays a form fieldset
_form_footer.php	Displays the form footer
_form_header.php	Displays the form header
_list.php	Displays the list

Template	Description
_list_actions.php	Displays the list actions
_list_batch_actions.php	Displays the list batch actions
_list_field_boolean.php	Displays a single boolean field in the list
_list_footer.php	Displays the list footer
_list_header.php	Displays the list header
_list_td_actions.php	Displays the object actions for a row
_list_td_batch_actions.php	Displays the checkbox for a row
_list_td_stacked.php	Displays the stacked layout for a row
_list_td_tabular.php	Displays a single field for the list
_list_th_stacked.php	Displays a single column name for the header
_list_th_tabular.php	Displays a single column name for the header
_pagination.php	Displays the list pagination
editSuccess.php	Displays the **edit** view
indexSuccess.php	Displays the **list** view
newSuccess.php	Displays the **new** view

Final Configuration

The final configuration for the Jobeet admin is as follows:

```
# apps/backend/modules/job/config/generator.yml
generator:
  class: sfDoctrineGenerator
  param:
    model_class:           JobeetJob
    theme:                 admin
    non_verbose_templates: true
    with_show:             false
    singular:              ~
    plural:                ~
    route_prefix:          jobeet_job
    with_doctrine_route:   1

    config:
      actions: ~
```

Listing 12-42

```
      fields:
        is_activated: { label: Activated?, help: Whether the user has
activated the job, or not }
        is_public:    { label: Public? }
      list:
        title:        Job Management
        layout:       stacked
        display:      [company, position, location, url,
is_activated, email]
        params: |
          %%is_activated%% <small>%%JobeetCategory%%</small> -
%%company%%
            (<em>%%email%%</em>) is looking for a %%=position%%
(%%location%%)
        max_per_page: 10
        sort:         [expires_at, desc]
        batch_actions:
          _delete:   ~
          extend:    ~
        object_actions:
          extend:    ~
          _edit:     ~
          _delete:   ~
        actions:
          deleteNeverActivated: { label: Delete never activated jobs }
        table_method: retrieveBackendJobList
      filter:
        display: [category_id, company, position, description,
is_activated, is_public, email, expires_at]
      form:
        class:        BackendJobeetJobForm
        display:
          Content: [category_id, type, company, logo, url, position,
location, description, how_to_apply, is_public, email]
          Admin:   [_generated_token, is_activated, expires_at]
      edit:
        title: Editing Job "%%company%% is looking for a %%position%%"
      new:
        title: Job Creation

# apps/backend/modules/category/config/generator.yml
generator:
  class: sfDoctrineGenerator
  param:
    model_class:            JobeetCategory
```

```
theme:                admin
non_verbose_templates: true
with_show:            false
singular:             ~
plural:               ~
route_prefix:         jobeet_category
with_doctrine_route:  1

config:
  actions: ~
  fields:  ~
  list:
    title:   Category Management
    display: [=name, slug]
    batch_actions: {}
    object_actions: {}
  filter:
    class: false
  form:
    actions:
      _delete: ~
      _list:   ~
      _save:   ~
  edit:
    title: Editing Category "%%name%%"
  new:
    title: New Category
```

With just these two configuration files, we have developed a great backend interface for Jobeet in a matter of minutes.

 You already know that when something is configurable in a YAML file, there is also the possibility to use plain PHP code. For the admin generator, you can edit the **apps/backend/modules/job/lib/ jobGeneratorConfiguration.class.php** file. It gives you the same options as the YAML file but with a PHP interface. To learn the method names, have a look at the generated base class in **cache/backend/dev/modules/autoJob/ lib/BaseJobGeneratorConfiguration.class.php**.

See you Tomorrow

In just one hour, we have built a fully featured backend interface for the Jobeet project. And all in all, we have written less than 50 lines of PHP code. Not too bad for so many features!

Tomorrow, we will see how to secure the backend application with a username and a password. This will also be the occasion to talk about the symfony user class.

Day 13

The User

Yesterday was packed with a lot of information. With very few PHP lines of code, the symfony admin generator allows the developer to create backend interfaces in a matter of minutes.

Today, we will discover how symfony manages persistent data between HTTP requests. As you might know, the HTTP protocol is stateless, which means that each request is independent from its preceding or proceeding ones. Modern websites need a way to persist data between requests to enhance the user experience.

A user session can be identified using a cookie. In symfony, the developer does not need to manipulate the session directly, but rather uses the **sfUser** object, which represents the application end user.

User Flashes

We have already seen the user object in action with flashes. A ~flash|Flash Message~ is an ephemeral message stored in the user session that will be automatically deleted after the very next request. It is very useful when you need to display a message to the user after a redirect. The admin generator uses flashes a lot to display feedback to the user whenever a job is saved, deleted, or extended.

A flash is set by using the **setFlash()** method of **sfUser**:

Listing
13-1
```
// apps/frontend/modules/job/actions/actions.class.php
public function executeExtend(sfWebRequest $request)
{
  $request->checkCSRFProtection();

  $job = $this->getRoute()->getObject();
  $this->forward404Unless($job->extend());

  $this->getUser()->setFlash('notice', sprintf('Your job validity has
been extended until %s.',
$job->getDateTimeObject('expires_at')->format('m/d/Y')));

  $this->redirect('job_show_user', $job);
}
```

The first argument is the identifier of the flash and the second one is the message to display. You can define whatever flashes you want, but **notice** and **error** are two of the more common ones (they are used extensively by the admin generator).

It is up to the developer to include the flash message in the templates. For Jobeet, they are output by the **layout.php**:

Listing
13-2
```
// apps/frontend/templates/layout.php
<?php if ($sf_user->hasFlash('notice')): ?>
  <div class="flash_notice"><?php echo $sf_user->getFlash('notice')
?></div>
<?php endif; ?>
```

```php
<?php if ($sf_user->hasFlash('error')): ?>
  <div class="flash_error"><?php echo $sf_user->getFlash('error')
?></div>
<?php endif; ?>
```

In a template, the user is accessible via the special **sf_user** variable.

 Some symfony objects are always accessible in the templates, without the need to explicitly pass them from the action: **sf_request**, **sf_user**, and **sf_response**.

User Attributes

Unfortunately, the Jobeet user stories have no requirement that includes storing something in the user session. So let's add a new requirement: to ease job browsing, the last three jobs viewed by the user should be displayed in the menu with links to come back to the job page later on.

When a user access a job page, the displayed job object needs to be added in the user history and stored in the session:

Listing 13-3

```php
// apps/frontend/modules/job/actions/actions.class.php
class jobActions extends sfActions
{
  public function executeShow(sfWebRequest $request)
  {
    $this->job = $this->getRoute()->getObject();

    // fetch jobs already stored in the job history
    $jobs = $this->getUser()->getAttribute('job_history', array());

    // add the current job at the beginning of the array
    array_unshift($jobs, $this->job->getId());

    // store the new job history back into the session
    $this->getUser()->setAttribute('job_history', $jobs);
  }

  // ...
}
```

We could have feasibly stored the **JobeetJob** objects directly into the session. This is strongly discouraged because the session variables are serialized between requests. And when the session is loaded, the **JobeetJob** objects are de-serialized and can be "stalled" if they have been modified or deleted in the meantime.

getAttribute(), setAttribute()

Given an identifier, the **sfUser::getAttribute()** method fetches values from the user session. Conversely, the **setAttribute()** method stores any PHP variable in the session for a given identifier.

The **getAttribute()** method also takes an optional default value to return if the identifier is not yet defined.

 The default value taken by the **getAttribute()** method is a shortcut for:

Listing 13-4

```
if (!$value = $this->getAttribute('job_history'))
{
  $value = array();
}
```

The myUser class

To better respect the separation of concerns, let's move the code to the **myUser** class. The **myUser** class overrides the default symfony base **sfUser**[55] class with application specific behaviors:

Listing 13-5

```
// apps/frontend/modules/job/actions/actions.class.php
class jobActions extends sfActions
{
  public function executeShow(sfWebRequest $request)
  {
    $this->job = $this->getRoute()->getObject();

    $this->getUser()->addJobToHistory($this->job);
  }

  // ...
}
```

---

55. http://www.symfony-project.org/api/1_4/sfUser

```
// apps/frontend/lib/myUser.class.php
class myUser extends sfBasicSecurityUser
{
  public function addJobToHistory(JobeetJob $job)
  {
    $ids = $this->getAttribute('job_history', array());

    if (!in_array($job->getId(), $ids))
    {
      array_unshift($ids, $job->getId());

      $this->setAttribute('job_history', array_slice($ids, 0, 3));
    }
  }
}
```

The code has also been changed to take into account all the requirements:

- `!in_array($job->getId(), $ids)`: A job cannot be stored twice in the history
- `array_slice($ids, 0, 3)`: Only the latest three jobs viewed by the user are displayed

In the layout, add the following code before the **$sf_content** variable is output:

```
// apps/frontend/templates/layout.php
<div id="job_history">
  Recent viewed jobs:
  <ul>
    <?php foreach ($sf_user->getJobHistory() as $job): ?>
      <li>
        <?php echo link_to($job->getPosition().' -
'.$job->getCompany(), 'job_show_user', $job) ?>
      </li>
    <?php endforeach; ?>
  </ul>
</div>

<div class="content">
  <?php echo $sf_content ?>
</div>
```

Listing
13-6

The layout uses a new **getJobHistory()** method to retrieve the current job history:

Listing
13-7

```php
// apps/frontend/lib/myUser.class.php
class myUser extends sfBasicSecurityUser
{
  public function getJobHistory()
  {
    $ids = $this->getAttribute('job_history', array());

    if (!empty($ids))
    {
      return Doctrine::getTable('JobeetJob')
        ->createQuery('a')
        ->whereIn('a.id', $ids)
        ->execute();
    }
    else
    {
      return array();
    }
  }

  // ...
}
```

sfParameterHolder

To complete the job history API, let's add a method to reset the history:

Listing
13-8

```php
// apps/frontend/lib/myUser.class.php
class myUser extends sfBasicSecurityUser
{
  public function resetJobHistory()
  {
    $this->getAttributeHolder()->remove('job_history');
  }
```

```
    // ...
}
```

The user attributes are managed by an object of class **sfParameterHolder**. The **getAttribute()** and **setAttribute()** methods are proxy methods for **getParameterHolder()->get()** and **getParameterHolder()->set()**. As the **remove()** method has no proxy method in **sfUser**, you need to use the parameter holder object directly.

 The **sfParameterHolder**[56] class is also used by **sfRequest** to store its parameters.

Application Security

Authentication

Like many other symfony features, security is managed by a YAML file, **security.yml**. For instance, you can find the default configuration for the backend application in the **config/** directory:

```
# apps/backend/config/security.yml
default:
  is_secure: false
```

Listing
13.9

If you switch the **is_secure** entry to **true**, the entire backend application will require the user to be authenticated.

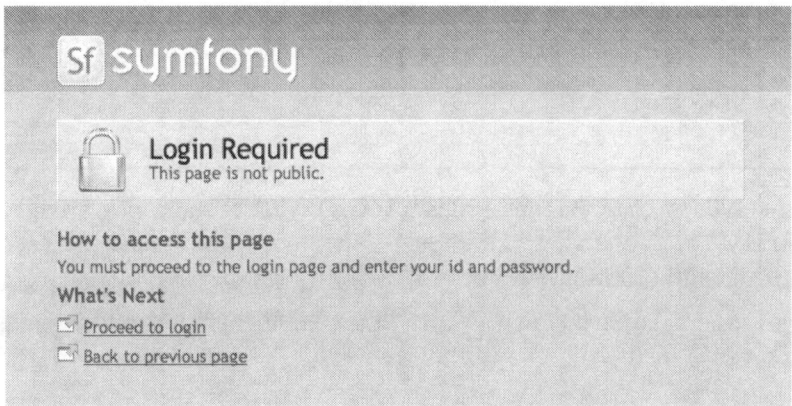

---

56. http://www.symfony-project.org/api/1_4/sfParameterHolder

In a YAML file, a Boolean can be expressed with the strings **true** and **false**.

If you have a look at the logs in the web debug toolbar, you will notice that the **executeLogin()** method of the **defaultActions** class is called for every page you try to access.

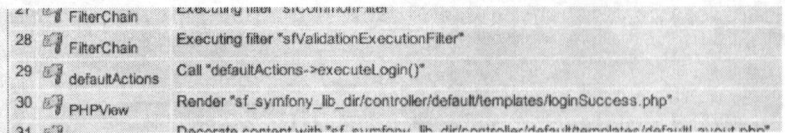

When an un-authenticated user tries to access a secured action, symfony forwards the request to the **login** action configured in **settings.yml**:

Listing 13-10
```
all:
  .actions:
    login_module: default
    login_action: login
```

 It is not possible to secure the login action to avoid infinite recursion.

 As we saw during day 4, the same configuration file can be defined in several places. This is also the case for **security.yml**. To only secure or un-secure a single action or a whole module, create a **security.yml** in the **config/** directory of the module:

Listing 13-11
```
index:
  is_secure: false

all:
  is_secure: true
```

By default, the **myUser** class extends **sfBasicSecurityUser**[57], and not **sfUser**. **sfBasicSecurityUser** provides additional methods to manage user authentication and authorization.

To manage user authentication, use the **isAuthenticated()** and **setAuthenticated()** methods:

---

57. http://www.symfony-project.org/api/1_4/sfBasicSecurityUser

```
if (!$this->getUser()->isAuthenticated())
{
  $this->getUser()->setAuthenticated(true);
}
```

Listing
13-12

Authorization

When a user is authenticated, the access to some actions can be even more restricted by defining **credentials**. A user must have the required credentials to access the page:

```
default:
  is_secure:   false
  credentials: admin
```

Listing
13-13

The credential system of symfony is quite simple and powerful. A credential can represent anything you need to describe the application security model (like groups or permissions).

Complex Credentials

The credentials entry of security.yml supports Boolean operations to describe complex credentials requirements.

If a user must have credential A **and** B, wrap the credentials with square brackets:

```
index:
  credentials: [A, B]
```

Listing
13-14

If a user must have credential A **or** B, wrap them with two pairs of square brackets:

```
index:
  credentials: [[A, B]]
```

Listing
13-15

You can even mix and match brackets to describe any kind of Boolean expression with any number of credentials.

To manage the user credentials, sfBasicSecurityUser provides several methods:

```
// Add one or more credentials
$user->addCredential('foo');
$user->addCredentials('foo', 'bar');
```

Listing
13-16

```
// Check if the user has a credential
echo $user->hasCredential('foo');                       =>      true

// Check if the user has both credentials
echo $user->hasCredential(array('foo', 'bar'));         =>      true

// Check if the user has one of the credentials
echo $user->hasCredential(array('foo', 'bar'), false); =>      true

// Remove a credential
$user->removeCredential('foo');
echo $user->hasCredential('foo');                       =>      false

// Remove all credentials (useful in the logout process)
$user->clearCredentials();
echo $user->hasCredential('bar');                       =>      false
```

For the Jobeet backend, we won't use any credentials as we only have one profile: the administrator.

Plugins

As we don't like to reinvent the wheel, we won't develop the login action from scratch. Instead, we will install a **symfony plugin**.

One of the great strengths of the symfony framework is the plugin ecosystem. As we will see in coming days, it is very easy to create a plugin. It is also quite powerful, as a plugin can contain anything from configuration to modules and assets.

Today, we will install sfDoctrineGuardPlugin[58] to secure the backend application

Listing 13-17
```
$ php symfony plugin:install sfDoctrineGuardPlugin
```

The **plugin:install** task installs a plugin by name. All plugins are stored under the **plugins/** directory and each one has its own directory named after the plugin name.

 PEAR must be installed for the **plugin:install** task to work.

---

58. http://www.symfony-project.org/plugins/sfDoctrineGuardPlugin

When you install a plugin with the **plugin:install** task, symfony installs the latest stable version of it. To install a specific version of a plugin, pass the **--release** option.

The plugin page[59] lists all available version grouped by symfony version.

As a plugin is self-contained into a directory, you can also download the package[60] from the symfony website and unarchive it, or alternatively make an **svn:externals** link to its Subversion repository[61].

The **plugin:install** task automatically enables the plugin(s) it installs by automatically updating the **ProjectConfiguration.class.php** file. But if you install a plugin via Subversion or by downloading its archive, you need to enable it by hand in **ProjectConfiguration.class.php**:

```
// config/ProjectConfiguration.class.php
class ProjectConfiguration extends sfProjectConfiguration
{
  public function setup()
  {
    $this->enablePlugins('sfDoctrinePlugin', 'sfDoctrineGuardPlugin');
  }
}
```

Listing 13-18

Backend Security

Each plugin has a README[62] file that explains how to configure it.

Let's see how to configure the new plugin. As the plugin provides several new model classes to manage users, groups, and permissions, you need to rebuild your model:

```
$ php symfony doctrine:build --all --and-load
```

Listing 13-19

 Remember that the **doctrine:build --all --and-load** task removes all existing tables before re-creating them. To avoid this, you can build the

---

59. http://www.symfony-project.org/plugins/
sfDoctrineGuardPlugin?tab=plugin_all_releases
60. http://www.symfony-project.org/plugins/
sfDoctrineGuardPlugin?tab=plugin_installation
61. http://svn.symfony-project.com/plugins/sfDoctrineGuardPlugin
62. http://www.symfony-project.org/plugins/sfGuardPlugin?tab=plugin_readme

models, forms, and filters, and then, create the new tables by executing the generated SQL statements stored in **data/sql/**.

As **sfDoctrineGuardPlugin** adds several methods to the user class, you need to change the base class of **myUser** to **sfGuardSecurityUser**:

Listing 13-20

```php
// apps/backend/lib/myUser.class.php
class myUser extends sfGuardSecurityUser
{
}
```

sfDoctrineGuardPlugin provides a **signin** action in the **sfGuardAuth** module to authenticate users.

Edit the **settings.yml** file to change the default action used for the login page:

Listing 13-21

```yaml
# apps/backend/config/settings.yml
all:
  .settings:
    enabled_modules: [default, sfGuardAuth]

    # ...

  .actions:
    login_module:    sfGuardAuth
    login_action:    signin

    # ...
```

As plugins are shared amongst all applications of a project, you need to explicitly enable the modules you want to use by adding them in the **enabled_modules** setting.

The last step is to create an administrator user:

```
$ php symfony guard:create-user fabien SecretPass
$ php symfony guard:promote fabien
```

Listing
13-22

 The sfGuardPlugin provides tasks to manage users, groups, and permissions from the command line. Use the **list** task to list all task belonging to the guard namespace:

```
$ php symfony list guard
```

Listing
13-23

When the user is not authenticated, we need to hide the menu bar:

```
// apps/backend/templates/layout.php
<?php if ($sf_user->isAuthenticated()): ?>
  <div id="menu">
    <ul>
      <li><?php echo link_to('Jobs', '@jobeet_job_job') ?></li>
      <li><?php echo link_to('Categories',
'@jobeet_category_category') ?></li>
    </ul>
  </div>
<?php endif; ?>
```

Listing
13-24

And when the user is authenticated, we need to add a logout link in the menu:

```
// apps/backend/templates/layout.php
<li><?php echo link_to('Logout', '@sf_guard_signout') ?></li>
```

Listing
13-25

 To list all routes provided by sfGuardPlugin, use the **app:routes** task.

To polish the Jobeet backend even more, let's add a new module to manage the administrator users. Thankfully, sfGuardPlugin provides such a module. As for the sfGuardAuth module, you need to enable it in **settings.yml**:

```
// apps/backend/config/settings.yml
all:
  .settings:
    enabled_modules: [default, sfGuardAuth, sfGuardUser]
```

Listing
13-26

Add a link in the menu:

Listing
13-27

```
// apps/backend/templates/layout.php
<li><?php echo link_to('Users', '@sf_guard_user') ?></li>
```

We are done!

User Testing

Today's tutorial is not over as we have not yet talked about user testing. As the symfony browser simulates cookies, it is quite easy to test user behaviors by using the built-in **sfTesterUser**[63] tester.

Let's update the functional tests for the menu feature we have added today. Add the following code at the end of the **job** module functional tests:

Listing 13-28

```
// test/functional/frontend/jobActionsTest.php
$browser->
  info('4 - User job history')->

  loadData()->
  restart()->

  info(' 4.1 - When the user access a job, it is added to its
history')->
  get('/')->
  click('Web Developer', array(), array('position' => 1))->
  get('/')->
  with('user')->begin()->
    isAttribute('job_history',
array($browser->getMostRecentProgrammingJob()->getId()))->
  end()->

  info(' 4.2 - A job is not added twice in the history')->
  click('Web Developer', array(), array('position' => 1))->
  get('/')->
```

---

63. http://symfony-project.org/api/1_4/sfTesterUser

```
  with('user')->begin()->
    isAttribute('job_history',
array($browser->getMostRecentProgrammingJob()->getId()))->
  end()
;
```

To ease testing, we first reload the fixtures data and restart the browser to start with a clean session.

The **isAttribute()** method checks a given user attribute.

 The **sfTesterUser** tester also provides **isAuthenticated()** and **hasCredential()** methods to test user authentication and autorizations.

See you Tomorrow

The symfony user classes are a nice way to abstract the PHP session management. Coupled with the great symfony plugin system and the **sfGuardPlugin** plugin, we have been able to secure the Jobeet backend in a matter of minutes. And we have even added a clean interface to manage our administrator users for free, thanks to the modules provided by the plugin.

Day 14

Feeds

Yesterday, you started developing your first very own symfony application. Don't stop now. As you learn more on symfony, try to add new features to your application, host it somewhere, and share it with the community.

Let's move on to something completely different today.

If you are looking for a job, you will probably want to be informed as soon as a new job is posted. Because it is not very convenient to check the website every other hour, we will add several job feeds today to keep our Jobeet users up-to-date.

Formats

The symfony framework has native support for formats and mime-types. This means that the same Model and Controller can have different templates based on the requested format. The default format is HTML but symfony supports ~several other formats|Built-in Formats~ out of the box like **txt**, **js**, **css**, **json**, **xml**, **rdf**, or **atom**.

The format can be set by using the **setRequestFormat()** method of the request object:

```
$request->setRequestFormat('xml');
```

Listing 14-1

But most of the time, the format is embedded in the URL. In this case, symfony will set it for you if the special **sf_format** variable is used in the corresponding route. For the job list, the list URL is:

```
http://jobeet.localhost/frontend_dev.php/job
```

Listing 14-2

This URL is equivalent to:

Listing
14-3 `http://jobeet.localhost/frontend_dev.php/job.html`

Both URLs are equivalent because the routes generated by the
sfDoctrineRouteCollection class have the **sf_format** as the extension and
because `html` is the default format. You can check it for yourself by running the
app:routes task:

```
~/work/jobeet $ ./symfony app:routes frontend
>> app       Current routes for application "frontend"
Name        Method Pattern
category    ANY    /category/:slug
job         GET    /job.:sf_format
job_new     GET    /job/new.:sf_format
job_create  POST   /job.:sf_format
job_edit    GET    /job/:token/edit.:sf_format
job_update  PUT    /job/:token.:sf_format
job_delete  DELETE /job/:token.:sf_format
job_show    GET    /job/:token.:sf_format
job_publish PUT    /job/:token/publish.:sf_format
job_extend  PUT    /job/:token/extend.:sf_format
job_show_user GET  /job/:company_slug/:location_slug/:id/:position_slug
homepage    ANY    /
~/work/jobeet $
```

Feeds

Latest Jobs Feed

Supporting different formats is as easy as creating different templates. To create an
Atom feed[64] for the latest jobs, create an **indexSuccess.atom.php** template:

Listing
14-4
```php
<!-- apps/frontend/modules/job/templates/indexSuccess.atom.php -->
<?xml version="1.0" encoding="utf-8"?>
<feed xmlns="http://www.w3.org/2005/Atom">
  <title>Jobeet</title>
  <subtitle>Latest Jobs</subtitle>
  <link href="" rel="self"/>
  <link href=""/>
  <updated></updated>
  <author><name>Jobeet</name></author>
  <id>Unique Id</id>

  <entry>
    <title>Job title</title>
    <link href="" />
```

---

64. `http://en.wikipedia.org/wiki/Atom_(standard)`

```
    <id>Unique id</id>
    <updated></updated>
    <summary>Job description</summary>
    <author><name>Company</name></author>
  </entry>
</feed>
```

Template Names

As html is the most common format used for web applications, it can be omitted from the template name. Both indexSuccess.php and indexSuccess.html.php templates are equivalent and symfony uses the first one it finds.

Why are default templates suffixed with Success? An action can return a value to indicate which template to render. If the action returns nothing, it is equivalent to the following code:

```
return sfView::SUCCESS; // == 'Success'
```
Listing 14-5

If you want to change the suffix, just return something else:

```
return sfView::ERROR; // == 'Error'
```
Listing 14-6

```
return 'Foo';
```

As seen in a previous day, the name of the template can also be changed by using the setTemplate() method:

```
$this->setTemplate('foo');
```
Listing 14-7

By default, symfony will change the response Content-Type according to the format, and for all non-HTML formats, the layout is disabled. For an Atom feed, symfony changes the Content-Type to application/atom+xml; charset=utf-8.

In the Jobeet footer, update the link to the feed:

```
<!-- apps/frontend/templates/layout.php -->
<li class="feed">
  <a href="<?php echo url_for('@job?sf_format=atom') ?>">Full feed</a>
</li>
```
Listing 14-8

The internal URI is the same as for the job list with the sf_format added as a variable.

Add a `<link>` tag in the head section of the layout to allow automatic discover by the browser of our feed:

Listing
14-9

```
<!-- apps/frontend/templates/layout.php -->
<link rel="alternate" type="application/atom+xml" title="Latest Jobs"
  href="<?php echo url_for('@job?sf_format=atom', true) ?>" />
```

For the link **href** attribute, an URL (Absolute) is used thanks to the second argument of the **url_for()** helper.

Replace the Atom template header with the following code:

Listing
14-10

```
<!-- apps/frontend/modules/job/templates/indexSuccess.atom.php -->
<title>Jobeet</title>
<subtitle>Latest Jobs</subtitle>
<link href="<?php echo url_for('@job?sf_format=atom', true) ?>"
rel="self"/>
<link href="<?php echo url_for('@homepage', true) ?>"/>
<updated><?php echo gmstrftime('%Y-%m-%dT%H:%M:%SZ',
Doctrine::getTable('JobeetJob')->getLatestPost()->getDateTimeObject('created_at')
?></updated>
<author>
  <name>Jobeet</name>
</author>
<id><?php echo sha1(url_for('@job?sf_format=atom', true)) ?></id>
```

Notice the usage of the **U** as an argument to **format()** to get the date as a timestamp. To get the date of the latest post, create the **getLatestPost()** method:

Listing
14-11

```
// lib/model/doctrine/JobeetJobTable.class.php
class JobeetJobTable extends Doctrine_Table
{
  public function getLatestPost()
  {
    $q = Doctrine_Query::create()
      ->from('JobeetJob j');
    $this->addActiveJobsQuery($q);

    return $q->fetchOne();
  }

  // ...
}
```

The feed entries can be generated with the following code:

Listing
14-12

```php
<!-- apps/frontend/modules/job/templates/indexSuccess.atom.php -->
<?php use_helper('Text') ?>
<?php foreach ($categories as $category): ?>
  <?php foreach
($category->getActiveJobs(sfConfig::get('app_max_jobs_on_homepage'))
as $job): ?>
    <entry>
      <title>
        <?php echo $job->getPosition() ?> (<?php echo
$job->getLocation() ?>)
      </title>
      <link href="<?php echo url_for('job_show_user', $job, true) ?>"
/>
      <id><?php echo sha1($job->getId()) ?></id>
      <updated><?php echo gmstrftime('%Y-%m-%dT%H:%M:%SZ',
$job->getDateTimeObject('created_at')->format('U')) ?></updated>
      <summary type="xhtml">
        <div xmlns="http://www.w3.org/1999/xhtml">
          <?php if ($job->getLogo()): ?>
            <div>
              <a href="<?php echo $job->getUrl() ?>">
                <img src="http://<?php echo $sf_request->getHost().'/
uploads/jobs/'.$job->getLogo() ?>"
                  alt="<?php echo $job->getCompany() ?> logo" />
              </a>
            </div>
          <?php endif; ?>

          <div>
            <?php echo simple_format_text($job->getDescription()) ?>
          </div>

          <h4>How to apply?</h4>

          <p><?php echo $job->getHowToApply() ?></p>
        </div>
      </summary>
      <author>
        <name><?php echo $job->getCompany() ?></name>
      </author>
    </entry>
  <?php endforeach; ?>
<?php endforeach; ?>
```

The getHost() method of the request object ($sf_request) returns the current host, which comes in handy for creating an absolute link for the company logo.

 When creating a feed, debugging is easier if you use command line tools like curl[65] or wget[66], as you see the actual content of the feed.

Latest Jobs in a Category Feed

One of the goals of Jobeet is to help people find more targeted jobs. So, we need to provide a feed for each category.

First, let's update the **category** route to add support for different formats:

Listing 14-13

```
// apps/frontend/config/routing.yml
category:
  url:     /category/:slug.:sf_format
  class:   sfDoctrineRoute
  param:   { module: category, action: show, sf_format: html }
  options: { model: JobeetCategory, type: object }
  requirements:
    sf_format: (?:html|atom)
```

Now, the **category** route will understand both the **html** and **atom** formats. Update the links to category feeds in the templates:

---

65. http://curl.haxx.se/
66. http://www.gnu.org/software/wget/

```
<!-- apps/frontend/modules/job/templates/indexSuccess.php -->
<div class="feed">
  <a href="<?php echo url_for('category', array('sf_subject' =>
$category, 'sf_format' => 'atom')) ?>">Feed</a>
</div>

<!-- apps/frontend/modules/category/templates/showSuccess.php -->
<div class="feed">
  <a href="<?php echo url_for('category', array('sf_subject' =>
$category, 'sf_format' => 'atom')) ?>">Feed</a>
</div>
```

Listing
14-14

The last step is to create the **showSuccess.atom.php** template. But as this feed will
also list jobs, we can refactor the code that generates the feed entries by creating a
_list.atom.php partial. As for the **html** format, partials are format specific:

Listing
14-15

```
<!-- apps/frontend/job/templates/_list.atom.php -->
<?php use_helper('Text') ?>

<?php foreach ($jobs as $job): ?>
  <entry>
    <title><?php echo $job->getPosition() ?> (<?php echo
$job->getLocation() ?>)</title>
    <link href="<?php echo url_for('job_show_user', $job, true) ?>" />
    <id><?php echo sha1($job->getId()) ?></id>
      <updated><?php echo gmstrftime('%Y-%m-%dT%H:%M:%SZ',
$job->getDateTimeObject('created_at')->format('U')) ?></updated>
    <summary type="xhtml">
     <div xmlns="http://www.w3.org/1999/xhtml">
       <?php if ($job->getLogo()): ?>
         <div>
           <a href="<?php echo $job->getUrl() ?>">
             <img src="http://<?php echo $sf_request->getHost().'/
uploads/jobs/'.$job->getLogo() ?>"
               alt="<?php echo $job->getCompany() ?> logo" />
           </a>
         </div>
       <?php endif; ?>

       <div>
         <?php echo simple_format_text($job->getDescription()) ?>
       </div>

       <h4>How to apply?</h4>
```

```
        <p><?php echo $job->getHowToApply() ?></p>
      </div>
    </summary>
    <author>
      <name><?php echo $job->getCompany() ?></name>
    </author>
  </entry>
<?php endforeach; ?>
```

You can use the _list.atom.php partial to simplify the job feed template:

Listing
14-16
```
<!-- apps/frontend/modules/job/templates/indexSuccess.atom.php -->
<?xml version="1.0" encoding="utf-8"?>
<feed xmlns="http://www.w3.org/2005/Atom">
  <title>Jobeet</title>
  <subtitle>Latest Jobs</subtitle>
  <link href="<?php echo url_for('@job?sf_format=atom', true) ?>"
rel="self"/>
  <link href="<?php echo url_for('@homepage', true) ?>"/>
  <updated><?php echo gmstrftime('%Y-%m-%dT%H:%M:%SZ',
Doctrine::getTable('JobeetJob')->getLatestPost()->getDateTimeObject('created_at')
?></updated>
  <author>
    <name>Jobeet</name>
  </author>
  <id><?php echo sha1(url_for('@job?sf_format=atom', true)) ?></id>

<?php foreach ($categories as $category): ?>
  <?php include_partial('job/list', array('jobs' =>
$category->getActiveJobs(sfConfig::get('app_max_jobs_on_homepage'))))
?>
<?php endforeach; ?>
</feed>
```

Eventually, create the showSuccess.atom.php template:

Listing
14-17
```
<!-- apps/frontend/modules/category/templates/showSuccess.atom.php -->
<?xml version="1.0" encoding="utf-8"?>
<feed xmlns="http://www.w3.org/2005/Atom">
  <title>Jobeet (<?php echo $category ?>)</title>
  <subtitle>Latest Jobs</subtitle>
  <link href="<?php echo url_for('category', array('sf_subject' =>
$category, 'sf_format' => 'atom'), true) ?>" rel="self" />
  <link href="<?php echo url_for('category', array('sf_subject' =>
$category), true) ?>" />
```

```
  <updated><?php echo gmstrftime('%Y-%m-%dT%H:%M:%SZ',
$category->getLatestPost()->getDateTimeObject('created_at')->format('U'))
?></updated>
  <author>
    <name>Jobeet</name>
  </author>
  <id><?php echo sha1(url_for('category', array('sf_subject' =>
$category), true)) ?></id>

  <?php include_partial('job/list', array('jobs' =>
$pager->getResults())) ?>
</feed>
```

As for the main job feed, we need the date of the latest job for a category:

Listing
14-18

```
// lib/model/doctrine/JobeetCategory.class.php
class JobeetCategory extends BaseJobeetCategory
{
  public function getLatestPost()
  {
    $jobs = $this->getActiveJobs(1);

    return $jobs[0];
  }

  // ...
}
```

See you Tomorrow

As with many symfony features, the native format support allows you to add feeds to your websites without effort.

Today, we have enhanced the job seeker experience. Tomorrow, we will see how to provide greater exposure to the job posters by providing a Web Service.

Day 15

Web Services

With the addition of feeds on Jobeet, job seekers can now be informed of new jobs in real-time.

On the other side of the fence, when you post a job, you will want to have the greatest exposure possible. If your job is syndicated on a lot of small websites, you will have a better chance to find the right person. That's the power of the long tail[67]. Affiliates will be able to publish the latest posted jobs on their websites thanks to the web services we will develop today.

Affiliates

As per day 2 requirements:

"Story F7: An affiliate retrieves the current active job list"

The Fixtures

Let's create a new fixture file for the affiliates:

Listing 15-1

```
# data/fixtures/affiliates.yml
JobeetAffiliate:
  sensio_labs:
    url:       http://www.sensio-labs.com/
    email:     fabien.potencier@example.com
    is_active: true
    token:     sensio_labs
    JobeetCategories: [programming]
```

---

67. http://en.wikipedia.org/wiki/The_Long_Tail

```
symfony:
  url:       http://www.symfony-project.org/
  email:     fabien.potencier@example.org
  is_active: false
  token:     symfony
  JobeetCategories: [design, programming]
```

Creating records for many-to-many relationships is as simple as defining an array with the key which is the name of the relationship. The content of the array is the object names as defined in the fixture files. You can link objects from different files, but the names must be defined first.

In the fixture file, the tokens are hardcoded to simplify the testing, but when an actual user applies for an account, the token will need to be generated:

Listing
15-2

```
// lib/model/doctrine/JobeetAffiliate.php
class JobeetAffiliate extends BaseJobeetAffiliate
{
  public function preValidate($event)
  {
    $object = $event->getInvoker();

    if (!$object->getToken())
    {
      $object->setToken(sha1($object->getEmail().rand(11111, 99999)));
    }
  }

  // ...
}
```

You can now reload the data:

Listing
15-3

```
$ php symfony doctrine:data-load
```

The Job Web Service

As always, when you create a new resource, it's a good habit to define the URL first:

Listing
15-4

```
# apps/frontend/config/routing.yml
api_jobs:
  url:     /api/:token/jobs.:sf_format
  class:   sfDoctrineRoute
```

```
param:    { module: api, action: list }
options: { model: JobeetJob, type: list, method: getForToken }
requirements:
  sf_format: (?:xml|json|yaml)
```

For this route, the special **sf_format** variable ends the URL and the valid values
are **xml**, **json**, or **yaml**.

The **getForToken()** method is called when the action retrieves the collection of
objects related to the route. As we need to check that the affiliate is activated, we
need to override the default behavior of the route:

```
// lib/model/doctrine/JobeetJobTable.class.php
class JobeetJobTable extends Doctrine_Table
{
  public function getForToken(array $parameters)
  {
    $affiliate = Doctrine::getTable('JobeetAffiliate')
        ➥ ->findOneByToken($parameters['token']);
    if (!$affiliate || !$affiliate->getIsActive())
    {
      throw new sfError404Exception(sprintf('Affiliate with token "%s"
does not exist or is not activated.', $parameters['token']));
    }

    return $affiliate->getActiveJobs();
  }

  // ...
}
```

Listing 15-5

If the token does not exist in the database, we throw a **sfError404Exception**
exception. This exception class is then automatically converted to a **~404|404
Error~** response. This is the simplest way to generate a **404** page from a model
class.

The **getForToken()** method uses one new method named **getActiveJobs()** and
returns the list of currently active jobs:

```
// lib/model/doctrine/JobeetAffiliate.class.php
class JobeetAffiliate extends BaseJobeetAffiliate
{
  public function getActiveJobs()
  {
    $q = Doctrine_Query::create()
      ->select('j.*')
```

Listing 15-6

```
        ->from('JobeetJob j')
        ->leftJoin('j.JobeetCategory c')
        ->leftJoin('c.JobeetAffiliates a')
        ->where('a.id = ?', $this->getId());

    $q = Doctrine::getTable('JobeetJob')->addActiveJobsQuery($q);

    return $q->execute();
  }

  // ...
}
```

The last step is to create the **api** action and templates. Bootstrap the module with the **generate:module** task:

*Listing
15-7*
```
$ php symfony generate:module frontend api
```

 As we won't use the default **index** action, you can remove it from the action class, and remove the associated template **indexSucess.php**.

The Action

All formats share the same **list** action:

*Listing
15-8*
```
// apps/frontend/modules/api/actions/actions.class.php
public function executeList(sfWebRequest $request)
{
  $this->jobs = array();
  foreach ($this->getRoute()->getObjects() as $job)
  {
    $this->jobs[$this->generateUrl('job_show_user', $job, true)] =
    ➥ $job->asArray($request->getHost());
  }
}
```

Instead of passing an array of **JobeetJob** objects to the templates, we pass an array of strings. As we have three different templates for the same action, the logic to process the values has been factored out in the **JobeetJob::asArray()** method:

*Listing
15-9*
```
// lib/model/doctrine/JobeetJob.class.php
class JobeetJob extends BaseJobeetJob
{
```

```php
  public function asArray($host)
  {
    return array(
      'category'     => $this->getJobeetCategory()->getName(),
      'type'         => $this->getType(),
      'company'      => $this->getCompany(),
      'logo'         => $this->getLogo() ? 'http://'.$host.'/uploads/
jobs/'.$this->getLogo() : null,
      'url'          => $this->getUrl(),
      'position'     => $this->getPosition(),
      'location'     => $this->getLocation(),
      'description'  => $this->getDescription(),
      'how_to_apply' => $this->getHowToApply(),
      'expires_at'   => $this->getCreatedAt(),
    );
  }

  // ...
}
```

The xml Format

Supporting the **xml** format is as simple as creating a template:

Listing
15-10

```php
<!-- apps/frontend/modules/api/templates/listSuccess.xml.php -->
<?xml version="1.0" encoding="utf-8"?>
<jobs>
<?php foreach ($jobs as $url => $job): ?>
  <job url="<?php echo $url ?>">
<?php foreach ($job as $key => $value): ?>
    <<?php echo $key ?>><?php echo $value ?></<?php echo $key ?>>
<?php endforeach; ?>
  </job>
<?php endforeach; ?>
</jobs>
```

The json Format

Support the JSON format[68] is similar:

Listing
15-11

```php
<!-- apps/frontend/modules/api/templates/listSuccess.json.php -->
[
<?php $nb = count($jobs); $i = 0; foreach ($jobs as $url => $job):
```

---

68. http://json.org/

```
++$i ?>
{
  "url": "<?php echo $url ?>",
<?php $nb1 = count($job); $j = 0; foreach ($job as $key => $value):
++$j ?>
  "<?php echo $key ?>": <?php echo json_encode($value).($nb1 == $j ?
'' : ',') ?>

<?php endforeach; ?>
}<?php echo $nb == $i ? '' : ',' ?>

<?php endforeach; ?>
]
```

The yaml Format

For built-in formats, symfony does some configuration in the background, like changing the content type, or disabling the layout.

As the YAML format is not in the list of the built-in request formats, the response content type can be changed and the layout disabled in the action:

Listing 15-12
```
class apiActions extends sfActions
{
  public function executeList(sfWebRequest $request)
  {
    $this->jobs = array();
    foreach ($this->getRoute()->getObjects() as $job)
    {
      $this->jobs[$this->generateUrl('job_show_user', $job, true)] =
        ➥ $job->asArray($request->getHost());
    }

    switch ($request->getRequestFormat())
    {
      case 'yaml':
        $this->setLayout(false);
        $this->getResponse()->setContentType('text/yaml');
        break;
    }
  }
}
```

In an action, the **setLayout()** method changes the default layout or disables it when set to **false**.

The template for YAML reads as follows:

Listing
15-13

```
<!-- apps/frontend/modules/api/templates/listSuccess.yaml.php -->
<?php foreach ($jobs as $url => $job): ?>
-
  url: <?php echo $url ?>

<?php foreach ($job as $key => $value): ?>
  <?php echo $key ?>: <?php echo sfYaml::dump($value) ?>

<?php endforeach; ?>
<?php endforeach; ?>
```

If you try to call the web service with a non-valid token, you will have a 404 XML page for the XML format, and a 404 JSON page for the JSON format. But for the YAML format, symfony does not know what to render.

Whenever you create a format, a custom error template must be created. The template will be used for 404 pages, and all other exceptions.

As the exception should be different in the production and development environment, two files are needed (**config/error/exception.yaml.php** for debugging, and **config/error/error.yaml.php** for production):

Listing
15-14

```
// config/error/exception.yaml.php
<?php echo sfYaml::dump(array(
  'error'      => array(
    'code'     => $code,
    'message'  => $message,
    'debug'    => array(
      'name'   => $name,
      'message' => $message,
      'traces' => $traces,
    ),
)), 4) ?>

// config/error/error.yaml.php
<?php echo sfYaml::dump(array(
  'error'      => array(
    'code'     => $code,
    'message'  => $message,
))) ?>
```

Before trying it, you must create a layout for YAML format:

Listing
15-15

```
// apps/frontend/templates/layout.yaml.php
<?php echo $sf_content ?>
```

```
~/work/jobeet $ curl http://jobeet.localhost/frontend_dev.php/api/sensio_lab/jobs.yaml
error:
  code: 404
  message: 'Affiliate with token "sensio_lab" does not exist or is not activated.'
  debug:
    name: sfError404Exception
    message: 'Affiliate with token "sensio_lab" does not exist or is not activated.'
    traces:
      - 'at () in SF_ROOT_DIR/lib/model/JobeetJobPeer.php line 12'
      - 'at JobeetJobPeer::getForToken(array(''token'' =&gt; ''sensio_lab'', ''sf_format''
      - 'at call_user_func(array(''JobeetJobPeer'', ''getForToken''), array(''token'' =&gt
      - 'at sfObjectRoute->getObjectForParameters(array(''module'' =&gt; ''api'', ''action
sfPropelPlugin/lib/routing/sfPropelRoute.class.php line 100'
      - 'at sfPropelRoute->getObjectsForParameters(array(''module'' =&gt; ''api'', ''actio
/sfObjectRoute.class.php line 141'
      - 'at sfObjectRoute->getObjects() in SF_ROOT_DIR/apps/frontend/modules/api/actions/a
```

 Overriding the 404 error and exception templates for built-in templates is as simple as creating a file in the **config/error/** directory.

Web Service Tests

To test the web service, copy the affiliate fixtures from **data/fixtures/** to the **test/fixtures/** directory and replace the content of the auto-generated **apiActionsTest.php** file with the following content:

Listing 15-16

```php
// test/functional/frontend/apiActionsTest.php
include(dirname(__FILE__).'/../../bootstrap/functional.php');

$browser = new JobeetTestFunctional(new sfBrowser());
$browser->loadData();

$browser->
  info('1 - Web service security')->

  info('  1.1 - A token is needed to access the service')->
  get('/api/foo/jobs.xml')->
  with('response')->isStatusCode(404)->

  info('  1.2 - An inactive account cannot access the web service')->
  get('/api/symfony/jobs.xml')->
  with('response')->isStatusCode(404)->

  info('2 - The jobs returned are limited to the categories configured
for the affiliate')->
```

```
get('/api/sensio_labs/jobs.xml')->
with('request')->isFormat('xml')->
with('response')->checkElement('job', 32)->

info('3 - The web service supports the JSON format')->
get('/api/sensio_labs/jobs.json')->
with('request')->isFormat('json')->
with('response')->matches('/"category"\: "Programming"/')->

info('4 - The web service supports the YAML format')->
get('/api/sensio_labs/jobs.yaml')->
with('response')->begin()->
  isHeader('content-type', 'text/yaml; charset=utf-8')->
  matches('/category\: Programming/')->
end()
;
```

In this test, you will notice two new methods:

- isFormat(): It tests the format of a request
- matches(): For non-HTML format, if checks that the response verifies the regex passed as an argument

The Affiliate Application Form

Now that the web service is ready to be used, let's create the account creation form for affiliates. We will yet again describe the classic process of adding a new feature to an application.

Routing

You guess it. The route is the first thing we create:

Listing
15-17

```
# apps/frontend/config/routing.yml
affiliate:
  class:    sfDoctrineRouteCollection
  options:
    model: JobeetAffiliate
    actions: [new, create]
    object_actions: { wait: get }
```

It is a classic Doctrine collection route with a new configuration option: **actions**. As we don't need all the seven default actions defined by the route, the **actions** option instructs the route to only match for the **new** and **create** actions. The additional **wait** route will be used to give the soon-to-be affiliate some feedback about his account.

Bootstrapping

The classic second step is to generate a module:

Listing
15-18

```
$ php symfony doctrine:generate-module frontend affiliate
JobeetAffiliate --non-verbose-templates
```

Templates

The **doctrine:generate-module** task generate the classic seven actions and their corresponding templates. In the **templates/** directory, remove all the files but the **_form.php** and **newSuccess.php** ones. And for the files we keep, replace their content with the following:

Listing
15-19

```
<!-- apps/frontend/modules/affiliate/templates/newSuccess.php -->
<?php use_stylesheet('job.css') ?>

<h1>Become an Affiliate</h1>

<?php include_partial('form', array('form' => $form)) ?>

<!-- apps/frontend/modules/affiliate/templates/_form.php -->
<?php include_stylesheets_for_form($form) ?>
<?php include_javascripts_for_form($form) ?>

<?php echo form_tag_for($form, 'affiliate') ?>
  <table id="job_form">
    <tfoot>
      <tr>
        <td colspan="2">
          <input type="submit" value="Submit" />
        </td>
      </tr>
    </tfoot>
    <tbody>
      <?php echo $form ?>
    </tbody>
  </table>
</form>
```

Create the **waitSuccess.php** template:

Listing
15-20

```
<!-- apps/frontend/modules/affiliate/templates/waitSuccess.php -->
<h1>Your affiliate account has been created</h1>

<div style="padding: 20px">
  Thank you!
  You will receive an email with your affiliate token
  as soon as your account will be activated.
</div>
```

Last, change the link in the footer to point to the **affiliate** module:

Listing
15-21

```
// apps/frontend/templates/layout.php
<li class="last">
  <a href="<?php echo url_for('@affiliate_new') ?>">Become an
affiliate</a>
</li>
```

Actions

Here again, as we will only use the creation form, open the **actions.class.php** file and remove all methods but **executeNew()**, **executeCreate()**, and **processForm()**.

For the **processForm()** action, change the redirect URL to the **wait** action:

Listing
15-22

```
// apps/frontend/modules/affiliate/actions/actions.class.php
$this->redirect($this->generateUrl('affiliate_wait',
$jobeet_affiliate));
```

The **wait** action is simple as we don't need to pass anything to the template:

Listing
15-23

```
// apps/frontend/modules/affiliate/actions/actions.class.php
public function executeWait()
{
}
```

The affiliate cannot choose its token, nor can he activates his account right away. Open the **JobeetAffiliateForm** file to customize the form:

Listing
15-24

```
// lib/form/doctrine/JobeetAffiliateForm.class.php
class JobeetAffiliateForm extends BaseJobeetAffiliateForm
{
  public function configure()
```

```
  {
    unset($this['is_active'], $this['token'], $this['created_at'],
$this['updated_at']);


$this->widgetSchema['jobeet_categories_list']->setOption('expanded',
true);

$this->widgetSchema['jobeet_categories_list']->setLabel('Categories');


$this->validatorSchema['jobeet_categories_list']->setOption('required',
true);

    $this->widgetSchema['url']->setLabel('Your website URL');
    $this->widgetSchema['url']->setAttribute('size', 50);

    $this->widgetSchema['email']->setAttribute('size', 50);

    $this->validatorSchema['email'] = new
sfValidatorEmail(array('required' => true));
  }
}
```

The form framework supports ~many-to-many relationship|Many to Many Relationships (Forms)~ like any other column. By default, such a relation is rendered as a drop-down box thanks to the **sfWidgetFormChoice** widget. As seen during day 10, we have changed the rendered tag by using the **expanded** option.

As emails and URLs tend to be quite longer than the default size of an input tag, default HTML attributes can be set by using the **setAttribute()** method.

Tests

The last step is to write some functional tests for the new feature.

Replace the generated tests for the **affiliate** module by the following code:

Listing
15-25

```
// test/functional/frontend/affiliateActionsTest.php
include(dirname(__FILE__).'/../../bootstrap/functional.php');

$browser = new JobeetTestFunctional(new sfBrowser());
$browser->loadData();

$browser->
  info('1 - An affiliate can create an account')->

  get('/affiliate/new')->
  click('Submit', array('jobeet_affiliate' => array(
    'url'                        => 'http://www.example.com/',
    'email'                      => 'foo@example.com',
    'jobeet_categories_list'     =>
array(Doctrine::getTable('JobeetCategory')->findOneBySlug('programming')->getId()),
  )))->
  isRedirected()->
  followRedirect()->
  with('response')->checkElement('#content h1', 'Your affiliate
account has been created')->

  info('2 - An affiliate must at least select one category')->

  get('/affiliate/new')->
```

```
    click('Submit', array('jobeet_affiliate' => array(
      'url'   => 'http://www.example.com/',
      'email' => 'foo@example.com',
    )))->
    with('form')->isError('jobeet_categories_list')
;
```

The Affiliate Backend

For the backend, an **affiliate** module must be created for affiliates to be
activated by the administrator:

Listing
15-26

```
$ php symfony doctrine:generate-admin backend JobeetAffiliate
--module=affiliate
```

To access the newly created module, add a link in the main menu with the number
of affiliate that need to be activated:

Listing
15-27

```
<!-- apps/backend/templates/layout.php -->
<li>
  <a href="<?php echo url_for('@jobeet_affiliate_affiliate') ?>">
    Affiliates - <strong><?php echo
Doctrine::getTable('JobeetAffiliate')->countToBeActivated() ?></strong>
  </a>
</li>

// lib/model/doctrine/JobeetAffiliateTable.class.php
class JobeetAffiliateTable extends Doctrine_Table
{
  public function countToBeActivated()
  {
    $q = $this->createQuery('a')
      ->where('a.is_active = ?', 0);

    return $q->count();
  }

  // ...

}
```

As the only action needed in the backend is to activate or deactivate accounts, change the default generator **config** section to simplify the interface a bit and add a link to activate accounts directly from the list view:

Listing
15-28

```
# apps/backend/modules/affiliate/config/generator.yml
config:
  fields:
    is_active: { label: Active? }
  list:
    title:    Affiliate Management
    display: [is_active, url, email, token]
    sort:    [is_active]
    object_actions:
      activate:   ~
      deactivate: ~
    batch_actions:
      activate:   ~
      deactivate: ~
    actions: {}
  filter:
    display: [url, email, is_active]
```

To make administrators more productive, change the default filters to only show affiliates to be activated:

Listing
15-29

```
// apps/backend/modules/affiliate/lib/
affiliateGeneratorConfiguration.class.php
class affiliateGeneratorConfiguration extends
BaseAffiliateGeneratorConfiguration
{
  public function getFilterDefaults()
  {
    return array('is_active' => '0');
  }
}
```

The only other code to write is for the **activate, deactivate** actions:

Listing
15-30

```
// apps/backend/modules/affiliate/actions/actions.class.php
class affiliateActions extends autoAffiliateActions
{
  public function executeListActivate()
  {
    $this->getRoute()->getObject()->activate();
```

```php
    $this->redirect('@jobeet_affiliate_affiliate');
  }

  public function executeListDeactivate()
  {
    $this->getRoute()->getObject()->deactivate();

    $this->redirect('@jobeet_affiliate_affiliate');
  }

  public function executeBatchActivate(sfWebRequest $request)
  {
    $q = Doctrine_Query::create()
      ->from('JobeetAffiliate a')
      ->whereIn('a.id', $request->getParameter('ids'));

    $affiliates = $q->execute();

    foreach ($affiliates as $affiliate)
    {
      $affiliate->activate();
    }

    $this->redirect('@jobeet_affiliate_affiliate');
  }

  public function executeBatchDeactivate(sfWebRequest $request)
  {
    $q = Doctrine_Query::create()
      ->from('JobeetAffiliate a')
      ->whereIn('a.id', $request->getParameter('ids'));

    $affiliates = $q->execute();

    foreach ($affiliates as $affiliate)
    {
      $affiliate->deactivate();
    }

    $this->redirect('@jobeet_affiliate_affiliate');
  }
}

// lib/model/doctrine/JobeetAffiliate.class.php
class JobeetAffiliate extends BaseJobeetAffiliate
```

```
{
  public function activate()
  {
    $this->setIsActive(true);

    return $this->save();
  }

  public function deactivate()
  {
    $this->setIsActive(false);

    return $this->save();
  }

  // ...
}
```

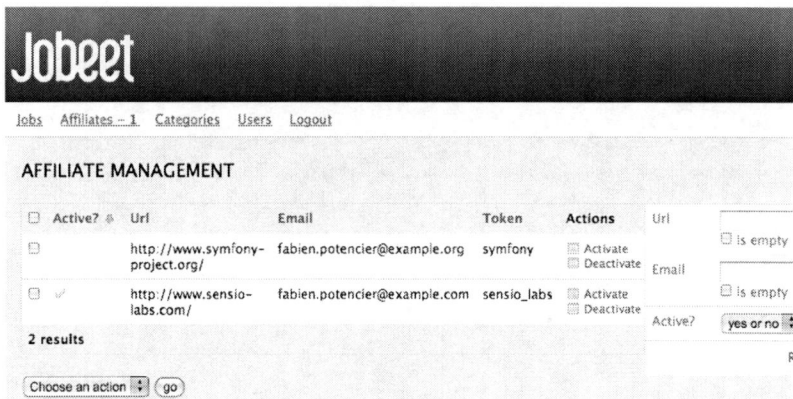

See you Tomorrow

Thanks to the REST architecture of symfony, it is quite easy to implement web services for your projects. Although, we wrote code for a read-only web service today, you have enough symfony knowledge to implement a read-write web service.

The implementation of the affiliate account creation form in the frontend and its backend counterpart was really easy as you are now familiar with the process of adding new features to your project.

If you remember requirements from day 2:

"The affiliate can also limit the number of jobs to be returned, and refine his query by specifying a category."

The implementation of this feature is so easy that we will let you do it tonight.

Whenever an affiliate account is activated by the administrator, an email should be sent to the affiliate to confirm his subscription and give him his token. Sending emails is the topic we will talk about tomorrow.

Day 16

The Mailer

Yesterday, we added a read-only web service to Jobeet. Affiliates can now create an account but it needs to be activated by the administrator before it can be used. In order for the affiliate to get its token, we still need to implement the email notification. That's what we will start doing today.

The symfony framework comes bundled with one of the best PHP emailing solution: Swift Mailer[69]. Of course, the library is fully integrated with symfony, with some cool features added on top of its default features.

 Symfony 1.3/1.4 uses Swift Mailer version 4.1.

Sending simple Emails

Let's start by sending a simple email to notify the affiliate when his account has been confirmed and to give him the affiliate token.

Replace the **activate** action with the following code:

```
// apps/backend/modules/affiliate/actions/actions.class.php
class affiliateActions extends autoAffiliateActions
{
  public function executeListActivate()
  {
    $affiliate = $this->getRoute()->getObject();
    $affiliate->activate();
```

Listing 16-1

---

69. http://www.swiftmailer.org/

```
    // send an email to the affiliate
    $message = $this->getMailer()->compose(
      array('jobeet@example.com' => 'Jobeet Bot'),
      $affiliate->getEmail(),
      'Jobeet affiliate token',
      <<<EOF
Your Jobeet affiliate account has been activated.

Your token is {$affiliate->getToken()}.

The Jobeet Bot.
EOF
    );

    $this->getMailer()->send($message);

    $this->redirect('@jobeet_affiliate_affiliate');
  }

  // ...
}
```

 For the code to work properly, you should change the jobeet@example.com email address to a real one.

Email management in symfony is centered around a mailer object, which can be retrieved from an action with the getMailer() method.

The compose() method takes four arguments and returns an email message object:

- the sender email address (from);
- the recipient email address(es) (to);
- the subject of the message;
- the body of the message.

Sending the message is then as simple as calling the send() method on the mailer instance and passing the message as an argument. As a shortcut, you can only compose and send an email in one go by using the composeAndSend() method.

 The email message is an instance of the Swift_Message class. Refer to the Swift Mailer official documentation[70] to learn more about this object, and how to do more advanced stuff like attaching files.

---

70. http://www.swiftmailer.org/docs

Configuration

By default, the **send()** method tries to use a local SMTP server to send the message to the recipient. Of course, as many things in symfony, this is totally configurable.

Factories

During the previous days, we have already talked about symfony core objects like the **user**, **request**, **response**, or the **routing**. These objects are automatically created, configured, and managed by the symfony framework. They are always accessible from the **sfContext** object, and like many things in the framework, they are configurable via a configuration file: **factories.yml**. This file is configurable by environment.

When the **sfContext** initializes the core factories, it reads the **factories.yml** file for the class names (**class**) and the parameters (**param**) to pass to the constructor:

Listing
16-2

```
response:
  class: sfWebResponse
  param:
    send_http_headers: false
```

In the above snippet, to create the response factory, symfony instantiates a **sfWebResponse** object and passes the **send_http_headers** option as a parameter.

The sfContext class

The sfContext object contains references to symfony core objects like the request, the response, the user, and so on. As sfContext acts like a singleton, you can use the sfContext::getInstance() statement to get it from anywhere and then have access to any symfony core objects:

Listing
16-3

```
$mailer = sfContext::getInstance()->getMailer();
```

Whenever you want to use the sfContext::getInstance() in one of your class, think twice as it introduces a strong coupling. It is quite always better to pass the object you need as an argument.

You can even use sfContext as a registry and add your own objects using the set() methods. It takes a name and an object as arguments and the get() method can be used later on to retrieve an object by name:

Listing
16-4

```
sfContext::getInstance()->set('job', $job);
$job = sfContext::getInstance()->get('job');
```

Delivery Strategy

Like many other core symfony objects, the mailer is a factory. So, it is configured in the factories.yml configuration file. The default configuration reads as follows:

Listing
16-5

```
mailer:
  class: sfMailer
  param:
    logging:           %SF_LOGGING_ENABLED%
    charset:           %SF_CHARSET%
    delivery_strategy: realtime
    transport:
      class: Swift_SmtpTransport
      param:
        host:       localhost
        port:       25
        encryption: ~
        username:   ~
        password:   ~
```

When creating a new application, the local factories.yml configuration file overrides the default configuration with some sensible defaults for the env and test environments:

```
test:
  mailer:
    param:
      delivery_strategy: none

dev:
  mailer:
    param:
      delivery_strategy: none
```

Listing
16-6

The **delivery_strategy** setting tells symfony how to deliver emails. By default, symfony comes with four different strategies:

- **realtime**: Messages are sent in realtime.
- **single_address**: Messages are sent to a single address.
- **spool**: Messages are stored in a queue.
- **none**: Messages are simply ignored.

Whatever the strategy, emails are always logged and available in the "mailer" panel in the web debug toolbar.

Mail Transport

Mail messages are actually sent by a transport. The transport is configured in the **factories.yml** configuration file, and the default configuration uses the SMTP server of the local machine:

```
transport:
  class: Swift_SmtpTransport
  param:
    host:       localhost
    port:       25
    encryption: ~
    username:   ~
    password:   ~
```

Listing
16-7

Swift Mailer comes bundled with three different transport classes:

- **Swift_SmtpTransport**: Uses a SMTP server to send messages.
- **Swift_SendmailTransport**: Uses **sendmail** to send messages.
- **Swift_MailTransport**: Uses the native PHP **mail()** function to send messages.

The "Transport Types"[71] section of the Swift Mailer official documentation describes all you need to know about the built-in transport classes and their different parameters.

Testing Emails

Now that we have seen how to send an email with the symfony mailer, let's write some functional tests to ensure we did the right thing. By default, symfony registers a **mailer** tester (**sfMailerTester**) to ease mail testing in functional tests.

Replace the **affiliate** functional test file for the backend application with the following code:

Listing 16-8

```
// test/functional/backend/affiliateActionsTest.php
include(dirname(__FILE__).'/../../bootstrap/functional.php');

$browser = new JobeetTestFunctional(new sfBrowser());
$browser->loadData();

$browser->
  info('1 - When validating an affiliate, an email must be sent with
its token')->

  get('/affiliate/new')->
  click('activate', array(), array('position' => 1))->
  with('mailer')->begin()->
    checkHeader('Subject', '/Jobeet affiliate token/')->
    checkBody('/Your token is symfony/')->
  end()
;
```

For the previous code to work, you need to copy yesterday's fixture file (**data/fixtures/030_affiliates.yml**) in the **test/fixtures/** directory.

Each sent email can be tested with the help of the **checkHeader()** and **checkBody()** methods. The second argument of **checkHeader()** and the first argument of **checkBody()** can be one of the following:

- a string to check an exact match;
- a regular expression to check the value against it;

---

71. http://swiftmailer.org/docs/transport-types

- a negative regular expression (a regular expression starting with a !) to check that the value does not match.

 By default, checks are done on the first email sent. If several emails have been sent, you can choose the one you want to test with the `withMessage()` method. The `withMessage()` takes a recipient as its first argument. It also takes a second argument to indicate which email you want to test if several ones have been sent to the same recipient.

 Like other built-in testers, you can see the raw message by calling the `debug()` method.

See you Tomorrow

Tomorrow, we will implement the last missing feature of the Jobeet website, the search engine.

Day 17

Search

Two days ago, we added some feeds to keep Jobeet users up-to-date with new job posts. Today, we will continue to improve the user experience by implementing the latest main feature of the Jobeet website: the search engine.

The Technology

Before we jump in head first, let's talk a bit about the history of symfony. We advocate a lot of best practices, like tests and refactoring, and we also try to apply them to the framework itself. For instance, we like the famous "Don't reinvent the wheel" motto. As a matter of fact, the symfony framework started its life four years ago as the glue between two existing Open-Source softwares: Mojavi and Propel. And every time we need to tackle a new problem, we look for an existing library that does the job well before coding one ourself from scratch.

Today, we want to add a search engine to Jobeet, and the Zend Framework provides a great library, called Zend Lucene[72], which is a port of the well-know Java Lucene project. Instead of creating yet another search engine for Jobeet, which is quite a complex task, we will use Zend Lucene.

On the Zend Lucene documentation page, the library is described as follows:

> ... *a general purpose text search engine written entirely in PHP 5. Since it stores its index on the filesystem and does not require a database server, it can add search capabilities to almost any PHP-driven website. Zend_Search_Lucene supports the following features:*

---

72. `http://framework.zend.com/manual/en/zend.search.lucene.html`

- *Ranked searching - best results returned first*
- *Many powerful query types: phrase queries, boolean queries, wildcard queries, proximity queries, range queries and many others*
- *Search by specific field (e.g., title, author, contents)*

 This chapter is not a tutorial about the Zend Lucene library, but how to integrate it into the Jobeet website; or more generally, how to integrate third-party libraries into a symfony project. If you want more information about this technology, please refer to the Zend Lucene documentation[73].

Installing and Configuring the Zend Framework

The Zend Lucene library is part of the Zend Framework. We will only install the Zend Framework into the **lib/vendor/** directory, alongside the symfony framework itself.

First, download the Zend Framework[74] and un-archive the files so that you have a **lib/vendor/Zend/** directory.

 The following explanations have been tested with the 1.9 version of the Zend Framework.

 You can clean up the directory by removing everything but the following files and directories:

- Exception.php
- Loader/
- Autoloader.php
- Search/

Then, add the following code to the **ProjectConfiguration** class to provide a simple way to register the Zend autoloader:

Listing 17-1
```
// config/ProjectConfiguration.class.php
class ProjectConfiguration extends sfProjectConfiguration
```

73. http://framework.zend.com/manual/en/zend.search.lucene.html
74. http://framework.zend.com/download/overview

```
{
  static protected $zendLoaded = false;

  static public function registerZend()
  {
    if (self::$zendLoaded)
    {
      return;
    }

    set_include_path(sfConfig::get('sf_lib_dir').'/
vendor'.PATH_SEPARATOR.get_include_path());
    require_once sfConfig::get('sf_lib_dir').'/vendor/Zend/Loader/
Autoloader.php';
    Zend_Loader_Autoloader::getInstance();
    self::$zendLoaded = true;
  }

  // ...
}
```

Indexing

The Jobeet search engine should be able to return all jobs matching keywords entered by the user. Before being able to search anything, an index has to be built for the jobs; for Jobeet, it will be stored in the **data/** directory.

Zend Lucene provides two methods to retrieve an index depending whether one already exists or not. Let's create a helper method in the **JobeetJobTable** class that returns an existing index or creates a new one for us:

Listing
17-2

```
// lib/model/doctrine/JobeetJobTable.class.php
static public function getLuceneIndex()
{
  ProjectConfiguration::registerZend();

  if (file_exists($index = self::getLuceneIndexFile()))
  {
    return Zend_Search_Lucene::open($index);
  }
  else
  {
    return Zend_Search_Lucene::create($index);
  }
}
```

```
}

static public function getLuceneIndexFile()
{
  return sfConfig::get('sf_data_dir').'/
job.'.sfConfig::get('sf_environment').'.index';
}
```

The save() method

Each time a job is created, updated, or deleted, the index must be updated. Edit
JobeetJob to update the index whenever a job is serialized to the database:

Listing
17-3
```
public function save(Doctrine_Connection $conn = null)
{
  // ...

  $ret = parent::save($conn);

  $this->updateLuceneIndex();

  return $ret;
}
```

And create the **updateLuceneIndex()** method that does the actual work:

Listing
17-4
```
// lib/model/doctrine/JobeetJob.class.php
public function updateLuceneIndex()
{
  $index = $this->getTable()->getLuceneIndex();

  // remove existing entries
  foreach ($index->find('pk:'.$this->getId()) as $hit)
  {
    $index->delete($hit->id);
  }

  // don't index expired and non-activated jobs
  if ($this->isExpired() || !$this->getIsActivated())
  {
    return;
  }

  $doc = new Zend_Search_Lucene_Document();
```

```
  // store job primary key to identify it in the search results
  $doc->addField(Zend_Search_Lucene_Field::Keyword('pk',
$this->getId()));

  // index job fields
  $doc->addField(Zend_Search_Lucene_Field::UnStored('position',
$this->getPosition(), 'utf-8'));
  $doc->addField(Zend_Search_Lucene_Field::UnStored('company',
$this->getCompany(), 'utf-8'));
  $doc->addField(Zend_Search_Lucene_Field::UnStored('location',
$this->getLocation(), 'utf-8'));
  $doc->addField(Zend_Search_Lucene_Field::UnStored('description',
$this->getDescription(), 'utf-8'));

  // add job to the index
  $index->addDocument($doc);
  $index->commit();
}
```

As Zend Lucene is not able to update an existing entry, it is removed first if the job already exists in the index.

Indexing the job itself is simple: the primary key is stored for future reference when searching jobs and the main columns (**position**, **company**, **location**, and **description**) are indexed but not stored in the index as we will use the real objects to display the results.

Doctrine Transactions

What if there is a problem when indexing a job or if the job is not saved into the database? Both Doctrine and Zend Lucene will throw an exception. But under some circumstances, we might have a job saved in the database without the corresponding indexing. To prevent this from happening, we can wrap the two updates in a transaction and rollback in case of an error:

Listing 17-5

```
// lib/model/doctrine/JobeetJob.class.php
public function save(Doctrine_Connection $conn = null)
{
  // ...

  $conn = $conn ? $conn : $this->getTable()->getConnection();
  $conn->beginTransaction();
  try
  {
    $ret = parent::save($conn);
```

```
    $this->updateLuceneIndex();

    $conn->commit();

    return $ret;
  }
  catch (Exception $e)
  {
    $conn->rollBack();
    throw $e;
  }
}
```

delete()

We also need to override the **delete()** method to remove the entry of the deleted job from the index:

Listing 17-6
```
// lib/model/doctrine/JobeetJob.class.php
public function delete(Doctrine_Connection $conn = null)
{
  $index = $this->getTable()->getLuceneIndex();

  foreach ($index->find('pk:'.$this->getId()) as $hit)
  {
    $index->delete($hit->id);
  }

  return parent::delete($conn);
}
```

Searching

Now that we have everything in place, you can reload the fixture data to index them:

Listing 17-7
```
$ php symfony doctrine:data-load --env=dev
```

The task is run with the **--env** option as the index is environment dependent and the default environment for tasks is **cli**.

For Unix-like users: as the index is modified from the command line and also from the web, you must change the index directory permissions accordingly depending on your configuration: check that both the command line user you use and the web server user can write to the index directory.

 You might have some warnings about the **ZipArchive** class if you don't have the **zip** extension compiled in your PHP. It's a known bug of the **Zend_Loader** class.

Implementing the search in the frontend is a piece of cake. First, create a route:

Listing
17-8

```
job_search:
  url:    /search
  param: { module: job, action: search }
```

And the corresponding action:

Listing
17-9

```php
// apps/frontend/modules/job/actions/actions.class.php
class jobActions extends sfActions
{
  public function executeSearch(sfWebRequest $request)
  {
    if (!$query = $request->getParameter('query'))
    {
      return $this->forward('job', 'index');
    }

    $this->jobs = Doctrine::getTable('JobeetJob')
      -> ->getForLuceneQuery($query);
  }

  // ...
}
```

The template is also quite straightforward:

Listing
17-10

```php
// apps/frontend/modules/job/templates/searchSuccess.php
<?php use_stylesheet('jobs.css') ?>

<div id="jobs">
  <?php include_partial('job/list', array('jobs' => $jobs)) ?>
</div>
```

The search itself is delegated to the **getForLuceneQuery()** method:

Listing
17-11

```php
// lib/model/doctrine/JobeetJobTable.class.php
public function getForLuceneQuery($query)
{
  $hits = $this->getLuceneIndex()->find($query);

  $pks = array();
  foreach ($hits as $hit)
  {
    $pks[] = $hit->pk;
  }

  if (empty($pks))
  {
    return array();
  }

  $q = $this->createQuery('j')
    ->whereIn('j.id', $pks)
    ->limit(20);
  $q = $this->addActiveJobsQuery($q);

  return $q->execute();
}
```

After we get all results from the Lucene index, we filter out the inactive jobs, and limit the number of results to **20**.

To make it work, update the layout:

Listing
17-12

```php
// apps/frontend/templates/layout.php
<h2>Ask for a job</h2>
<form action="<?php echo url_for('@job_search') ?>" method="get">
  <input type="text" name="query" value="<?php echo
$sf_request->getParameter('query') ?>" id="search_keywords" />
  <input type="submit" value="search" />
  <div class="help">
    Enter some keywords (city, country, position, ...)
  </div>
</form>
```

Zend Lucene defines a rich query language that supports operations like Booleans, wildcards, fuzzy search, and much more. Everything is documented in the Zend Lucene manual[75]

Unit Tests

What kind of unit tests do we need to create to test the search engine? We obviously won't test the Zend Lucene library itself, but its integration with the `JobeetJob` class.

Add the following tests at the end of the `JobeetJobTest.php` file and don't forget to update the number of tests at the beginning of the file to **7**:

Listing 17-13

```
// test/unit/model/JobeetJobTest.php
$t->comment('->getForLuceneQuery()');
$job = create_job(array('position' => 'foobar', 'is_activated' =>
false));
$job->save();
$jobs =
Doctrine::getTable('JobeetJob')->getForLuceneQuery('position:foobar');
$t->is(count($jobs), 0, '::getForLuceneQuery() does not return non
activated jobs');

$job = create_job(array('position' => 'foobar', 'is_activated' =>
true));
$job->save();
$jobs =
Doctrine::getTable('JobeetJob')->getForLuceneQuery('position:foobar');
$t->is(count($jobs), 1, '::getForLuceneQuery() returns jobs matching
the criteria');
$t->is($jobs[0]->getId(), $job->getId(), '::getForLuceneQuery()
returns jobs matching the criteria');

$job->delete();
$jobs =
Doctrine::getTable('JobeetJob')->getForLuceneQuery('position:foobar');
$t->is(count($jobs), 0, '::getForLuceneQuery() does not return deleted
jobs');
```

---

75. http://framework.zend.com/manual/en/zend.search.lucene.query-api.html

We test that a non activated job, or a deleted one does not show up in the search results; we also check that jobs matching the given criteria do show up in the results.

Tasks

Eventually, we need to create a task to cleanup the index from stale entries (when a job expires for example) and optimize the index from time to time. As we already have a cleanup task, let's update it to add those features:

Listing
17-14

```php
// lib/task/JobeetCleanupTask.class.php
protected function execute($arguments = array(), $options = array())
{
  $databaseManager = new sfDatabaseManager($this->configuration);

  // cleanup Lucene index
  $index = Doctrine::getTable('JobeetJob')->getLuceneIndex();

  $q = Doctrine_Query::create()
    ->from('JobeetJob j')
    ->where('j.expires_at < ?', date('Y-m-d'));

  $jobs = $q->execute();
  foreach ($jobs as $job)
  {
    if ($hit = $index->find('pk:'.$job->getId()))
    {
      $index->delete($hit->id);
    }
  }

  $index->optimize();

  $this->logSection('lucene', 'Cleaned up and optimized the job
index');

  // Remove stale jobs
  $nb = Doctrine::getTable('JobeetJob')->cleanup($options['days']);

  $this->logSection('doctrine', sprintf('Removed %d stale jobs', $nb));
}
```

The task removed all expired jobs from the index and then optimizes it thanks to the Zend Lucene built-in `optimize()` method.

See you Tomorrow

Today, we implemented a full search engine with many features in less than an hour. Every time you want to add a new feature to your projects, check that it has not yet been solved somewhere else. First, check if something is not implemented natively in the symfony framework[76]. Then, check the symfony plugins[77]. And don't forget to check the Zend Framework libraries[78] and the ezComponent[79] ones too.

Tomorrow, we will use some unobtrusive JavaScripts to enhance the responsiveness of the search engine by updating the results in real-time as the user types in the search box. Of course, this will be the occasion to talk about how to use AJAX with symfony.

---

76. http://www.symfony-project.org/api/1_4/
77. http://www.symfony-project.org/plugins/
78. http://framework.zend.com/manual/en/
79. http://ezcomponents.org/docs

Day 18

AJAX

Yesterday, we implemented a very powerful search engine for Jobeet, thanks to the Zend Lucene library.

Today, to enhance the responsiveness of the search engine, we will take advantage of AJAX[80] to convert the search engine to a live one.

As the form should work with and without JavaScript enabled, the live search feature will be implemented using unobtrusive JavaScript[81]. Using unobtrusive JavaScript also allows for a better separation of concerns in the client code between HTML, CSS, and the JavaScript behaviors.

Installing jQuery

Instead of reinventing the wheel and managing the many differences between browsers, we will use a JavaScript library, jQuery. The symfony framework itself is agnostic and can work with any JavaScript library.

Go to the jQuery[82] website, download the latest version, and put the `.js` file under `web/js/`.

---

80. http://en.wikipedia.org/wiki/AJAX
81. http://en.wikipedia.org/wiki/Unobtrusive_JavaScript
82. http://jquery.com/

Including jQuery

As we will need jQuery on all pages, update the layout to include it in the `<head>`. Be careful to insert the `use_javascript()` function before the `include_javascripts()` call:

Listing 18-1
```
<!-- apps/frontend/templates/layout.php -->

  <?php use_javascript('jquery-1.2.6.min.js') ?>
  <?php include_javascripts() ?>
</head>
```

We could have included the jQuery file directly with a `<script>` tag, but using the `use_javascript()` helper ensures that the same JavaScript file won't be included twice.

 For performance reasons[83], you might also want to move the `include_javascripts()` helper call just before the ending `</body>` tag.

Adding Behaviors

Implementing a live search means that each time the user types a letter in the search box, a call to the server needs to be triggered; the server will then return the needed information to update some regions of the page without refreshing the whole page.

Instead of adding the behavior with an `on*()` HTML attributes, the main principle behind jQuery is to add behaviors to the DOM after the page is fully loaded. This way, if you disable JavaScript support in your browser, no behavior is registered, and the form still works as before.

The first step is to intercept whenever a user types a key in the search box:

Listing 18-2
```
$('#search_keywords').keyup(function(key)
{
  if (this.value.length >= 3 || this.value == '')
  {
    // do something
  }
});
```

---

83. `http://developer.yahoo.com/performance/rules.html#js_bottom`

Don't add the code for now, as we will modify it heavily. The final JavaScript code will be added to the layout in the next section.

Every time the user types a key, jQuery executes the anonymous function defined in the above code, but only if the user has typed more than 3 characters or if he removed everything from the input tag.

Making an AJAX call to the server is as simple as using the **load()** method on the DOM element:

```
$('#search_keywords').keyup(function(key)
{
  if (this.value.length >= 3 || this.value == '')
  {
    $('#jobs').load(
      $(this).parents('form').attr('action'), { query: this.value +
'*' }
    );
  }
});
```

Listing
18-3

To manage the AJAX Call, the same action as the "normal" one is called. The needed changes in the action will be done in the next section.

Last but not least, if JavaScript is enabled, we will want to remove the search button:

```
$('.search input[type="submit"]').hide();
```

Listing
18-4

User Feedback

Whenever you make an AJAX call, the page won't be updated right away. The browser will wait for the server response to come back before updating the page. In the meantime, you need to provide visual feedback to the user to inform him that something is going on.

A convention is to display a loader icon during the AJAX call. Update the layout to add the loader image and hide it by default:

```
<!-- apps/frontend/templates/layout.php -->
<div class="search">
  <h2>Ask for a job</h2>
  <form action="<?php echo url_for('@job_search') ?>" method="get">
    <input type="text" name="query" value="<?php echo
```

Listing
18-5

```
$sf_request->getParameter('query') ?>" id="search_keywords" />
    <input type="submit" value="search" />
    <img id="loader" src="http://www.symfony-project.org/images/
loader.gif" style="vertical-align: middle; display: none" />
    <div class="help">
      Enter some keywords (city, country, position, ...)
    </div>
  </form>
</div>
```

 The default loader is optimized for the current layout of Jobeet. If you want to create your own, you will find a lot of free online services like http://www.ajaxload.info/.

Now that you have all the pieces needed to make the HTML work, create a **search.js** file that contains the JavaScript we have written so far:

Listing 18-6

```javascript
// web/js/search.js
$(document).ready(function()
{
  $('.search input[type="submit"]').hide();

  $('#search_keywords').keyup(function(key)
  {
    if (this.value.length >= 3 || this.value == '')
    {
      $('#loader').show();
      $('#jobs').load(
        $(this).parents('form').attr('action'),
        { query: this.value + '*' },
        function() { $('#loader').hide(); }
      );
    }
  });
});
```

You also need to update the layout to include this new file:

Listing 18-7

```php
<!-- apps/frontend/templates/layout.php -->
<?php use_javascript('search.js') ?>
```

Although the JavaScript we have written for the search engine is static, sometimes, you need to call some PHP code (to use the `url_for()` helper for instance).

JavaScript is just another format like HTML, and as seen some days ago, symfony makes format management quite easy. As the JavaScript file will contain behavior for a page, you can even have the same URL as the page for the JavaScript file, but ending with `.js`. For instance, if you want to create a file for the search engine behavior, you can modify the `job_search` route as follows and create a `searchSuccess.js.php` template:

```
job_search:
  url:   /search.:sf_format
  param: { module: job, action: search, sf_format: html }
  requirements:
    sf_format: (?:html|js)
```

Listing 18-8

AJAX in an Action

If JavaScript is enabled, jQuery will intercept all keys typed in the search box, and will call the **search** action. If not, the same **search** action is also called when the user submits the form by pressing the "enter" key or by clicking on the "search" button.

So, the **search** action now needs to determine if the call is made via AJAX or not. Whenever a request is made with an AJAX call, the `isXmlHttpRequest()` method of the request object returns **true**.

 The `isXmlHttpRequest()` method works with all major JavaScript libraries like Prototype, Mootools, or jQuery.

```php
// apps/frontend/modules/job/actions/actions.class.php
public function executeSearch(sfWebRequest $request)
{
  if (!$query = $request->getParameter('query'))
  {
    return $this->forward('job', 'index');
  }
```

Listing 18-9

```
$this->jobs =
Doctrine::getTable('JobeetJob')->getForLuceneQuery($query);

  if ($request->isXmlHttpRequest())
  {
    return $this->renderPartial('job/list', array('jobs' =>
$this->jobs));
  }
}
```

As jQuery won't reload the page but will only replace the **#jobs** DOM element with the response content, the page should not be decorated by the layout. As this is a common need, the layout is disabled by default when an AJAX request comes in.

Moreover, instead of returning the full template, we only need to return the content of the **job/list** partial. The **renderPartial()** method used in the action returns the partial as the response instead of the full template.

If the user removes all characters in the search box, or if the search returns no result, we need to display a message instead of a blank page. We will use the **renderText()** method to render a simple test string:

Listing
18-10

```
// apps/frontend/modules/job/actions/actions.class.php
public function executeSearch(sfWebRequest $request)
{
  if (!$query = $request->getParameter('query'))
  {
    return $this->forward('job', 'index');
  }

  $this->jobs =
Doctrine::getTable('JobeetJob')->getForLuceneQuery($query);

  if ($request->isXmlHttpRequest())
  {
    if ('*' == $query || !$this->jobs)
    {
      return $this->renderText('No results.');
    }
    else
    {
      return $this->renderPartial('job/list', array('jobs' =>
$this->jobs));
    }
```

```
    }
}
```

 You can also return a component in an action by using the `renderComponent()` method.

Testing AJAX

As the symfony browser cannot simulate JavaScript, you need to help it when testing AJAX calls. It mainly means that you need to manually add the header that jQuery and all other major JavaScript libraries send with the request:

```
// test/functional/frontend/jobActionsTest.php
$browser->setHttpHeader('X_REQUESTED_WITH', 'XMLHttpRequest');
$browser->
  info('5 - Live search')->

  get('/search?query=sens*')->
  with('response')->begin()->
    checkElement('table tr', 2)->
  end()
;
```

Listing 18-11

The `setHttpHeader()` method set an HTTP header for the very next request made with the browser.

See you Tomorrow

Yesterday, we used the Zend Lucene library to implement the search engine. Today, we have used jQuery to make it more responsive. The symfony framework provides all the fundamental tools to build MVC applications with ease, and also plays well with other components. As always, try to use the best tool for the job.

Tomorrow, we will see how to internationalize the Jobeet website.

Day 19

Internationalization and Localization

Yesterday, we finished the search engine feature by making it more fun with the addition of some AJAX goodness.

Today, we will talk about Jobeet **internationalization** (or i18n) and **localization** (or l10n).

From Wikipedia[84]:

> **Internationalization** *is the process of designing a software application so that it can be adapted to various* languages *and regions without engineering changes.*
>
> **Localization** *is the process of adapting software for a specific region or language by adding* locale-*specific components and* translating text.

As always, the symfony framework has not reinvented the wheel and its i18n and l10n supports is based on the ICU standard[85].

User

No internationalization is possible without a user. When your website is available in several languages or for different regions of the world, the user is responsible for choosing the one that fits him best.

 We have already talked about the symfony User class during day 13.

---

84. http://en.wikipedia.org/wiki/Internationalization
85. http://www.icu-project.org/

The User Culture

The i18n and l10n features of symfony are based on the **user culture**. The culture is the combination of the language and the country of the user. For instance, the culture for a user that speaks French is `fr` and the culture for a user from France is `fr_FR`.

You can manage the user culture by calling the `setCulture()` and `getCulture()` method on the User object:

Listing
19-1
```
// in an action
$this->getUser()->setCulture('fr_BE');
echo $this->getUser()->getCulture();
```

 The language is coded in two lowercase characters, according to the ISO 639-1 standard[86], and the country is coded in two uppercase characters, according to the ISO 3166-1 standard[87].

The Preferred Culture

By default, the user culture is the one configured in the `settings.yml` configuration file:

Listing
19-2
```
# apps/frontend/config/settings.yml
all:
  .settings:
    default_culture: it_IT
```

 As the culture is managed by the User object, it is stored in the user session. During development, if you change the default culture, you will have to clear your session cookie for the new setting to have any effect in your browser.

When a user starts a session on the Jobeet website, we can also determine the best culture, based on the information provided by the **Accept-Language** HTTP header.

The `getLanguages()` method of the request object returns an array of accepted languages for the current user, sorted by order of preference:

Listing
19-3
```
// in an action
$languages = $request->getLanguages();
```

86. http://en.wikipedia.org/wiki/ISO_639-1
87. http://en.wikipedia.org/wiki/ISO_3166-1

But most of the time, your website won't be available in the world's 136 major languages. The getPreferredCulture() method returns the best language by comparing the user preferred languages and the supported languages of your website:

Listing
19-4

```
// in an action
$language = $request->getPreferredCulture(array('en', 'fr'));
```

In the previous call, the returned language will be English or French according to the user preferred languages, or English (the first language in the array) if none match.

Culture in the URL

The Jobeet website will be available in English and French. As a URL can only represent a single resource, the culture must be embedded in the URL. In order to do that, open the routing.yml file, and add the special :sf_culture variable for all routes but the api_jobs and the homepage ones. For simple routes, add /:sf_culture to the front of the url. For collection routes, add a prefix_path option that starts with /:sf_culture.

Listing
19-5

```
# apps/frontend/config/routing.yml
affiliate:
  class: sfDoctrineRouteCollection
  options:
    model:          JobeetAffiliate
    actions:        [new, create]
    object_actions: { wait: get }
    prefix_path:    /:sf_culture/affiliate

category:
  url:     /:sf_culture/category/:slug.:sf_format
  class:   sfDoctrineRoute
  param:   { module: category, action: show, sf_format: html }
  options: { model: JobeetCategory, type: object }
  requirements:
    sf_format: (?:html|atom)

job_search:
  url:   /:sf_culture/search
  param: { module: job, action: search }

job:
```

```
class: sfDoctrineRouteCollection
options:
  model:          JobeetJob
  column:         token
  object_actions: { publish: put, extend: put }
  prefix_path:    /:sf_culture/job
requirements:
  token: \w+

job_show_user:
  url:      /:sf_culture/job/:company_slug/:location_slug/:id/
:position_slug
  class:    sfDoctrineRoute
  options:
    model: JobeetJob
    type: object
    method_for_query: retrieveActiveJob
  param:    { module: job, action: show }
  requirements:
    id:            \d+
    sf_method: get
```

When the **sf_culture** variable is used in a route, symfony will automatically use its value to change the culture of the user.

As we need as many homepages as languages we support (**/en/**, **/fr/**, ...), the default homepage (**/**) must redirect to the appropriate localized one, according to the user culture. But if the user has no culture yet, because he comes to Jobeet for the first time, the preferred culture will be chosen for him.

First, add the **isFirstRequest()** method to **myUser**. It returns **true** only for the very first request of a user session:

Listing
19-6

```
// apps/frontend/lib/myUser.class.php
public function isFirstRequest($boolean = null)
{
  if (is_null($boolean))
  {
    return $this->getAttribute('first_request', true);
  }
  else
  {
    $this->setAttribute('first_request', $boolean);
  }
}
```

Add a `localized_homepage` route:

Listing
19-7

```yaml
# apps/frontend/config/routing.yml
localized_homepage:
  url:    /:sf_culture/
  param: { module: job, action: index }
  requirements:
    sf_culture: (?:fr|en)
```

Change the **index** action of the **job** module to implement the logic to redirect the user to the "best" homepage on the first request of a session:

Listing
19-8

```php
// apps/frontend/modules/job/actions/actions.class.php
public function executeIndex(sfWebRequest $request)
{
  if (!$request->getParameter('sf_culture'))
  {
    if ($this->getUser()->isFirstRequest())
    {
      $culture = $request->getPreferredCulture(array('en', 'fr'));
      $this->getUser()->setCulture($culture);
      $this->getUser()->isFirstRequest(false);
    }
    else
    {
      $culture = $this->getUser()->getCulture();
    }

    $this->redirect('@localized_homepage');
  }

  $this->categories =
Doctrine::getTable('JobeetCategory')->getWithJobs();
}
```

If the **sf_culture** variable is not present in the request, it means that the user has come to the / URL. If this is the case and the session is new, the preferred culture is used as the user culture. Otherwise the user's current culture is used.

The last step is to redirect the user to the **localized_homepage** URL. Notice that the **sf_culture** variable has not been passed in the redirect call as symfony adds it automatically for you.

Now, if you try to go to the **/it/** URL, symfony will return a 404 error as we have restricted the **sf_culture** variable to **en**, or **fr**. Add this requirement to all the routes that embed the culture:

Listing
19.9
```
requirements:
  sf_culture: (?:fr|en)
```

Culture Testing

It is time to test our implementation. But before adding more tests, we need to fix the existing ones. As all URLs have changed, edit all functional test files in **test/functional/frontend/** and add **/en** in front of all URLs. Don't forget to also change the URLs in the **lib/test/JobeetTestFunctional.class.php** file. Launch the test suite to check that you have correctly fixed the tests:

Listing
19-10
```
$ php symfony test:functional frontend
```

The user tester provides an **isCulture()** method that tests the current user's culture. Open the **jobActionsTest** file and add the following tests:

Listing
19-11
```php
// test/functional/frontend/jobActionsTest.php
$browser->setHttpHeader('ACCEPT_LANGUAGE', 'fr_FR,fr,en;q=0.7');
$browser->
  info('6 - User culture')->

  restart()->

  info('  6.1 - For the first request, symfony guesses the best
culture')->
  get('/')->
  isRedirected()->followRedirect()->
  with('user')->isCulture('fr')->

  info('  6.2 - Available cultures are en and fr')->
  get('/it/')->
  with('response')->isStatusCode(404)
;

$browser->setHttpHeader('ACCEPT_LANGUAGE', 'en,fr;q=0.7');
$browser->
  info('  6.3 - The culture guessing is only for the first request')->

  get('/')->
  isRedirected()->followRedirect()->
  with('user')->isCulture('fr')
;
```

Language Switching

For the user to change the culture, a language form must be added in the layout. The form framework does not provide such a form out of the box but as the need is quite common for internationalized websites, the symfony core team maintains the **sfFormExtraPlugin**[88], which contains validators, widgets, and forms which cannot be included with the main symfony package as they are too specific or have external dependencies but are nonetheless very useful.

Install the plugin with the **plugin:install** task:

```
$ php symfony plugin:install sfFormExtraPlugin
```

Listing
19-12

 The **sfFormExtraPlugin** contains widgets that require external dependencies like JavaScript libraries. You will find a widget for rich date selectors, one for a WYSIWYG editor, and much more. Take the time to read the documentation as you will find a lot of useful stuff.

The **sfFormExtraPlugin** plugin provides a **sfFormLanguage** form to manage the language selection. Adding the language form can be done in the layout like this:

 The below code is not meant to be implemented. It is here to show you how you might be tempted to implement something in the wrong way. We will go on to show you how to implement it properly using symfony.

```
// apps/frontend/templates/layout.php
<div id="footer">
  <div class="content">
    <!-- footer content -->

    <?php $form = new sfFormLanguage(
      $sf_user,
      array('languages' => array('en', 'fr'))
      )
    ?>
    <form action="<?php echo url_for('@change_language') ?>">
      <?php echo $form ?><input type="submit" value="ok" />
    </form>
  </div>
</div>
```

Listing
19-13

---

88. http://www.symfony-project.org/plugins/sfFormExtraPlugin?tab=plugin_readme

Do you spot a problem? Right, the form object creation does not belong to the View layer. It must be created from an action. But as the code is in the layout, the form must be created for every action, which is far from practical. In such cases, you should use a **component**. A component is like a partial but with some code attached to it. Consider it a lightweight action.

Including a component from a template can be done by using the include_component() helper:

Listing
19-14

```
// apps/frontend/templates/layout.php
<div id="footer">
  <div class="content">
    <!-- footer content -->

    <?php include_component('language', 'language') ?>
  </div>
</div>
```

The helper takes the module and the action as arguments. The third argument can be used to pass parameters to the component.

Create a **language** module to host the component and the action that will actually change the user language:

Listing
19-15

```
$ php symfony generate:module frontend language
```

Components are to be defined in the **actions/components.class.php** file.

Create this file now:

Listing
19-16

```
// apps/frontend/modules/language/actions/components.class.php
class languageComponents extends sfComponents
{
  public function executeLanguage(sfWebRequest $request)
  {
    $this->form = new sfFormLanguage(
      $this->getUser(),
      array('languages' => array('en', 'fr'))
    );
  }
}
```

As you can see, a components class is quite similar to an actions class.

The template for a component uses the same naming convention as a partial would: an underscore (_) followed by the component name:

```
// apps/frontend/modules/language/templates/_language.php
<form action="<?php echo url_for('@change_language') ?>">
  <?php echo $form ?><input type="submit" value="ok" />
</form>
```

Listing
19-17

As the plugin does not provide the action that actually changes the user culture, edit the routing.yml file to create the change_language route:

```
# apps/frontend/config/routing.yml
change_language:
  url:    /change_language
  param: { module: language, action: changeLanguage }
```

Listing
19-18

And create the corresponding action:

```
// apps/frontend/modules/language/actions/actions.class.php
class languageActions extends sfActions
{
  public function executeChangeLanguage(sfWebRequest $request)
  {
    $form = new sfFormLanguage(
      $this->getUser(),
      array('languages' => array('en', 'fr'))
    );

    $form->process($request);

    return $this->redirect('@localized_homepage');
  }
}
```

Listing
19-19

The process() method of sfFormLanguage takes care of changing the user culture, based on the user form submission.

Internationalization

Languages, Charset, and Encoding

Different languages have different character sets. The English language is the simplest one as it only uses the ASCII characters, the French language is a bit more complex with accentuated characters like "é", and languages like Russian, Chinese, or Arabic are much more complex as all their characters are outside the ASCII range. Such languages are defined with totally different character sets.

When dealing with internationalized data, it is better to use the unicode norm. The idea behind unicode is to establish a universal set of characters that contains all characters for all languages. The problem with unicode is that a single character can be represented with as many as 21 octets. Therefore, for the web, we use UTF-8, which maps Unicode code points to variable-length sequences of octets. In UTF-8, most used languages have their characters coded with less than 3 octets.

UTF-8 is the default encoding used by symfony, and it is defined in the **settings.yml** configuration file:

*Listing
19-20*

```
# apps/frontend/config/settings.yml
all:
  .settings:
    charset: utf-8
```

Also, to enable the internationalization layer of symfony, you must set the **i18n** setting to **true** in **settings.yml**:

*Listing
19-21*

```
# apps/frontend/config/settings.yml
all:
  .settings:
    i18n: true
```

Templates

An internationalized website means that the user interface is translated into several languages.

In a template, all strings that are language dependent must be wrapped with the __() helper (notice that there is two underscores).

The __() helper is part of the **I18N** helper group, which contains helpers that ease i18n management in templates. As this helper group is not loaded by default, you need to either manually add it in each template with **use_helper('I18N')** as we already did for the **Text** helper group, or load it globally by adding it to the `standard_helpers` setting:

Listing
19-22

```yaml
# apps/frontend/config/settings.yml
all:
  .settings:
    standard_helpers: [Partial, Cache, I18N]
```

Here is how to use the __() helper for the Jobeet footer:

Listing
19-23

```php
// apps/frontend/templates/layout.php
<div id="footer">
  <div class="content">
    <span class="symfony">
      <img src="http://www.symfony-project.org/images/jobeet-mini.png"
/>
      powered by <a href="http://www.symfony-project.org/">
      <img src="http://www.symfony-project.org/images/symfony.gif"
alt="symfony framework" /></a>
    </span>
    <ul>
      <li>
        <a href=""><?php echo __('About Jobeet') ?></a>
      </li>
      <li class="feed">
        <?php echo link_to(__('Full feed'), '@job?sf_format=atom') ?>
      </li>
      <li>
        <a href=""><?php echo __('Jobeet API') ?></a>
      </li>
      <li class="last">
        <?php echo link_to(__('Become an affiliate'),
'@affiliate_new') ?>
      </li>
    </ul>
    <?php include_component('language', 'language') ?>
  </div>
</div>
```

 The __() helper can take the string for the default language or you can also use a unique identifier for each string. It is just a matter of taste. For Jobeet, we will use the former strategy so templates are more readable.

When symfony renders a template, each time the __() helper is called, symfony looks for a translation for the current user's culture. If a translation is found, it is used, if not, the first argument is returned as a fallback value.

All translations are stored in a catalogue. The i18n framework provides a lot of different strategies to store the translations. We will use the "XLIFF"[89] format, which is a standard and the most flexible one. It is also the store used by the admin generator and most symfony plugins.

 Other catalogue stores are gettext, MySQL, and SQLite. As always, have a look at the i18n API[90] for more details.

i18n:extract

Instead of creating the catalogue file by hand, use the built-in i18n:extract task:

Listing 19-24
```
$ php symfony i18n:extract frontend fr --auto-save
```

The i18n:extract task finds all strings that need to be translated in fr in the frontend application and creates or updates the corresponding catalogue. The --auto-save option saves the new strings in the catalogue. You can also use the --auto-delete option to automatically remove strings that do not exist anymore.

In our case, it populates the file we have created:

Listing 19-25
```xml
<!-- apps/frontend/i18n/fr/messages.xml -->
<?xml version="1.0" encoding="UTF-8"?>
<!DOCTYPE xliff PUBLIC "-//XLIFF//DTD XLIFF//EN"
  "http://www.oasis-open.org/committees/xliff/documents/xliff.dtd">
<xliff version="1.0">
  <file source-language="EN" target-language="fr" datatype="plaintext"
      original="messages" date="2008-12-14T12:11:22Z"
      product-name="messages">
    <header/>
    <body>
      <trans-unit id="1">
        <source>About Jobeet</source>
        <target/>
      </trans-unit>
      <trans-unit id="2">
        <source>Feed</source>
        <target/>
```

---

89. http://en.wikipedia.org/wiki/XLIFF
90. http://www.symfony-project.org/api/1_4/i18n

```
    </trans-unit>
    <trans-unit id="3">
      <source>Jobeet API</source>
      <target/>
    </trans-unit>
    <trans-unit id="4">
      <source>Become an affiliate</source>
      <target/>
    </trans-unit>
    </body>
  </file>
</xliff>
```

Each translation is managed by a **trans-unit** tag which has a unique **id** attribute. You can now edit this file and add translations for the French language:

Listing
19-26

```
<!-- apps/frontend/i18n/fr/messages.xml -->
<?xml version="1.0" encoding="UTF-8"?>
<!DOCTYPE xliff PUBLIC "-//XLIFF//DTD XLIFF//EN"
  "http://www.oasis-open.org/committees/xliff/documents/xliff.dtd">
<xliff version="1.0">
  <file source-language="EN" target-language="fr" datatype="plaintext"
      original="messages" date="2008-12-14T12:11:22Z"
      product-name="messages">
    <header/>
    <body>
      <trans-unit id="1">
        <source>About Jobeet</source>
        <target>A propos de Jobeet</target>
      </trans-unit>
      <trans-unit id="2">
        <source>Feed</source>
        <target>Fil RSS</target>
      </trans-unit>
      <trans-unit id="3">
        <source>Jobeet API</source>
        <target>API Jobeet</target>
      </trans-unit>
      <trans-unit id="4">
        <source>Become an affiliate</source>
        <target>Devenir un affilié</target>
      </trans-unit>
    </body>
  </file>
</xliff>
```

As XLIFF is a standard format, a lot of tools exist to ease the translation process. Open Language Tools[91] is an Open-Source Java project with an integrated XLIFF editor.

 As XLIFF is a file-based format, the same precedence and merging rules that exist for other symfony configuration files are also applicable. I18n files can exist in a project, an application, or a module, and the most specific file overrides translations found in the more global ones.

Translations with Arguments

The main principle behind internationalization is to translate whole sentences. But some sentences embed dynamic values. In Jobeet, this is the case on the homepage for the "more..." link:

Listing 19-27

```
<!-- apps/frontend/modules/job/templates/indexSuccess.php -->
<div class="more_jobs">
  and <?php echo link_to($count, 'category', $category) ?> more...
</div>
```

The number of jobs is a variable that must be replaced by a placeholder for translation:

Listing 19-28

```
<!-- apps/frontend/modules/job/templates/indexSuccess.php -->
<div class="more_jobs">
  <?php echo __('and %count% more...', array('%count%' =>
link_to($count, 'category', $category))) ?>
</div>
```

The string to be translated is now "and %count% more...", and the **%count%** placeholder will be replaced by the real number at runtime, thanks to the value given as the second argument to the __() helper.

Add the new string manually by inserting a **trans-unit** tag in the **messages.xml** file, or use the **i18n:extract** task to update the file automatically:

Listing 19-29

```
$ php symfony i18n:extract frontend fr --auto-save
```

After running the task, open the XLIFF file to add the French translation:

Listing 19-30

---

91. https://open-language-tools.dev.java.net/

```
<trans-unit id="5">
  <source>and %count% more...</source>
  <target>et %count% autres...</target>
</trans-unit>
```

The only requirement in the translated string is to use the **%count%** placeholder somewhere.

Some other strings are even more complex as they involve plurals. According to some numbers, the sentence changes, but not necessarily the same way for all languages. Some languages have very complex grammar rules for plurals, like Polish or Russian.

On the category page, the number of jobs in the current category is displayed:

```
<!-- apps/frontend/modules/category/templates/showSuccess.php -->
<strong><?php echo count($pager) ?></strong> jobs in this category
```

Listing 19-31

When a sentence has different translations according to a number, the `format_number_choice()` helper should be used:

```
<?php echo format_number_choice(
    '[0]No job in this category|[1]One job in this
category|(1,+Inf]%count% jobs in this category',
    array('%count%' => '<strong>'.count($pager).'</strong>'),
    count($pager)
  )
?>
```

Listing 19-32

The `format_number_choice()` helper takes three arguments:

- The string to use depending on the number
- An array of placeholder replacements
- The number to use to determine which text to use

The string that describes the different translations according to the number is formatted as follows:

- Each possibility is separated by a pipe character (|)
- Each string is composed of a range followed by the translation

The range can describe any range of numbers:

- **[1,2]**: Accepts values between 1 and 2, inclusive
- **(1,2)**: Accepts values between 1 and 2, excluding 1 and 2
- **{1,2,3,4}**: Only values defined in the set are accepted

- [-Inf,0): Accepts values greater or equal to negative infinity and strictly less than 0
- {n: n % 10 > 1 && n % 10 < 5}: Matches numbers like 2, 3, 4, 22, 23, 24

Translating the string is similar to other message strings:

Listing
19-33

```
<trans-unit id="6">
  <source>[0]No job in this category|[1]One job in this
category|(1,+Inf]%count% jobs in this category</source>
  <target>[0]Aucune annonce dans cette catégorie|[1]Une annonce dans
cette catégorie|(1,+Inf]%count% annonces dans cette catégorie</target>
</trans-unit>
```

Now that you know how to internationalize all kind of strings, take the time to add __() calls for all templates of the frontend application. We won't internationalize the backend application.

Forms

The form classes contain many strings that need to be translated, like labels, error messages, and help messages. All these strings are automatically internationalized by symfony, so you only need to provide translations in the XLIFF files.

 Unfortunately, the i18n:extract task does not yet parse form classes for untranslated strings.

Doctrine Objects

For the Jobeet website, we won't internationalize all tables as it does not make sense to ask the job posters to translate their job posts in all available languages. But the category table definitely needs to be translated.

The Doctrine plugin supports i18n tables out of the box. For each table that contains localized data, two tables need to be created: one for columns that are i18n-independent, and the other one with columns that need to be internationalized. The two tables are linked by a one-to-many relationship.

Update the schema.yml accordingly:

Listing
19-34

```
# config/doctrine/schema.yml
JobeetCategory:
  actAs:
    Timestampable: ~
```

```
I18n:
  fields: [name]
  actAs:
    Sluggable: { fields: [name], uniqueBy: [lang, name] }
columns:
  name: { type: string(255), notnull: true }
```

By turning on the I18n behavior, a model named JobeetCategoryTranslation
will be automatically created and the specified fields are moved to that model.

Notice we simply turn on the I18n behavior and move the Sluggable behavior
to be attached to the JobeetCategoryTranslation model which is automatically
created. The uniqueBy option tells the Sluggable behavior which fields determine
whether a slug is unique or not. In this case each slug must be unique for each lang
and name pair.

And update the fixtures for categories:

Listing
19-35

```
# data/fixtures/categories.yml
JobeetCategory:
  design:
    Translation:
      en:
        name: Design
      fr:
        name: design
  programming:
    Translation:
      en:
        name: Programming
      fr:
        name: Programmation
  manager:
    Translation:
      en:
        name: Manager
      fr:
        name: Manager
  administrator:
    Translation:
      en:
        name: Administrator
      fr:
        name: Administrateur
```

We also need to override the `findOneBySlug()` method in `JobeetCategoryTable`. Since Doctrine provides some magic finders for all columns in a model, we need to simply create the `findOneBySlug()` method so that we override the default magic functionality Doctrine provides.

We need to make a few changes so that the category is retrieved based on the english slug in the `JobeetCategoryTranslation` table.

Listing 19-36

```
// lib/model/doctrine/JobeetCategoryTable.cass.php
public function findOneBySlug($slug)
{
  $q = $this->createQuery('a')
    ->leftJoin('a.Translation t')
    ->andWhere('t.lang = ?', 'en')
    ->andWhere('t.slug = ?', $slug);
  return $q->fetchOne();
}
```

Rebuild the model:

Listing 19-37

```
$ php symfony doctrine:build --all --and-load --no-confirmation
$ php symfony cc
```

 As the **doctrine:build --all --and-load** removes all tables and data from the database, don't forget to re-create a user to access the Jobeet backend with the **guard:create-user** task. Alternatively, you can add a fixture file to add it automatically for you.

When using the **I18n** behavior, proxies are created between the `JobeetCategory` object and the `JobeetCategoryTranslation` object so all the old functions for retrieving the category name will still work and retrieve the value for the current culture.

Listing 19-38

```
$category = new JobeetCategory();
$category->setName('foo'); // sets the name for the current culture
$category->getName(); // gets the name for the current culture

$this->getUser()->setCulture('fr'); // from your actions class

$category->setName('foo'); // sets the name for French
echo $category->getName(); // gets the name for French
```

To reduce the number of database requests, join the JobeetCategoryTranslation in your queries. It will retrieve the main object and the i18n one in one request.

Listing
19-39

```
$categories = Doctrine_Query::create()
  ->from('JobeetCategory c')
  ->leftJoin('c.Translation t WITH t.lang = ?', $culture)
  ->execute();
```

The WITH keyword above will append a condition to the automatically added ON condition of the query. So, the ON condition of the join will end up being.

```
LEFT JOIN c.Translation t ON c.id = t.id AND t.lang = ?
```

Listing
19-40

As the **category** route is tied to the **JobeetCategory** model class and because the **slug** is now part of the **JobeetCategoryTranslation**, the route is not able to retrieve the **Category** object automatically. To help the routing system, let's create a method that will take care of object retrieval:

Since we already overrode the **findOneBySlug()** let's refactor a little bit more so these methods can be shared. We'll create a new **findOneBySlugAndCulture()** and **doSelectForSlug()** methods and change the **findOneBySlug()** method to simply use the **findOneBySlugAndCulture()** method.

Listing
19-41

```
// lib/model/doctrine/JobeetCategoryTable.class.php
public function doSelectForSlug($parameters)
{
  return $this->findOneBySlugAndCulture($parameters['slug'],
$parameters['sf_culture']);
}

public function findOneBySlugAndCulture($slug, $culture = 'en')
{
  $q = $this->createQuery('a')
    ->leftJoin('a.Translation t')
    ->andWhere('t.lang = ?', $culture)
    ->andWhere('t.slug = ?', $slug);
  return $q->fetchOne();
}

public function findOneBySlug($slug)
{
  return $this->findOneBySlugAndCulture($slug, 'en');
}
```

Then, use the **method** option to tell the **category** route to use the doSelectForSlug() method to retrieve the object:

Listing
19-42
```
# apps/frontend/config/routing.yml
category:
  url:     /:sf_culture/category/:slug.:sf_format
  class:   sfDoctrineRoute
  param:   { module: category, action: show, sf_format: html }
  options: { model: JobeetCategory, type: object, method:
doSelectForSlug }
  requirements:
    sf_format: (?:html|atom)
```

We need to reload the fixtures to regenerate the proper slugs for the categories:

Listing
19-43
```
$ php symfony doctrine:data-load
```

Now the **category** route is internationalized and the URL for a category embeds the translated category slug:

Listing
19-44
```
/frontend_dev.php/fr/category/programmation
/frontend_dev.php/en/category/programming
```

Admin Generator

For the backend, we want the French and the English translations to be edited in the same form:

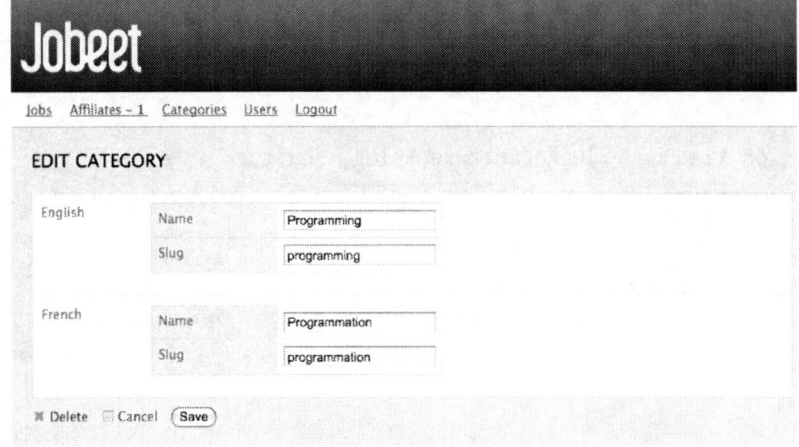

Embedding an i18n form can be done by using the **embedI18N()** method:

```
// lib/form/JobeetCategoryForm.class.php
class JobeetCategoryForm extends BaseJobeetCategoryForm
{
  public function configure()
  {
    unset(
      $this['jobeet_affiliates_list'],
      $this['created_at'], $this['updated_at']
    );

    $this->embedI18n(array('en', 'fr'));
    $this->widgetSchema->setLabel('en', 'English');
    $this->widgetSchema->setLabel('fr', 'French');
  }
}
```

Listing
19.45

The admin generator interface supports internationalization out of the box. It comes with translations for more than 20 languages, and it is quite easy to add a new one, or to customize an existing one. Copy the file for the language you want to customize from symfony (admin translations are to be found in **lib/vendor/symfony/lib/plugins/sfDoctrinePlugin/i18n/**) in the application **i18n** directory. As the file in your application will be merged with the symfony one, only keep the modified strings in the application file.

You will notice that the admin generator translation files are named like **sf_admin.fr.xml**, instead of **fr/messages.xml**. As a matter of fact, **messages** is the name of the default catalogue used by symfony, and can be changed to allow a better separation between different parts of your application. Using a catalogue other than the default one requires that you specify it when using the __() helper:

```
<?php echo __('About Jobeet', array(), 'jobeet') ?>
```

Listing
19.46

In the above __() call, symfony will look for the "About Jobeet" string in the **jobeet** catalogue.

Tests

Fixing tests is an integral part of the internationalization migration. First, update the test fixtures for categories by copying the fixtures we have define above in **test/fixtures/categories.yml**.

Rebuild the model for the **test** environment:

```
$ php symfony doctrine:build --all -and-load --no-confirmation
--env=test
```

Listing
19.47

You can now launch all tests to check that they are running fine:

Listing 19.48

```
$ php symfony test:all
```

 When we have developed the backend interface for Jobeet, we have not written functional tests. But whenever you create a module with the symfony command line, symfony also generate test stubs. These stubs are safe to remove.

Localization

Templates

Supporting different cultures also means supporting different way to format dates and numbers. In a template, several helpers are at your disposal to help take all these differences into account, based on the current user culture:

In the Date[92] helper group:

Helper	Description
format_date()	Formats a date
format_datetime()	Formats a date with a time (hours, minutes, seconds)
time_ago_in_words()	Displays the elapsed time between a date and now in words
distance_of_time_in_words()	Displays the elapsed time between two dates in words
format_daterange()	Formats a range of dates

In the Number[93] helper group:

Helper	Description
format_number()	Formats a number
format_currency()	Formats a currency

In the I18N[94] helper group:

---

92. http://www.symfony-project.org/api/1_4/DateHelper
93. http://www.symfony-project.org/api/1_4/NumberHelper

Helper	Description
format_country()	Displays the name of a country
format_language()	Displays the name of a language

Forms (I18n)

The form framework provides several widgets and validators for localized data:

- sfWidgetFormI18nDate[95]
- sfWidgetFormI18nDateTime[96]
- sfWidgetFormI18nTime[97]
- sfWidgetFormI18nChoiceCountry[98]
- sfWidgetFormI18nChoiceCurrency[99]
- sfWidgetFormI18nChoiceLanguage[100]
- sfWidgetFormI18nChoiceTimezone[101]
- sfValidatorI18nChoiceCountry[102]
- sfValidatorI18nChoiceLanguage[103]
- sfValidatorI18nChoiceTimezone[104]

See you Tomorrow

Internationalization and localization are first-class citizens in symfony. Providing a localized website to your users is very easy as symfony provides all the basic tools and even gives you command line tasks to make it fast.

Be prepared for a very special tutorial tomorrow as we will be moving a lot of files around and exploring a different approach to organizing a symfony project.

94. http://www.symfony-project.org/api/1_4/I18NHelper
95. http://www.symfony-project.org/api/1_4/sfWidgetFormI18nDate
96. http://www.symfony-project.org/api/1_4/sfWidgetFormI18nDateTime
97. http://www.symfony-project.org/api/1_4/sfWidgetFormI18nTime
98. http://www.symfony-project.org/api/1_4/sfWidgetFormI18nChoiceCountry
99. http://www.symfony-project.org/api/1_4/sfWidgetFormI18nChoiceCurrency
100. http://www.symfony-project.org/api/1_4/sfWidgetFormI18nChoiceLanguage
101. http://www.symfony-project.org/api/1_4/sfWidgetFormI18nChoiceTimezone
102. http://www.symfony-project.org/api/1_4/sfValidatorI18nChoiceCountry
103. http://www.symfony-project.org/api/1_4/sfValidatorI18nChoiceLanguage
104. http://www.symfony-project.org/api/1_4/sfValidatorI18nChoiceTimezone

Day 20

The Plugins

Yesterday you learned how to internationalize and localize your symfony applications. Once again, thanks to the ICU standard and a lot of helpers, symfony makes this really easy.

Today, we will talk about plugins: what they are, what you can bundle in a plugin, and what they can be used for.

Plugins

A symfony Plugin

A symfony plugin offers a way to package and distribute a subset of your project files. Like a project, a plugin can contain classes, helpers, configuration, tasks, modules, schemas, and even web assets.

Private Plugins

The first usage of plugins is to ease sharing code between your applications, or even between different projects. Recall that symfony applications only share the model. Plugins provide a way to share more components between applications.

If you need to reuse the same schema for different projects, or the same modules, move them to a plugin. As a plugin is just a directory, you can move it around quite easily by creating a SVN repository and using **svn:externals**, or by just copying the files from one project to another.

We call these "private plugins" because their usage is restricted to a single developer or a company. They are not publicly available.

You can even create a package out of your private plugins, create your own symfony plugin channel, and install them via the `plugin:install` task.

Public Plugins

Public plugins are available for the community to download and install. During this tutorial, we have used a couple of public plugins: `sfDoctrineGuardPlugin` and `sfFormExtraPlugin`.

They are exactly the same as private plugins. The only difference is that anybody can install them for their projects. You will learn later on how to publish and host a public plugin on the symfony website.

A Different Way to Organize Code

There is one more way to think about plugins and how to use them. Forget about re-usability and sharing. Plugins can be used as a different way to organize your code. Instead of organizing the files by layers: all models in the `lib/model/` directory, templates in the `templates/` directory, ...; the files are put together by feature: all the job files together (the model, modules, and templates), all the CMS files together, and so on.

Plugin File Structure

A plugin is just a directory structure with files organized in a pre-defined structure, according to the nature of the files. Today, we will move most of the code we have written for Jobeet in a `sfJobeetPlugin`. The basic layout we will use is as follows:

Listing 20-1
```
sfJobeetPlugin/
  config/
    sfJobeetPluginConfiguration.class.php // Plugin initialization
    routing.yml                           // Routing
    doctrine/
      schema.yml                          // Database schema
  lib/
    Jobeet.class.php                      // Classes
    helper/                               // Helpers
    filter/                               // Filter classes
    form/                                 // Form classes
    model/                                // Model classes
    task/                                 // Tasks
```

```
modules/
  job/                                 // Modules
    actions/
    config/
    templates/
  web/                                 // Assets like JS, CSS, and
images
```

The Jobeet Plugin

Bootstrapping a plugin is as simple as creating a new directory under **plugins/**.
For Jobeet, let's create a **sfJobeetPlugin** directory:

```
$ mkdir plugins/sfJobeetPlugin
```

*Listing
20-2*

 All plugins must end with **Plugin**. It is also a good habit to prefix them with **sf**, although it is not mandatory.

The Model

First, move the **config/doctrine/schema.yml** file to **plugins/sfJobeetPlugin/config/**:

```
$ mkdir plugins/sfJobeetPlugin/config/
$ mkdir plugins/sfJobeetPlugin/config/doctrine
$ mv config/doctrine/schema.yml plugins/sfJobeetPlugin/config/doctrine/
schema.yml
```

*Listing
20-3*

 All commands are for Unix like environments. If you use Windows, you can drag and drop files in the Explorer. And if you use Subversion, or any other tool to manage your code, use the built-in tools they provide (like **svn mv** to move files).

Move model, form, and filter files to **plugins/sfJobeetPlugin/lib/**:

```
$ mkdir plugins/sfJobeetPlugin/lib/
$ mv lib/model/ plugins/sfJobeetPlugin/lib/
$ mv lib/form/ plugins/sfJobeetPlugin/lib/
$ mv lib/filter/ plugins/sfJobeetPlugin/lib/
```

*Listing
20-4*

After you move the models, forms and filters the classes must be renamed, made abstract and prefixed with the word `Plugin`.

 Only prefix the auto-generated classes with `Plugin` and not all classes. For example do not prefix any classes you wrote by hand. Only the auto-generated ones require the prefix.

Here is an example where we move the `JobeetAffiliate` and `JobeetAffiliateTable` classes.

Listing 20-5
```
$ mv plugins/sfJobeetPlugin/lib/model/doctrine/
JobeetAffiliate.class.php plugins/sfJobeetPlugin/lib/model/doctrine/
PluginJobeetAffiliate.class.php
```

And the code should be updated:

Listing 20-6
```
abstract class PluginJobeetAffiliate extends BaseJobeetAffiliate
{
  public function preValidate($event)
  {
    $object = $event->getInvoker();

    if (!$object->getToken())
    {
      $object->setToken(sha1($object->getEmail().rand(11111, 99999)));
    }
  }

  // ...
}
```

Now lets move the `JobeetAffiliateTable` class:

Listing 20-7
```
$ mv plugins/sfJobeetPlugin/lib/model/doctrine/
JobeetAffiliateTable.class.php plugins/sfJobeetPlugin/lib/model/
doctrine/PluginJobeetAffiliateTable.class.php
```

The class definition should now look like the following:

Listing 20-8
```
abstract class PluginJobeetAffiliateTable extends Doctrine_Table
{
  // ...
}
```

Now do the same thing for the forms and filter classes. Rename them to include a prefix with the word `Plugin`.

Make sure to remove the `base` directory in `plugins/sfJobeetPlugin/lib/*/doctrine/` for `form`, `filter`, and `model` directories:

Listing
20.9

```
$ rm -rf plugins/sfJobeetPlugin/lib/form/doctrine/base
$ rm -rf plugins/sfJobeetPlugin/lib/filter/doctrine/base
$ rm -rf plugins/sfJobeetPlugin/lib/model/doctrine/base
```

Once you have moved, renamed and removed some forms, filters and model classes run the tasks to build the re-build all the classes:

Listing
20-10

```
$ php symfony doctrine:build --all-classes
```

Now you will notice some new directories created to hold the models created from the schema included with the `sfJobeetPlugin` at `lib/model/doctrine/sfJobeetPlugin/`.

This directory contains the top level models and the base classes generated from the schema. For example the model `JobeetJob` now has this class structure:

- `JobeetJob` (extends `PluginJobeetJob`) in `lib/model/doctrine/sfJobeetPlugin/JobeetJob.class.php`: Top level class where all project model functionality can be placed. This is where you can add and override functionality that comes with the plugin models.

- `PluginJobeetJob` (extends `BaseJobeetJob`) in `plugins/sfJobeetPlugin/lib/model/doctrine/PluginJobeetJob.class.php`: This class contains all the plugin specific functionality. You can override functionality in this class and the base by modifying the `JobeetJob` class.

- `BaseJobeetJob` (extends `sfDoctrineRecord`) in `lib/model/doctrine/sfJobeetPlugin/base/BaseJobeetJob.class.php`: Base class that is generated from the yaml schema file each time you run `doctrine:build --model`.

- `JobeetJobTable` (extends `PluginJobeetJobTable`) in `lib/model/doctrine/sfJobeetPlugin/JobeetJobTable.class.php`: Same as the `JobeetJob` class except this is the instance of `Doctrine_Table` that will be returned when you call `Doctrine::getTable('JobeetJob')`.

- `PluginJobeetJobTable` (extends `Doctrine_Table`) in `lib/model/doctrine/sfJobeetPlugin/JobeetJobTable.class.php`: This class contains all the plugin specific functionality for the instance of

`Doctrine_Table` that will be returned when you call `Doctrine::getTable('JobeetJob')`.

With this generated structure you have the ability to customize the models of a plugin by editing the top level **JobeetJob** class. You can customize the schema and add columns, add relationships by overriding the **setTableDefinition()** and **setUp()** methods.

 When you move the form classes, be sure to change the **configure()** method to a **setup()** method and call **parent::setup()**. Below is an example.

Listing 20-11
```
abstract class PluginJobeetAffiliateForm extends
BaseJobeetAffiliateForm
{
  public function setup()
  {
    parent::setup();
  }

  // ...
}
```

We need to make sure our plugin doesn't have the base classes for all Doctrine forms. These files are global for a project and will be re-generated with the **doctrine:build --forms** and **doctrine:build --filters**.

Remove the files from the plugin:

Listing 20-12
```
$ rm plugins/sfJobeetPlugin/lib/form/doctrine/
BaseFormDoctrine.class.php
$ rm plugins/sfJobeetPlugin/lib/filter/doctrine/
BaseFormFilterDoctrine.class.php
```

You can also move the **Jobeet.class.php** file to the plugin:

Listing 20-13
```
$ mv lib/Jobeet.class.php plugins/sfJobeetPlugin/lib/
```

As we have moved files around, clear the cache:

Listing 20-14
```
$ php symfony cc
```

 If you use a PHP accelerator like APC and things get weird at this point, restart Apache.

Now that all the model files have been moved to the plugin, run the tests to check that everything still works fine:

```
$ php symfony test:all
```

Listing
20-15

The Controllers and the Views

The next logical step is to move the modules to the plugin. To avoid module name collisions, it is always a good habit to prefix plugin module names with the plugin name:

```
$ mkdir plugins/sfJobeetPlugin/modules/
$ mv apps/frontend/modules/affiliate plugins/sfJobeetPlugin/modules/
sfJobeetAffiliate
$ mv apps/frontend/modules/api plugins/sfJobeetPlugin/modules/
sfJobeetApi
$ mv apps/frontend/modules/category plugins/sfJobeetPlugin/modules/
sfJobeetCategory
$ mv apps/frontend/modules/job plugins/sfJobeetPlugin/modules/
sfJobeetJob
$ mv apps/frontend/modules/language plugins/sfJobeetPlugin/modules/
sfJobeetLanguage
```

Listing
20-16

For each module, you also need to change the class name in all actions.class.php and components.class.php files (for instance, the affiliateActions class needs to be renamed to sfJobeetAffiliateActions).

The include_partial() and include_component() calls must also be changed in the following templates:

- sfJobeetAffiliate/templates/_form.php (change affiliate to sfJobeetAffiliate)
- sfJobeetCategory/templates/showSuccess.atom.php
- sfJobeetCategory/templates/showSuccess.php
- sfJobeetJob/templates/indexSuccess.atom.php
- sfJobeetJob/templates/indexSuccess.php
- sfJobeetJob/templates/searchSuccess.php
- sfJobeetJob/templates/showSuccess.php
- apps/frontend/templates/layout.php

Update the search and delete actions:

```
// plugins/sfJobeetPlugin/modules/sfJobeetJob/actions/actions.class.php
class sfJobeetJobActions extends sfActions
{
```

Listing
20-17

```php
  public function executeSearch(sfWebRequest $request)
  {
    if (!$query = $request->getParameter('query'))
    {
      return $this->forward('sfJobeetJob', 'index');
    }

    $this->jobs = Doctrine::getTable('JobeetJob')
      ➥ ->getForLuceneQuery($query);

    if ($request->isXmlHttpRequest())
    {
      if ('*' == $query || !$this->jobs)
      {
        return $this->renderText('No results.');
      }
      else
      {
        return $this->renderPartial('sfJobeetJob/list',
          ➥ array('jobs' => $this->jobs));
      }
    }
  }

  public function executeDelete(sfWebRequest $request)
  {
    $request->checkCSRFProtection();

    $jobeet_job = $this->getRoute()->getObject();
    $jobeet_job->delete();

    $this->redirect('sfJobeetJob/index');
  }

  // ...
}
```

Now, modify the **routing.yml** file to take these changes into account:

Listing 20-18
```yaml
# apps/frontend/config/routing.yml
affiliate:
  class:    sfDoctrineRouteCollection
  options:
    model:        JobeetAffiliate
    actions:      [new, create]
```

```
    object_actions: { wait: GET }
    prefix_path:    /:sf_culture/affiliate
    module:         sfJobeetAffiliate
  requirements:
    sf_culture: (?:fr|en)

api_jobs:
  url:     /api/:token/jobs.:sf_format
  class:   sfDoctrineRoute
  param:   { module: sfJobeetApi, action: list }
  options: { model: JobeetJob, type: list, method: getForToken }
  requirements:
    sf_format: (?:xml|json|yaml)

category:
  url:     /:sf_culture/category/:slug.:sf_format
  class:   sfDoctrineRoute
  param:   { module: sfJobeetCategory, action: show, sf_format: html }
  options: { model: JobeetCategory, type: object, method:
doSelectForSlug }
  requirements:
    sf_format: (?:html|atom)
    sf_culture: (?:fr|en)

job_search:
  url:   /:sf_culture/search
  param: { module: sfJobeetJob, action: search }
  requirements:
    sf_culture: (?:fr|en)

job:
  class:   sfDoctrineRouteCollection
  options:
    model:          JobeetJob
    column:         token
    object_actions: { publish: PUT, extend: PUT }
    prefix_path:    /:sf_culture/job
    module:         sfJobeetJob
  requirements:
    token: \w+
    sf_culture: (?:fr|en)

job_show_user:
  url:     /:sf_culture/job/:company_slug/:location_slug/:id/
:position_slug
```

```
      class:    sfDoctrineRoute
      options:
        model: JobeetJob
        type: object
        method_for_query: retrieveActiveJob
      param:    { module: sfJobeetJob, action: show }
      requirements:
        id:           \d+
        sf_method: GET
        sf_culture: (?:fr|en)

  change_language:
    url:    /change_language
    param: { module: sfJobeetLanguage, action: changeLanguage }

  localized_homepage:
    url:    /:sf_culture/
    param: { module: sfJobeetJob, action: index }
    requirements:
      sf_culture: (?:fr|en)

  homepage:
    url:    /
    param: { module: sfJobeetJob, action: index }
```

Eventually, enable the plugin by hand in **ProjectConfiguration.class.php** as it was not installed via the **plugin:install** task:

Listing 20-19
```
// config/ProjectConfiguration.class.php
class ProjectConfiguration extends sfProjectConfiguration
{
  public function setup()
  {
    $this->enablePlugins('sfDoctrinePlugin', 'sfDoctrineGuardPlugin',
'sfFormExtraPlugin', 'sfJobeetPlugin');
  }
}
```

If you try to browse the Jobeet website now, you will have exceptions telling you that the modules are not enabled. As plugins are shared amongst all applications in a project, you need to specifically enable the module you need for a given application in its **settings.yml** configuration file:

Listing 20-20
```
# apps/frontend/config/settings.yml
all:
```

```
.settings:
  enabled_modules:
    - default
    - sfJobeetAffiliate
    - sfJobeetApi
    - sfJobeetCategory
    - sfJobeetJob
    - sfJobeetLanguage
```

The last step of the migration is to fix the functional tests where we test for the module name.

The Tasks

Tasks can be moved to the plugin quite easily:

```
$ mv lib/task plugins/sfJobeetPlugin/lib/
```

The i18n Files

A plugin can also contain XLIFF files:

```
$ mv apps/frontend/i18n plugins/sfJobeetPlugin/
```
Listing 20-22

The Routing

A plugin can also contain routing rules:

```
$ mv apps/frontend/config/routing.yml plugins/sfJobeetPlugin/config/
```
Listing 20-23

The Assets

Even if it is a bit counter-intuitive, a plugin can also contain web assets like images, stylesheets, and JavaScripts. As we don't want to distribute the Jobeet plugin, it does not really make sense, but it is possible by creating a **plugins/ sfJobeetPlugin/web/** directory.

A plugin's assets must be accessible in the project's **web/** directory to be viewable from a browser. The **plugin:publish-assets** addresses this by creating symlinks under Unix system and by copying the files on the Windows platform:

```
$ php symfony plugin:publish-assets
```
Listing 20-24

The User

Moving the **myUser** class methods that deal with job history is a bit more involved. We could create a **JobeetUser** class and make **myUser** inherit from it. But there is a better way, especially if several plugins want to add new methods to the class.

Core symfony objects notify events during their life-cycle that you can listen to. In our case, we need to listen to the **user.method_not_found** event, which occurs when an undefined method is called on the **sfUser** object.

When symfony is initialized, all plugins are also initialized if they have a plugin configuration class:

Listing
20-25

```php
// plugins/sfJobeetPlugin/config/sfJobeetPluginConfiguration.class.php
class sfJobeetPluginConfiguration extends sfPluginConfiguration
{
  public function initialize()
  {
    $this->dispatcher->connect('user.method_not_found',
array('JobeetUser', 'methodNotFound'));
  }
}
```

Event notifications are managed by **sfEventDispatcher**[105], the event dispatcher object. Registering a listener is as simple as calling the **connect()** method. The **connect()** method connects an event name to a PHP callable.

 A PHP callable[106] is a PHP variable that can be used by the **call_user_func()** function and returns **true** when passed to the **is_callable()** function. A string represents a function, and an array can represent an object method or a class method.

With the above code in place, **myUser** object will call the static **methodNotFound()** method of the **JobeetUser** class whenever it is unable to find a method. It is then up to the **methodNotFound()** method to process the missing method or not.

Remove all methods from the **myUser** class and create the **JobeetUser** class:

Listing
20-26

```php
// apps/frontend/lib/myUser.class.php
class myUser extends sfBasicSecurityUser
{
}
```

---

105. http://www.symfony-project.org/api/1_4/sfEventDispatcher
106. http://www.php.net/manual/en/function.is-callable.php

```php
// plugins/sfJobeetPlugin/lib/JobeetUser.class.php
class JobeetUser
{
  static public function methodNotFound(sfEvent $event)
  {
    if (method_exists('JobeetUser', $event['method']))
    {
      $event->setReturnValue(call_user_func_array(
        array('JobeetUser', $event['method']),
        array_merge(array($event->getSubject()), $event['arguments'])
      ));

      return true;
    }
  }

  static public function isFirstRequest(sfUser $user, $boolean = null)
  {
    if (is_null($boolean))
    {
      return $user->getAttribute('first_request', true);
    }
    else
    {
      $user->setAttribute('first_request', $boolean);
    }
  }

  static public function addJobToHistory(sfUser $user, JobeetJob $job)
  {
    $ids = $user->getAttribute('job_history', array());

    if (!in_array($job->getId(), $ids))
    {
      array_unshift($ids, $job->getId());
      $user->setAttribute('job_history', array_slice($ids, 0, 3));
    }
  }

  static public function getJobHistory(sfUser $user)
  {
    $ids = $user->getAttribute('job_history', array());

    if (!empty($ids))
    {
```

```
      return Doctrine::getTable('JobeetJob')
        ->createQuery('a')
        ->whereIn('a.id', $ids)
        ->execute();
    } else {
      return array();
    }
  }

  static public function resetJobHistory(sfUser $user)
  {
    $user->getAttributeHolder()->remove('job_history');
  }
}
```

When the dispatcher calls the **methodNotFound()** method, it passes a **sfEvent**[107] object.

If the method exists in the **JobeetUser** class, it is called and its returned value is subsequently returned to the notifier. If not, symfony will try the next registered listener or throw an Exception.

The **getSubject()** method returns the notifier of the event, which in this case is the current **myUser** object.

The Default Structure vs. the Plugin Architecture

Using the plugin architecture allows you to organize your code in a different way:

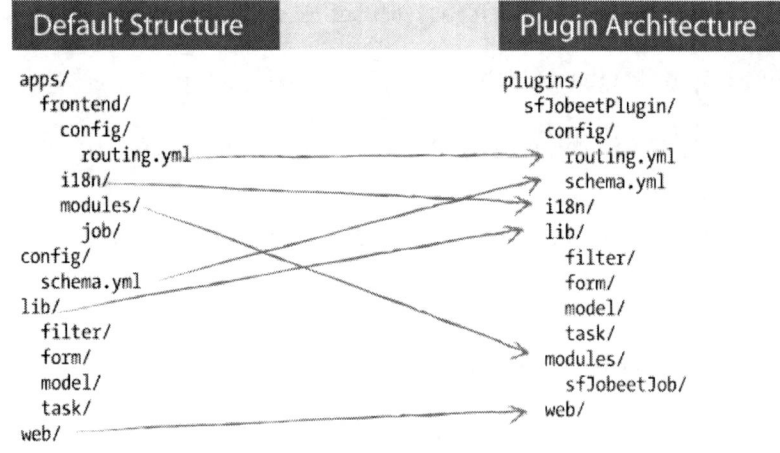

---

107. http://www.symfony-project.org/api/1_4/sfEvent

Using Plugins

When you start implementing a new feature, or if you try to solve a classic web problem, odds are that someone has already solved the same problem and perhaps packaged the solution as a symfony plugin. To you look for a public symfony plugin, go to the plugin section[108] of the symfony website.

As a plugin is self-contained in a directory, there are several way to install it:

- Using the `plugin:install` task (it only works if the plugin developer has created a plugin package and uploaded it on the symfony website)
- Downloading the package and manually un-archive it under the `plugins/` directory (it also need that the developer has uploaded a package)
- Creating a `svn:externals` in `plugins/` for the plugin (it only works if the plugin developer host its plugin on Subversion)

The last two ways are easy but lack some flexibility. The first way allows you to install the latest version according to the project symfony version, easily upgrade to the latest stable release, and to easily manage dependencies between plugins.

Contributing a Plugin

Packaging a Plugin

To create a plugin package, you need to add some mandatory files to the plugin directory structure. First, create a **README** file at the root of the plugin directory and explain how to install the plugin, what it provides, and what not. The **README** file must be formatted with the Markdown format[109]. This file will be used on the symfony website as the main piece of documentation. You can test the conversion of your README file to HTML by using the symfony plugin dingus[110].

---

108. `http://www.symfony-project.org/plugins/`
109. `http://daringfireball.net/projects/markdown/syntax`
110. `http://www.symfony-project.org/plugins/markdown_dingus`

If you find yourself frequently creating private and/or public plugins, consider taking advantage of some of the tasks in the sfTaskExtraPlugin[111]. This plugin, maintained by the core team, includes a number of tasks that help you streamline the plugin lifecycle:

- `generate:plugin`
- `plugin:package`

You also need to create a **LICENSE** file. Choosing a license is not an easy task, but the symfony plugin section only lists plugins that are released under a license similar to the symfony one (MIT, BSD, LGPL, and PHP). The content of the **LICENSE** file will be displayed under the license tab of your plugin's public page.

The last step is to create a **package.xml** file at the root of the plugin directory. This **package.xml** file follows the PEAR package syntax[112].

 The best way to learn the **package.xml** syntax is certainly to copy the one used by an existing plugin[113].

The **package.xml** file is composed of several parts as you can see in this template example:

```
<!-- plugins/sfJobeetPlugin/package.xml -->
<?xml version="1.0" encoding="UTF-8"?>
<package packagerversion="1.4.1" version="2.0"
    xmlns="http://pear.php.net/dtd/package-2.0"
    xmlns:tasks="http://pear.php.net/dtd/tasks-1.0"
    xmlns:xsi="http://www.w3.org/2001/XMLSchema-instance"
    xsi:schemaLocation="http://pear.php.net/dtd/tasks-1.0
    http://pear.php.net/dtd/tasks-1.0.xsd http://pear.php.net/dtd/
package-2.0
    http://pear.php.net/dtd/package-2.0.xsd"
>
  <name>sfJobeetPlugin</name>
  <channel>plugins.symfony-project.org</channel>
  <summary>A job board plugin.</summary>
  <description>A job board plugin.</description>
```

---

111. http://www.symfony-project.com/plugins/sfTaskExtraPlugin
112. http://pear.php.net/manual/en/guide-developers.php
113. http://svn.symfony-project.com/plugins/sfGuardPlugin/branches/1.2/package.xml

```xml
  <lead>
    <name>Fabien POTENCIER</name>
    <user>fabpot</user>
    <email>fabien.potencier@symfony-project.com</email>
    <active>yes</active>
  </lead>
  <date>2008-12-20</date>
  <version>
    <release>1.0.0</release>
    <api>1.0.0</api>
  </version>
  <stability>
    <release>stable</release>
    <api>stable</api>
  </stability>
  <license uri="http://www.symfony-project.com/license">
    MIT license
  </license>
  <notes />

  <contents>
    <!-- CONTENT -->
  </contents>

  <dependencies>
   <!-- DEPENDENCIES -->
  </dependencies>

  <phprelease>
</phprelease>

<changelog>
  <!-- CHANGELOG -->
</changelog>
</package>
```

The **<contents>** tag contains the files that need to be put into the package:

```xml
<contents>
  <dir name="/">
    <file role="data" name="README" />
    <file role="data" name="LICENSE" />

    <dir name="config">
      <file role="data" name="config.php" />
```

*Listing
20-28*

```
        <file role="data" name="schema.yml" />
      </dir>

      <!-- ... -->
    </dir>
  </contents>
```

The `<dependencies>` tag references all dependencies the plugin might have: PHP,
symfony, and also other plugins. This information is used by the `plugin:install`
task to install the best plugin version for the project environment and to also install
required plugin dependencies if any.

Listing
20-29
```
<dependencies>
  <required>
    <php>
      <min>5.0.0</min>
    </php>
    <pearinstaller>
      <min>1.4.1</min>
    </pearinstaller>
    <package>
      <name>symfony</name>
      <channel>pear.symfony-project.com</channel>
      <min>1.3.0</min>
      <max>1.5.0</max>
      <exclude>1.5.0</exclude>
    </package>
  </required>
</dependencies>
```

You should always declare a dependency on symfony, as we have done here.
Declaring a minimum and a maximum version allows the `plugin:install` to
know what symfony version is mandatory as symfony versions can have slightly
different APIs.

Declaring a dependency with another plugin is also possible:

Listing
20-30
```
<package>
  <name>sfFooPlugin</name>
  <channel>plugins.symfony-project.org</channel>
  <min>1.0.0</min>
  <max>1.2.0</max>
  <exclude>1.2.0</exclude>
</package>
```

The `<changelog>` tag is optional but gives useful information about what changed between releases. This information is available under the "Changelog" tab and also in the plugin feed[114].

Listing
20-31

```
<changelog>
  <release>
    <version>
      <release>1.0.0</release>
      <api>1.0.0</api>
    </version>
    <stability>
      <release>stable</release>
      <api>stable</api>
    </stability>
    <license uri="http://www.symfony-project.com/license">
      MIT license
    </license>
    <date>2008-12-20</date>
    <license>MIT</license>
    <notes>
       * fabien: First release of the plugin
    </notes>
  </release>
</changelog>
```

Hosting a Plugin on the symfony Website

If you develop a useful plugin and you want to share it with the symfony community, create a symfony account[115] if you don't have one already and then, create a new plugin[116].

You will automatically become the administrator for the plugin and you will see an "admin" tab in the interface. In this tab, you will find everything you need to manage your plugin and upload your packages.

 The plugin FAQ[117] contains a lot of useful information for plugin developers.

114. http://www.symfony-project.org/plugins/recently.rss
115. http://www.symfony-project.org/user/new
116. http://www.symfony-project.org/plugins/new
117. http://www.symfony-project.org/plugins/FAQ

See you Tomorrow

Creating plugins, and sharing them with the community is one of the best ways to contribute back to the symfony project. It is so easy, that the symfony plugin repository is full of useful, fun, but also ridiculous plugins.

Day 21

The Cache

Today, we will talk about caching. The symfony framework has many built-in cache strategies. For instance, the YAML configuration files are first converted to PHP and then cached on the filesystem. We have also seen that the modules generated by the admin generator are cached for better performance.

But today, we will talk about another cache: the HTML cache. To improve your website performance, you can cache whole HTML pages or just parts of them.

Creating a new Environment

By default, the template cache feature of symfony is enabled in the **settings.yml** configuration file for the **prod** environment, but not for the **test** and **dev** ones:

Listing
21-1

```
prod:
  .settings:
    cache: true

dev:
  .settings:
    cache: false

test:
  .settings:
    cache: false
```

As we need to test the cache feature before going to production, we can activate the cache for the **dev** environment or create a new environment. Recall that an environment is defined by its name (a string), an associated front controller, and optionally a set of specific configuration values.

To play with the cache system on Jobeet, we will create a **cache** environment, similar to the **prod** environment, but with the log and debug information available in the **dev** environment.

Create the front controller associated with the new **cache** environment by copying the **dev** front controller web/frontend_dev.php to web/frontend_cache.php:

Listing 21-2

```
// web/frontend_cache.php
if (!in_array(@$_SERVER['REMOTE_ADDR'], array('127.0.0.1', '::1')))
{
  die('You are not allowed to access this file. Check
'.basename(__FILE__).' for more information.');
}

require_once(dirname(__FILE__).'/../config/
ProjectConfiguration.class.php');

$configuration =
ProjectConfiguration::getApplicationConfiguration('frontend', 'cache',
true);
sfContext::createInstance($configuration)->dispatch();
```

That's all there is to it. The new **cache** environment is now useable. The only difference is the second argument of the getApplicationConfiguration() method which is the environment name, **cache**.

You can test the **cache** environment in your browser by calling its front controller:

Listing 21-3

```
http://jobeet.localhost/frontend_cache.php/
```

 The front controller script begins with a code that ensures that the front controller is only called from a local IP address. This security measure is to protect the front controller from being called on the production servers. We will talk about this in more details in tomorrow's tutorial.

For now, the **cache** environment inherits from the default configuration. Edit the **settings.yml** configuration file to add the **cache** environment specific configuration:

Listing 21-4

```
# apps/frontend/config/settings.yml
cache:
  .settings:
    error_reporting: <?php echo (E_ALL | E_STRICT)."\n" ?>
    web_debug:        true
```

```
cache:          true
etag:           false
```

In these settings, the symfony template cache feature has been activated with the **cache** setting and the web debug toolbar has been enabled with the **web_debug** setting.

As the default configuration caches all settings in the cache, you need to clear it before being able to see the changes in your browser:

```
$ php symfony cc
```

Listing
21-5

Now, if you refresh your browser, the web debug toolbar should be present in the top right corner of the page, as it is the case for the **dev** environment.

Cache Configuration

The symfony template cache can be configured with the **cache.yml** configuration file. The default configuration for the application is to be found in **apps/frontend/config/cache.yml**:

```
default:
  enabled:     false
  with_layout: false
  lifetime:    86400
```

Listing
21-6

By default, as all pages can contain dynamic information, the cache is globally disabled (**enabled: off**). We don't need to change this setting, because we will enable the cache on a page by page basis.

The **lifetime** setting defines the server side life time of the cache in seconds (**86400** seconds equals one day).

 You can also work the other way around: enable the cache globally and then, disable it on specific pages that cannot be cached. It depends on which represents the less work for your application.

Page Cache

As the Jobeet homepage will probably be the most visited page of the website, instead of requesting the data from the database each time a user accesses it, it can be cached.

Create a **cache.yml** file for the **sfJobeetJob** module:

Listing
21-7

```
# plugins/sfJobeetPlugin/modules/sfJobeetJob/config/cache.yml
index:
  enabled:     true
  with_layout: true
```

 The **cache.yml** configuration file has the same properties than any other symfony configuration files like **view.yml**. It means for instance that you can enable the cache for all actions of a module by using the special **all** key.

If you refresh your browser, you will see that symfony has decorated the page with a box indicating that the content has been cached:

The box gives some precious information about the cache key for debugging, like the lifetime of the cache, and the age of it.

If you refresh the page again, the color of the box changed from green to yellow, indicating that the page has been retrieved from the cache:

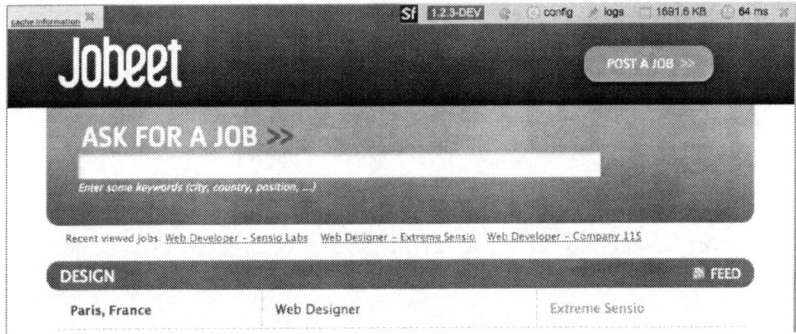

Also notice that no database request has been made in the second case, as shown in the web debug toolbar.

 Even if the language can be changed on a per-user basis, the cache still works as the language is embedded in the URL.

When a page is cacheable, and if the cache does not exist yet, symfony stores the response object in the cache at the end of the request. For all other future requests, symfony will send the cached response without calling the controller:

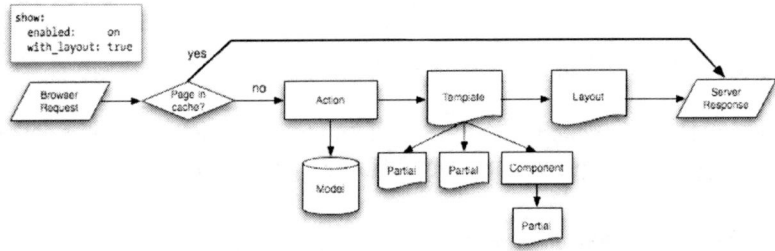

This has a great impact on performance as you can measure for yourself by using tools like JMeter[118].

 An incoming request with GET parameters or submitted with the POST, PUT, or DELETE method will never be cached by symfony, regardless of the configuration.

The job creation page can also be cached:

```
# plugins/sfJobeetPlugin/modules/sfJobeetJob/config/cache.yml
new:
  enabled:    true
```

Listing 21-8

118. `http://jakarta.apache.org/jmeter/`

```
index:
  enabled:    true

all:
  with_layout: true
```

As the two pages can be cached with the layout, we have created an **all** section that defines the default configuration for the all **sfJobeetJob** module actions.

Clearing the Cache

If you want to clear the page cache, you can use the **cache:clear** task:

Listing 21-9
```
$ php symfony cc
```

The **cache:clear** task clears all the symfony caches stored under the main **cache/** directory. It also takes options to selectively clear some parts of the cache. To only clear the template cache for the **cache** environment, use the **--type** and **--env** options:

Listing 21-10
```
$ php symfony cc --type=template --env=cache
```

Instead of clearing the cache each time you make a change, you can also disable the cache by adding any query string to the URL, or by using the "Ignore cache" button from the web debug toolbar:

Action Cache

Sometimes, you cannot cache the whole page in the cache, but the action template itself can be cached. Put another way, you can cache everything but the layout.

For the Jobeet application, we cannot cache the whole page because of the "history job" bar.

Change the configuration for the **job** module cache accordingly:

Listing 21-11
```
# plugins/sfJobeetPlugin/modules/sfJobeetJob/config/cache.yml
new:
```

```
    enabled:      true

index:
  enabled:      true

all:
  with_layout: false
```

By changing the **with_layout** setting to **false**, you have disabled layout caching.
Clear the cache:

```
$ php symfony cc
```

Listing
21-12

Refresh your browser to see the difference:

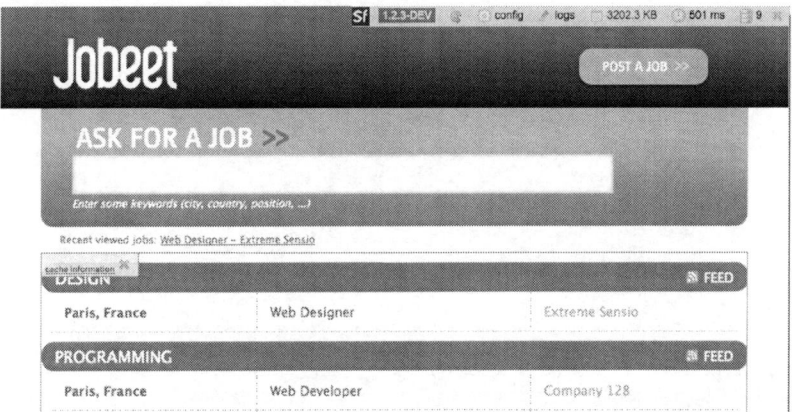

Even if the flow of the request is quite similar in the simplified diagram, caching without the layout is much more resource intensive.

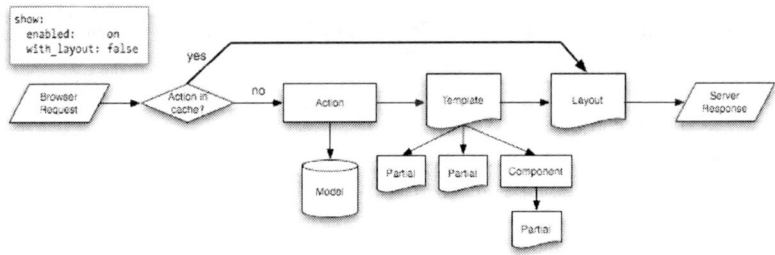

Partial and Component Cache

For highly dynamic websites, it is sometimes even impossible to cache the whole action template. For those cases, you need a way to configure the cache at the finer-grained level. Thankfully, partials and components can also be cached.

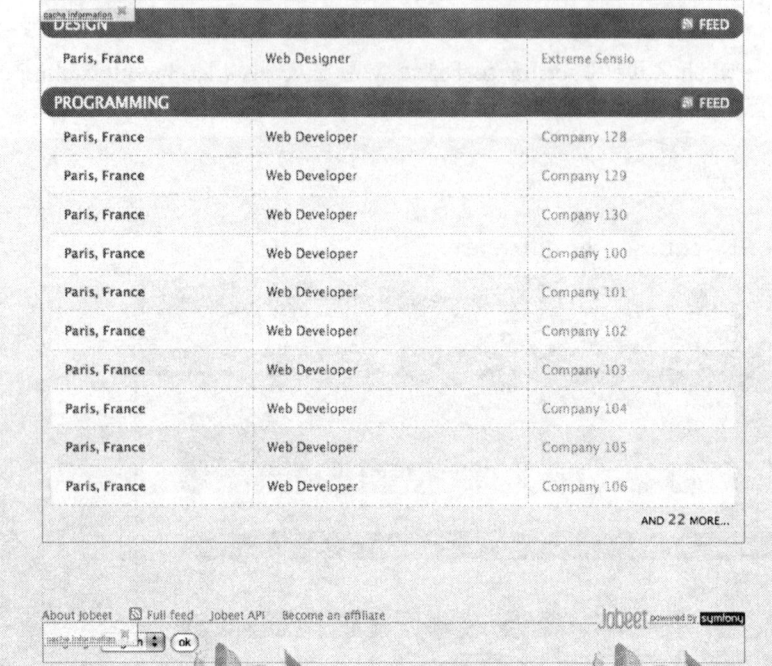

Let's cache the **language** component by creating a **cache.yml** file for the **sfJobeetLanguage** module:

Listing
21-13

```
# plugins/sfJobeetPlugin/modules/sfJobeetLanguage/config/cache.yml
_language:
  enabled: true
```

Configuring the cache for a partial or a component is as simple as adding an entry with its name. The **with_layout** option is not taken into account for this type of cache as it does not make any sense:

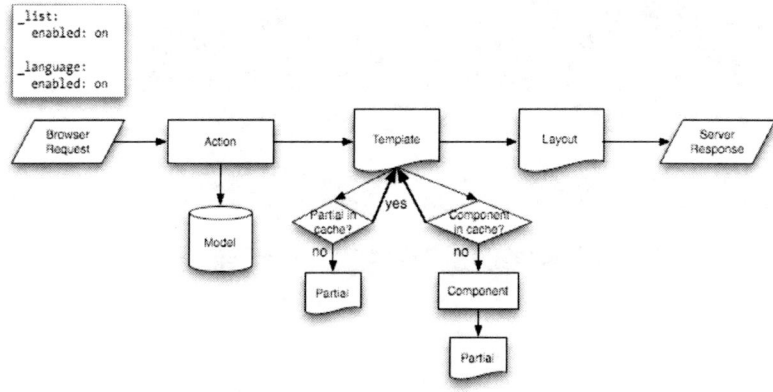

Listing 21-14

Forms in Cache

Storing the job creation page in the cache is problematic as it contains a form. To better understand the problem, go to the "Post a Job" page in your browser to seed the cache. Then, clear your session cookie, and try to submit a job. You must see an error message alerting you of a "CSRF attack":

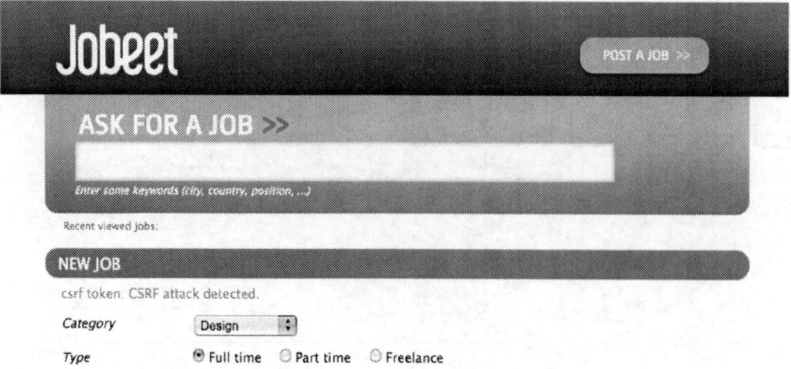

Why? As we have configured a CSRF secret when we created the frontend application, symfony embeds a CSRF token in all forms. To protect you against CSRF attacks, this token is unique for a given user and for a given form.

The first time the page is displayed, the generated HTML form is stored in the cache with the current user token. If another user comes afterwards, the page from the cache will be displayed with the first user CSRF token. When submitting the form, the tokens do not match, and an error is thrown.

How can we fix the problem as it seems legitimate to store the form in the cache? The job creation form does not depend on the user, and it does not change anything for the current user. In such a case, no CSRF protection is needed, and we can remove the CSRF token altogether:

Listing 21-15

```
// plugins/sfJobeetPlugin/lib/form/doctrine/
PluginJobeetJobForm.class.php
abstract PluginJobeetJobForm extends BaseJobeetJobForm
{
  public function configure()
  {
    $this->disableLocalCSRFProtection();
  }
}
```

After doing this change, clear the cache and re-try the same scenario as above to prove it works as expected now.

The same configuration must be applied to the language form as it is contained in the layout and will be stored in the cache. As the default **sfLanguageForm** is used, instead of creating a new class, just to remove the CSRF token, let's do it from the action and component of the **sfJobeetLanguage** module:

Listing 21-16

```
// plugins/sfJobeetPlugin/modules/sfJobeetLanguage/actions/
components.class.php
```

```
class sfJobeetLanguageComponents extends sfComponents
{
  public function executeLanguage(sfWebRequest $request)
  {
    $this->form = new sfFormLanguage($this->getUser(),
array('languages' => array('en', 'fr')));
    unset($this->form[$this->form->getCSRFFieldName()]);
  }
}

// plugins/sfJobeetPlugin/modules/sfJobeetLanguage/actions/
actions.class.php
class sfJobeetLanguageActions extends sfActions
{
  public function executeChangeLanguage(sfWebRequest $request)
  {
    $form = new sfFormLanguage($this->getUser(), array('languages' =>
array('en', 'fr')));
    unset($form[$form->getCSRFFieldName()]);

    // ...
  }
}
```

The getCSRFFieldName() returns the name of the field that contains the CSRF token. By unsetting this field, the widget and the associated validator are removed.

Removing the Cache

Each time a user posts and activates a job, the homepage must be refreshed to list the new job.

As we don't need the job to appear in real-time on the homepage, the best strategy is to lower the cache life time to something acceptable:

Listing 21-17

```
# plugins/sfJobeetPlugin/modules/sfJobeetJob/config/cache.yml
index:
  enabled:  true
  lifetime: 600
```

Instead of the default configuration of one day, the cache for the homepage will be automatically removed every ten minutes.

But if you want to update the homepage as soon as a user activates a new job, edit the **executePublish()** method of the **sfJobeetJob** module to add manual cache cleaning:

Listing 21-18

```php
// plugins/sfJobeetPlugin/modules/sfJobeetJob/actions/actions.class.php
public function executePublish(sfWebRequest $request)
{
  $request->checkCSRFProtection();

  $job = $this->getRoute()->getObject();
  $job->publish();

  if ($cache = $this->getContext()->getViewCacheManager())
  {
    $cache->remove('sfJobeetJob/index?sf_culture=*');
    $cache->remove('sfJobeetCategory/
show?id='.$job->getJobeetCategory()->getId());
  }

  $this->getUser()->setFlash('notice', sprintf('Your job is now online
for %s days.', sfConfig::get('app_active_days')));

  $this->redirect('job_show_user', $job);
}
```

The cache is managed by the **sfViewCacheManager** class. The **remove()** method removes the cache associated with an internal URI. To remove cache for all possible parameters of a variable, use the * as the value. The **sf_culture=*** we have used in the code above means that symfony will remove the cache for the English and the French homepage.

As the cache manager is **null** when the cache is disabled, we have wrapped the cache removing in an **if** block.

Testing the Cache

Before starting, we need to change the configuration for the **test** environment to enable the cache layer:

Listing 21-19

```yaml
# apps/frontend/config/settings.yml
test:
  .settings:
    error_reporting: <?php echo ((E_ALL | E_STRICT) ^ E_NOTICE)."\n" ?>
    cache:             true
```

```
web_debug:        false
etag:             false
```

Let's test the job creation page:

Listing 21-20

```
// test/functional/frontend/jobActionsTest.php
$browser->
  info('  7 - Job creation page')->

  get('/fr/')->
  with('view_cache')->isCached(true, false)->

  createJob(array('category_id' =>
Doctrine::getTable('CategoryTranslation')->findOneBySlug('programming')->getId()),
true)->

  get('/fr/')->
  with('view_cache')->isCached(true, false)->
  with('response')->checkElement('.category_programming .more_jobs',
'/23/')
;
```

The **view_cache** tester is used to test the cache. The **isCached()** method takes two booleans:

- Whether the page must be in cache or not
- Whether the cache is with layout or not

 Even with all the tools provided by the functional test framework, it is sometimes easier to diagnose problems within the browser. It is quite easy to accomplish. Just create a front controller for the **test** environment. The logs stored in **log/frontend_test.log** can also be very helpful.

See you Tomorrow

Like many other symfony features, the symfony cache sub-framework is very flexible and allows the developer to configure the cache at a very fine-grained level.

Tomorrow, we will talk about the last step of an application life-cycle: the deployment to the production servers.

Day 22

The Deployment

With the configuration of the cache system yesterday, the Jobeet website is ready to be deployed on the production servers.

During twenty-two days, we have developed Jobeet on a development machine, and for most of you, it probably means your local machine; except if you develop on the production server directly, which is of course a very bad idea. Now, it is time to move the website to a production server.

Today, we will see what needs to be done before going to production, what kind of deploying strategies you can use, and also the tools you need for a successful deployment.

Preparing the Production Server

Before deploying the project to production, we need to be sure the production server is configured correctly. You can re-read day 1, where we explained how to configure the web server.

In this section, we assume that you have already installed the web server, the database server, and PHP 5.2.4 or later.

 If you don't have an SSH access to the web server, skip the part where you need to have access to the command line.

Server Configuration

First, you need to check that PHP is installed with all the needed extensions and is correctly configured. As for day 1, we will use the check_configuration.php script provided with symfony. As we won't install symfony on the production server, download the file directly from the symfony website:

^{Listing}
²²⁻¹
```
http://trac.symfony-project.org/browser/branches/1.4/data/bin/
check_configuration.php?format=raw
```

Copy the file to the web root directory and run it from your browser **and** from the command line:

^{Listing}
²²⁻²
```
$ php check_configuration.php
```

Fix any fatal error the script finds and repeat the process until everything works fine in **both** environments.

PHP Accelerator

For the production server, you probably want the best performance possible. Installing a PHP accelerator[119] will give you the best improvement for your money.

 From Wikipedia: A PHP accelerator works by caching the compiled bytecode of PHP scripts to avoid the overhead of parsing and compiling source code on each request.

APC[120] is one of the most popular one, and it is quite simple to install it:

^{Listing}
²²⁻³
```
$ pecl install APC
```

Depending on your Operating System, you will also be able to install it with the OS native package manager.

 Take some time to learn how to configure APC[121].

---

119. http://en.wikipedia.org/wiki/PHP_accelerator
120. http://www.php.net/apc
121. http://www.php.net/manual/en/apc.configuration.php

The symfony Libraries

Embedding symfony

One of the great strengths of symfony is that a project is self-contained. All the files needed for the project to work are under the main root project directory. And you can move around the project in another directory without changing anything in the project itself as symfony only uses relative paths. It means that the directory on the production server does not have to be the same as the one on your development machine.

The only absolute path that can possibly be found is in the **config/ ProjectConfiguration.class.php** file; but we took care of it during day 1. Check that it actually contains a relative path to the symfony core autoloader:

```
// config/ProjectConfiguration.class.php
require_once dirname(__FILE__).'/../lib/vendor/symfony/lib/autoload/
sfCoreAutoload.class.php';
```

Listing 22.4

Upgrading symfony

Even if everything is self-contained in a single directory, upgrading symfony to a newer release is nonetheless insanely easy.

You will want to upgrade symfony to the latest minor release from time to time, as we constantly fix bugs and possibly security issues. The good news is that all symfony versions are maintained for at least a year and during the maintenance period, we never ever add new features, even the smallest one. So, it is always fast, safe, and secure to upgrade from one minor release to another.

Upgrading symfony is as simple as changing the content of the **lib/vendor/ symfony/** directory. If you have installed symfony with the archive, remove the current files and replace them with the newest ones.

If you use Subversion for your project, you can also link your project to the latest symfony 1.4 tag:

```
$ svn propedit svn:externals lib/vendor/
  # symfony http://svn.symfony-project.com/tags/RELEASE_1_4_0/
```

Listing 22.5

Upgrading symfony is then as simple as changing the tag to the latest symfony version.

You can also use the 1.4 branch to have fixes in real-time:

Listing 22-6
```
$ svn propedit svn:externals lib/vendor/
  # symfony http://svn.symfony-project.com/branches/1.4/
```

Now, each time you do an **svn up**, you will have the latest symfony 1.4 version.

When upgrading to a new version, you are advised to always clear the cache, especially in the production environment:

Listing 22-7
```
$ php symfony cc
```

 If you also have an FTP access to the production server, you can simulate a **symfony cc** by simply removing all the files and directories under the **cache/** directory.

You can even test a new symfony version without replacing the existing one. If you just want to test a new release, and want to be able to rollback easily, install symfony in another directory (**lib/vendor/symfony_test** for instance), change the path in the **ProjectConfiguration** class, clear the cache, and you are done. Rollbacking is as simple as removing the directory, and change back the path in **ProjectConfiguration**.

Tweaking the Configuration

Database Configuration

Most of the time, the production database has different credentials than the local one. Thanks to the symfony environments, it is quite simple to have a different configuration for the production database:

Listing 22-8
```
$ php symfony configure:database
    ➥ "mysql:host=localhost;dbname=prod_dbname" prod_user prod_pass
```

You can also edit the **databases.yml** configuration file directly.

Assets

As Jobeet uses plugins that embed assets, symfony created relative symbolic links in the **web/** directory. The **plugin:publish-assets** task regenerates or creates them if you install plugins without the **plugin:install** task:

Listing 22-9
```
$ php symfony plugin:publish-assets
```

Customizing Error Pages

Before going to production, it is better to customize default symfony pages, like the "Page Not Found" page, or the default exception page.

We have already configured the error page for the YAML format during day 16, by creating an **error.yaml.php** and an **exception.yaml.php** files in the **config/error/** directory. The **error.yaml.php** file is used by symfony in the **prod** environment, whereas **exception.yaml.php** is used in the **dev** environment.

So, to customize the default exception page for the HTML format, create two files: **config/error/error.html.php** and **config/error/exception.html.php**.

The **404** page (page not found) can be customized by changing the **error_404_module** and **error_404_action** settings:

Listing 22-10

```
# apps/frontend/config/settings.yml
all:
  .actions:
    error_404_module: default
    error_404_action: error404
```

Customizing the Directory Structure

To better structure and standardize your code, symfony has a default directory structure with pre-defined names. But sometimes, you don't have the choice but to change the structure because of some external constraints.

Configuring the directory names can be done in the **config/ProjectConfiguration.class.php** class.

The Web Root Directory

On some web hosts, you cannot change the web root directory name. Let's say that on your web host, it is named **public_html/** instead of **web/**:

Listing 22-11

```php
// config/ProjectConfiguration.class.php
class ProjectConfiguration extends sfProjectConfiguration
{
  public function setup()
  {
    $this->setWebDir($this->getRootDir().'/public_html');
  }
}
```

The setWebDir() method takes the absolute path of the web root directory. If you also move this directory elsewhere, don't forget to edit the controller scripts to check that paths to the config/ProjectConfiguration.class.php file are still valid:

Listing 22-12

```
require_once(dirname(__FILE__).'/../config/
ProjectConfiguration.class.php');
```

The Cache and Log Directory

The symfony framework only writes in two directories: cache/ and log/. For security reasons, some web hosts do not set write permissions in the main directory. If this is the case, you can move these directories elsewhere on the filesystem:

Listing 22-13

```
// config/ProjectConfiguration.class.php
class ProjectConfiguration extends sfProjectConfiguration
{
  public function setup()
  {
    $this->setCacheDir('/tmp/symfony_cache');
    $this->setLogDir('/tmp/symfony_logs');
  }
}
```

As for the setWebDir() method, setCacheDir() and setLogDir() take an absolute path to the cache/ and log/ directories respectively.

Customizing symfony core Objects (aka factories)

During day 16, we talked a bit about the symfony factories. Being able to customize the factories means that you can use a custom class for symfony core objects instead of the default one. You can also change the default behavior of these classes by changing the parameters send to them.

Let's take a look at some classic customizations you may want to do.

Cookie Name

To handle the user session, symfony uses a cookie. This cookie has a default name of symfony, which can be changed in factories.yml. Under the all key, add the following configuration to change the cookie name to jobeet:

```
# apps/frontend/config/factories.yml
storage:
  class: sfSessionStorage
  param:
    session_name: jobeet
```

Listing
22-14

Session Storage

The default session storage class is **sfSessionStorage**. It uses the filesystem to store the session information. If you have several web servers, you would want to store the sessions in a central place, like a database table:

```
# apps/frontend/config/factories.yml
storage:
  class: sfPDOSessionStorage
  param:
    session_name: jobeet
    db_table:     session
    database:     doctrine
    db_id_col:    id
    db_data_col:  data
    db_time_col:  time
```

Listing
22-15

Session Timeout

By default, the user session timeout if **1800** seconds. This can be changed by editing the **user** entry:

```
# apps/frontend/config/factories.yml
user:
  class: myUser
  param:
    timeout: 1800
```

Listing
22-16

Logging

By default, there is no logging in the **prod** environment because the logger class name is **sfNoLogger**:

```
# apps/frontend/config/factories.yml
prod:
  logger:
    class:    sfNoLogger
    param:
```

Listing
22-17

```
        level:   err
        loggers: ~
```

You can for instance enable logging on the filesystem by changing the logger class name to sfFileLogger:

Listing
22-18

```
# apps/frontend/config/factories.yml
logger:
  class: sfFileLogger
  param:
    level: error
    file:   %SF_LOG_DIR%/%SF_APP%_%SF_ENVIRONMENT%.log
```

 In the factories.yml configuration file, %XXX% strings are replaced with their corresponding value from the sfConfig object. So, %SF_APP% in a configuration file is equivalent to sfConfig::get('sf_app') in PHP code. This notation can also be used in the app.yml configuration file. It is very useful when you need to reference a path in a configuration file without hardcoding the path (SF_ROOT_DIR, SF_WEB_DIR, ...).

Deploying

What to deploy?

When deploying the Jobeet website to the production server, we need to be careful not to deploy unneeded files or override files uploaded by our users, like the company logos.

In a symfony project, there are three directories to exclude from the transfer: cache/, log/, and web/uploads/. Everything else can be transfered as is.

For security reasons, you also don't want to transfer the "non-production" front controllers, like the frontend_dev.php, backend_dev.php and frontend_cache.php scripts.

Deploying Strategies

In this section, we will assume that you have full control over the production server(s). If you can only access the server with a FTP account, the only deployment solution possible is to transfer all files every time you deploy.

The simplest way to deploy your website is to use the built-in **project:deploy** task. It uses **SSH** and **rsync** to connect and transfer the files from one computer to another one.

Servers for the **project:deploy** task can be configured in the **config/ properties.ini** configuration file:

```
# config/properties.ini
[production]
  host=www.jobeet.org
  port=22
  user=jobeet
  dir=/var/www/jobeet/
```

Listing
22-19

To deploy to the newly configured **production** server, use the **project:deploy** task:

```
$ php symfony project:deploy production
```

Listing
22-20

 Before running the **project:deploy** task for the first time, you need to connect to the server manually to add the key in the known hosts file.

 If the command does not work as expected, you can pass the **-t** option to see the real-time output of the **rsync** command.

If you run this command, symfony will only simulate the transfer. To actually deploy the website, add the **--go** option:

```
$ php symfony project:deploy production --go
```

Listing
22-21

 Even if you can provide the SSH password in the **properties.ini** file, it is better to configure your server with a SSH key to allow password-less connections.

By default, symfony won't transfer the directories we have talked about in the previous section, nor it will transfer the **dev** front controller script. That's because the **project:deploy** task exclude files and directories are configured in the **config/rsync_exclude.txt** file:

```
# config/rsync_exclude.txt
.svn
/web/uploads/*
```

Listing
22-22

```
/cache/*
/log/*
/web/*_dev.php
```

For Jobeet, we need to add the **frontend_cache.php** file:

Listing
22-23

```
# config/rsync_exclude.txt
.svn
/web/uploads/*
/cache/*
/log/*
/web/*_dev.php
/web/frontend_cache.php
```

 You can also create a **config/rsync_include.txt** file to force some files or directories to be transfered.

Even if the **project:deploy** task is very flexible, you might want to customize it even further. As deploying can be very different based on your server configuration and topology, don't hesitate to extend the default task.

Each time you deploy a website to production, don't forget to at least clear the configuration cache on the production server:

Listing
22-24

```
$ php symfony cc --type=config
```

If you have changed some routes, you will also need to clear the routing cache:

Listing
22-25

```
$ php symfony cc --type=routing
```

 Clearing the cache selectively allows to keep some parts of the cache, such as the template cache.

See you Tomorrow

The deployment of a project is the very last step of the symfony development life-cycle. It does not mean that you are done. This is quite the contrary. A website is something that has a life by itself. You will probably have to fix bugs and you will also want to add new features over time. But thanks to the symfony structure and the tools at your disposal, upgrading your website is simple, fast, and safe.

Tomorrow is the last day of the Jobeet tutorial. It will be time to take a step back and have a look at what you learned during the twenty-three days of Jobeet.

Day 23

Another Look at symfony

Today is the last stop of our trip to the wonderful world of symfony. During these twenty-three days, you learned symfony by example: from the design patterns used by the framework, to the powerful built-in features. You are not a symfony master yet, but you have all the needed knowledge to start building your symfony applications with confidence.

As we wrap up the Jobeet tutorial, let's have another look at the framework. Forget Jobeet for an hour, and recall all the features you learned during the last three weeks.

What is symfony?

The symfony framework is a set of cohesive but decoupled sub-frameworks *(page 183)*, that forms a full-stack MVC framework *(page 65)* (Model, View, Controller).

Before coding head first, take some time to read the symfony history and philosophy *(page 23)*. Then, check the framework prerequisites *(page 25)* and use the `check_configuration.php` script *(page 26)* to validate your configuration.

Eventually, install symfony *(page 26)*. After some time you will also want to upgrade *(page 361)* to the latest version of the framework.

The framework also provides tools to ease deployment *(page 366)*.

The Model

The Model part of symfony can be done with the help of the Doctrine ORM[122]. Based on the database description *(page 52)*, it generates classes for objects *(page 56)*, forms *(page 163)*, and filters *(page 222)*. Doctrine also generates the SQL *(page 56)* statements used to create the tables in the database.

The database configuration can be done with a task *(page 55)* or by editing a configuration file *(page 55)*. Beside its configuration, it is also possible to inject initial data, thanks to fixture files *(page 58)*. You can even make these files dynamic *(page 113)*.

Doctrine objects can also be easily internationalized *(page 316)*.

The View

By default, the View layer of the MVC architecture uses plain PHP files as templates.

Templates can use helpers *(page 70)* for recurrent tasks like creating a URL *(page 96)* or a link *(page 96)*.

A template can be decorated by a layout *(page 67)* to abstract the header and footer of pages. To make views even more reusable, you can define slots *(page 79)*, partials *(page 123)*, and components *(page 307)*.

To speed up things, you can use the cache sub-framework *(page 347)* to cache a whole page *(page 348)*, just the action *(page 350)*, or even just partials or components *(page 352)*. You can also remove the cache *(page 355)* manually.

The Controller

The Controller part is managed by front controllers *(page 37)* and actions *(page 61)*.

Tasks can be used to create simple modules *(page 121)*, CRUD modules *(page 61)*, or even to generate fullly working admin modules *(page 200)* for model classes.

Admin modules allows you to built a fully functional application without coding anything.

To abstract the technical implementation of a website, symfony uses a routing *(page 88)* sub-framework that generates pretty URLs *(page 87)*. To make implementing

---

122. `http://www.doctrine-project.org/`

web services even easier, symfony supports formats *(page 245)* out of the box. You can also create your own formats *(page 260)*.

An action can be forwarded *(page 83)* to another one, or redirected *(page 97)*.

Configuration

The symfony framework makes it easy to have different configuration settings for different environments. An environment *(page 37)* is a set of settings that allows different behaviors on the development or production servers. You can also create new environments *(page 345)*.

The symfony configuration files can be defined at different levels *(page 73)* and most of them are environment aware *(page 140)*:

- `app.yml` *(page 107)*
- `cache.yml` *(page 347)*
- `databases.yml` *(page 55)*
- `factories.yml` *(page 275)*
- `generator.yml` *(page 203)*
- `routing.yml` *(page 88)*
- `schema.yml` *(page 52)*
- `security.yml` *(page 235)*
- `settings.yml` *(page 194)*
- `view.yml` *(page 70)*

The configuration files mostly use the YAML format *(page 54)*.

Instead of using the default directory structure and organize your application files by layers, you can also organize them by feature, and bundle them in a plugin *(page 326)*. Speaking of the default directory structure, you can also customize it *(page 363)* according to your needs.

Debugging

From logging *(page 104)* to the web debug toolbar *(page 104)*, and meaningful exceptions *(page 37)*, symfony provides a lot of useful tools to help the developer debug problems faster.

Main symfony Objects

The symfony framework provides quite a few core objects that abstract recurrent needs in web projects: the request *(page 84)*, the response *(page 85)*, the user *(page 232)*, the logging *(page 365)*, the routing *(page 88)*, the mailer *(page 273)*, and the view cache manager *(page 276)*.

These core objects are managed by the `sfContext` object *(page 276)*, and they are configured via the factories *(page 275)*.

The user manages user authentication *(page 235)*, authorization *(page 237)*, flashes *(page 229)*, and attributes *(page 231)* to be serialized in the session.

Security

The symfony framework has built-in protections against XSS *(page 31)* and CSRF *(page 31)*. These settings can be configured from the command line *(page 31)*, or by editing a configuration file *(page 196)*.

The form framework also provides built-in security features *(page 194)*.

Forms

As managing forms is one of the most tedious task for a web developer, symfony provides a form sub-framework *(page 161)*. The form framework comes bundled with a lot of widgets[123] and validators[124]. One of the strength of the form sub-framework is that templates are very easily customizable *(page 171)*.

If you use Doctrine, the form framework also makes it easy to generate forms and filters *(page 163)* based on your models.

Internationalization and Localization

Internationalization *(page 310)* and localization *(page 322)* are supported by symfony, thanks to the ICU standard. The user culture *(page 302)* determines the language and the country of the user. It can be defined by the user itself, or embedded in the URL *(page 303)*.

---

123. `http://www.symfony-project.org/api/1_4/widget`
124. `http://www.symfony-project.org/api/1_4/validator`

Tests

The lime library, used for **unit tests**, provides a lot of testing methods *(page 130)*. The Doctrine objects can also be tested *(page 139)* from a dedicated database *(page 139)* and with dedicated fixtures *(page 140)*.

Unit tests can be run one at a time *(page 131)* or all together *(page 143)*.

Functional tests are written with the `sfFunctionalTest` *(page 147)* class, which uses a browser simulator *(page 146)* and allows symfony core objects introspection through Testers *(page 147)*. Testers exist for the request object *(page 149)*, the response object *(page 149)*, the user object *(page 242)*, the current form object *(page 185)*, the cache layer *(page 356)* and the Doctrine objects *(page 186)*.

You can also use debugging tools for the response *(page 158)* and forms *(page 185)*.

As for the unit tests, functional tests can be run one by one *(page 149)* or all together *(page 158)*.

You can also run all tests together *(page 158)*.

Plugins

The symfony framework only provides the foundation for your web applications and relies on plugins *(page 339)* to add more features. In this tutorial, we have talked about `sfGuardPlugin` *(page 238)*, `sfFormExtraPlugin` *(page 307)*, and `sfTaskExtraPlugin` *(page 339)*.

A plugin must be activated *(page 0)* after installation.

Plugins are the best way to contribute back *(page 339)* to the symfony project.

Tasks

The symfony CLI provides a lot of tasks, and the most useful have been discussed in this tutorial:

- `app:routes` *(page 100)*
- `cache:clear` *(page 350)*
- `configure:database` *(page 55)*
- `generate:project` *(page 30)*
- `generate:app` *(page 31)*
- `generate:module` *(page 121)*
- `help` *(page 56)*
- `i18n:extract` *(page 312)*

- `list` *(page 239)*
- `plugin:install` *(page 238)*
- `plugin:publish-assets` *(page 335)*
- `project:deploy` *(page 366)*
- `doctrine:build-all` *(page 56)*
- `doctrine:build-all-reload` *(page 121)*
- `doctrine:build --forms` *(page 163)*
- `doctrine:build-model` *(page 56)*
- `doctrine:build-sql` *(page 56)*
- `doctrine:data-load` *(page 58)*
- `doctrine:generate-admin` *(page 200)*
- `doctrine:generate-module` *(page 61)*
- `doctrine:insert-sql` *(page 56)*
- `test:all` *(page 158)*
- `test:coverage` *(page 134)*
- `test:functional` *(page 149)*
- `test:unit` *(page 131)*

You can also create your own tasks *(page 196)*.

See you soon

Learning by Practicing

The symfony framework, as does any piece of software, has a learning curve. In the learning process, the first step is to learn from practical examples with a book like this one. The second step is to **practice**. Nothing will ever replace practicing.

That's what you can start doing today. Think about the simplest web project that still provides some value: a todo list manager, a simple blog, a time or currency converter, whatever... Choose one and start implementing it with the knowledge you have today. Use the task help messages to learn the different options, browse the code generated by symfony, use a text editor that has PHP auto-completion support like Eclipse[125], and refer to the reference guide[126] to browse all the configuration provided by the framework.

Enjoy all the free material you have at your disposal to learn more about symfony.

---

125. `http://www.eclipse.org/`
126. `http://www.symfony-project.org/reference/1_4/`

The community

Before you leave, I would like to talk about one last thing about symfony. The framework has a lot of great features and a lot of free documentation. But, one of the most valuable asset an Open-Source can have is its community. And symfony has one of the most amazing and active community around. If you start using symfony for your projects, consider joining the symfony community:

- Subscribe to the user mailing-list[127]
- Subscribe to the official blog feed[128]
- Subscribe to the symfony planet feed[129]
- Come and chat on the #symfony IRC[130] channel on freenode

127. http://groups.google.com/group/symfony-users
128. http://feeds.feedburner.com/symfony/blog
129. http://feeds.feedburner.com/symfony/planet
130. irc://irc.freenode.net/symfony

Appendices

Appendix A

License

Attribution-Share Alike 3.0 Unported License

THE WORK (AS DEFINED BELOW) IS PROVIDED UNDER THE TERMS OF THIS CREATIVE COMMONS PUBLIC LICENSE ("CCPL" OR "LICENSE"). THE WORK IS PROTECTED BY COPYRIGHT AND/OR OTHER APPLICABLE LAW. ANY USE OF THE WORK OTHER THAN AS AUTHORIZED UNDER THIS LICENSE OR COPYRIGHT LAW IS PROHIBITED.

BY EXERCISING ANY RIGHTS TO THE WORK PROVIDED HERE, YOU ACCEPT AND AGREE TO BE BOUND BY THE TERMS OF THIS LICENSE. TO THE EXTENT THIS LICENSE MAY BE CONSIDERED TO BE A CONTRACT, THE LICENSOR GRANTS YOU THE RIGHTS CONTAINED HERE IN CONSIDERATION OF YOUR ACCEPTANCE OF SUCH TERMS AND CONDITIONS.

1. Definitions

    a. **"Adaptation"** means a work based upon the Work, or upon the Work and other pre-existing works, such as a translation, adaptation, derivative work, arrangement of music or other alterations of a literary or artistic work, or phonogram or performance and includes cinematographic adaptations or any other form in which the Work may be recast, transformed, or adapted including in any form recognizably derived from the original, except that a work that constitutes a Collection will not be considered an Adaptation for the purpose of this License. For the avoidance of doubt, where the Work is a musical work, performance or phonogram, the synchronization of the Work in timed-relation with a moving image ("synching") will be considered an Adaptation for the purpose of this License.

b. **"Collection"** means a collection of literary or artistic works, such as encyclopedias and anthologies, or performances, phonograms or broadcasts, or other works or subject matter other than works listed in Section 1(f) below, which, by reason of the selection and arrangement of their contents, constitute intellectual creations, in which the Work is included in its entirety in unmodified form along with one or more other contributions, each constituting separate and independent works in themselves, which together are assembled into a collective whole. A work that constitutes a Collection will not be considered an Adaptation (as defined below) for the purposes of this License.

c. **"Creative Commons Compatible License"** means a license that is listed at http://creativecommons.org/compatiblelicenses that has been approved by Creative Commons as being essentially equivalent to this License, including, at a minimum, because that license: (i) contains terms that have the same purpose, meaning and effect as the License Elements of this License; and, (ii) explicitly permits the relicensing of adaptations of works made available under that license under this License or a Creative Commons jurisdiction license with the same License Elements as this License.

d. **"Distribute"** means to make available to the public the original and copies of the Work or Adaptation, as appropriate, through sale or other transfer of ownership.

e. **"License Elements"** means the following high-level license attributes as selected by Licensor and indicated in the title of this License: Attribution, ShareAlike.

f. **"Licensor"** means the individual, individuals, entity or entities that offer(s) the Work under the terms of this License.

g. **"Original Author"** means, in the case of a literary or artistic work, the individual, individuals, entity or entities who created the Work or if no individual or entity can be identified, the publisher; and in addition (i) in the case of a performance the actors, singers, musicians, dancers, and other persons who act, sing, deliver, declaim, play in, interpret or otherwise perform literary or artistic works or expressions of folklore; (ii) in the case of a phonogram the producer being the person or legal entity who first fixes the sounds of a performance or other sounds; and, (iii) in the case of broadcasts, the organization that transmits the broadcast.

h. **"Work"** means the literary and/or artistic work offered under the terms of this License including without limitation any production in the literary, scientific and artistic domain, whatever may be the mode or form of its expression including digital form, such as a book, pamphlet and other writing; a lecture, address, sermon or other work of the same nature; a dramatic or dramatico-musical work; a choreographic work or entertainment in dumb show; a musical composition with or without words; a cinematographic work to which are assimilated works expressed by a process analogous to cinematography; a work of drawing, painting, architecture, sculpture, engraving or lithography; a photographic work to which are assimilated works expressed by a process analogous to photography; a work of applied art; an illustration, map, plan, sketch or three-dimensional work relative to geography, topography, architecture or science; a performance; a broadcast; a phonogram; a compilation of data to the extent it is protected as a copyrightable work; or a work performed by a variety or circus performer to the extent it is not otherwise considered a literary or artistic work.

i. **"You"** means an individual or entity exercising rights under this License who has not previously violated the terms of this License with respect to the Work, or who has received express permission from the Licensor to exercise rights under this License despite a previous violation.

j. **"Publicly Perform"** means to perform public recitations of the Work and to communicate to the public those public recitations, by any means or process, including by wire or wireless means or public digital performances; to make available to the public Works in such a way that members of the public may access these Works from a place and at a place individually chosen by them; to perform the Work to the public by any means or process and the communication to the public of the performances of the Work, including by public digital performance; to broadcast and rebroadcast the Work by any means including signs, sounds or images.

k. **"Reproduce"** means to make copies of the Work by any means including without limitation by sound or visual recordings and the right of fixation and reproducing fixations of the Work, including storage of a protected performance or phonogram in digital form or other electronic medium.

2. Fair Dealing Rights

Nothing in this License is intended to reduce, limit, or restrict any uses free from copyright or rights arising from limitations or exceptions that are provided for in connection with the copyright protection under copyright law or other applicable laws.

3. License Grant

Subject to the terms and conditions of this License, Licensor hereby grants You a worldwide, royalty-free, non-exclusive, perpetual (for the duration of the applicable copyright) license to exercise the rights in the Work as stated below:

a. to Reproduce the Work, to incorporate the Work into one or more Collections, and to Reproduce the Work as incorporated in the Collections;

b. to create and Reproduce Adaptations provided that any such Adaptation, including any translation in any medium, takes reasonable steps to clearly label, demarcate or otherwise identify that changes were made to the original Work. For example, a translation could be marked "The original work was translated from English to Spanish," or a modification could indicate "The original work has been modified.";

c. to Distribute and Publicly Perform the Work including as incorporated in Collections; and,

d. to Distribute and Publicly Perform Adaptations.

e. For the avoidance of doubt:

i. **Non-waivable Compulsory License Schemes**. In those jurisdictions in which the right to collect royalties through any statutory or compulsory licensing scheme cannot be waived, the Licensor reserves the exclusive right to collect such royalties for any exercise by You of the rights granted under this License;

ii. **Waivable Compulsory License Schemes**. In those jurisdictions in which the right to collect royalties through any statutory or compulsory licensing scheme can be waived, the Licensor waives the exclusive right to collect such royalties for any exercise by You of the rights granted under this License; and,

iii. **Voluntary License Schemes**. The Licensor waives the right to collect royalties, whether individually or, in the event that the Licensor is a member of a collecting society that administers voluntary licensing schemes, via that society, from any exercise by You of the rights granted under this License.

The above rights may be exercised in all media and formats whether now known or hereafter devised. The above rights include the right to make such modifications as are technically necessary to exercise the rights in other media and formats. Subject to Section 8(f), all rights not expressly granted by Licensor are hereby reserved.

4. Restrictions

The license granted in Section 3 above is expressly made subject to and limited by the following restrictions:

a. You may Distribute or Publicly Perform the Work only under the terms of this License. You must include a copy of, or the Uniform Resource Identifier (URI) for, this License with every copy of the Work You

Distribute or Publicly Perform. You may not offer or impose any terms on the Work that restrict the terms of this License or the ability of the recipient of the Work to exercise the rights granted to that recipient under the terms of the License. You may not sublicense the Work. You must keep intact all notices that refer to this License and to the disclaimer of warranties with every copy of the Work You Distribute or Publicly Perform. When You Distribute or Publicly Perform the Work, You may not impose any effective technological measures on the Work that restrict the ability of a recipient of the Work from You to exercise the rights granted to that recipient under the terms of the License. This Section 4(a) applies to the Work as incorporated in a Collection, but this does not require the Collection apart from the Work itself to be made subject to the terms of this License. If You create a Collection, upon notice from any Licensor You must, to the extent practicable, remove from the Collection any credit as required by Section 4(c), as requested. If You create an Adaptation, upon notice from any Licensor You must, to the extent practicable, remove from the Adaptation any credit as required by Section 4(c), as requested.

b. You may Distribute or Publicly Perform an Adaptation only under the terms of: (i) this License; (ii) a later version of this License with the same License Elements as this License; (iii) a Creative Commons jurisdiction license (either this or a later license version) that contains the same License Elements as this License (e.g., Attribution-ShareAlike 3.0 US)); (iv) a Creative Commons Compatible License. If you license the Adaptation under one of the licenses mentioned in (iv), you must comply with the terms of that license. If you license the Adaptation under the terms of any of the licenses mentioned in (i), (ii) or (iii) (the "Applicable License"), you must comply with the terms of the Applicable License generally and the following provisions: (I) You must include a copy of, or the URI for, the Applicable License with every copy of each Adaptation You Distribute or Publicly Perform; (II) You may not offer or impose any terms on the Adaptation that restrict the terms of the Applicable License or the ability of the recipient of the Adaptation to exercise the rights granted to that recipient under the terms of the Applicable License; (III) You must keep intact all notices that refer to the Applicable License and to the disclaimer of warranties with every copy of the Work as included in the Adaptation You Distribute or Publicly Perform; (IV) when You Distribute or Publicly Perform the Adaptation, You may not impose any effective technological measures on the Adaptation that restrict the ability of a recipient of the Adaptation from You to exercise the rights granted to that recipient under the terms of the Applicable License. This Section 4(b) applies to the Adaptation as incorporated in a Collection, but this does not require the Collection apart from the Adaptation itself to be made subject to the terms of the Applicable License.

c. If You Distribute, or Publicly Perform the Work or any Adaptations or Collections, You must, unless a request has been made pursuant to Section 4(a), keep intact all copyright notices for the Work and provide, reasonable to the medium or means You are utilizing: (i) the name of the Original Author (or pseudonym, if applicable) if supplied, and/or if the Original Author and/or Licensor designate another party or parties (e.g., a sponsor institute, publishing entity, journal) for attribution ("Attribution Parties") in Licensor's copyright notice, terms of service or by other reasonable means, the name of such party or parties; (ii) the title of the Work if supplied; (iii) to the extent reasonably practicable, the URI, if any, that Licensor specifies to be associated with the Work, unless such URI does not refer to the copyright notice or licensing information for the Work; and (iv) , consistent with Ssection 3(b), in the case of an Adaptation, a credit identifying the use of the Work in the Adaptation (e.g., "French translation of the Work by Original Author," or "Screenplay based on original Work by Original Author"). The credit required by this Section 4(c) may be implemented in any reasonable manner; provided, however, that in the case of a Adaptation or Collection, at a minimum such credit will appear, if a credit for all contributing authors of the Adaptation or Collection appears, then as part of these credits and in a manner at least as prominent as the credits for the other contributing authors. For the avoidance of doubt, You may only use the credit required by this Section for the purpose of attribution in the manner set out above and, by exercising Your rights under this License, You may not implicitly or explicitly assert or imply any connection with, sponsorship or endorsement by the Original Author, Licensor and/or Attribution Parties, as appropriate, of You or Your use of the Work, without the separate, express prior written permission of the Original Author, Licensor and/or Attribution Parties.

d. Except as otherwise agreed in writing by the Licensor or as may be otherwise permitted by applicable law, if You Reproduce, Distribute or Publicly Perform the Work either by itself or as part of any Adaptations or Collections, You must not distort, mutilate, modify or take other derogatory action in relation to the Work which would be prejudicial to the Original Author's honor or reputation. Licensor agrees that in those jurisdictions (e.g. Japan), in which any exercise of the right granted in Section 3(b) of this License (the right to make Adaptations) would be deemed to be a distortion, mutilation, modification or other derogatory action prejudicial to the Original Author's honor and reputation, the Licensor will waive or not assert, as appropriate, this Section, to the fullest extent permitted by the applicable national law, to enable You to reasonably exercise Your right under Section 3(b) of this License (right to make Adaptations) but not otherwise.

5. Representations, Warranties and Disclaimer

UNLESS OTHERWISE MUTUALLY AGREED TO BY THE PARTIES IN WRITING, LICENSOR OFFERS THE WORK AS-IS AND MAKES NO REPRESENTATIONS OR WARRANTIES OF ANY KIND CONCERNING THE WORK, EXPRESS, IMPLIED, STATUTORY OR OTHERWISE, INCLUDING, WITHOUT LIMITATION, WARRANTIES OF TITLE, MERCHANTIBILITY, FITNESS FOR A PARTICULAR PURPOSE, NONINFRINGEMENT, OR THE ABSENCE OF LATENT OR OTHER DEFECTS, ACCURACY, OR THE PRESENCE OF ABSENCE OF ERRORS, WHETHER OR NOT DISCOVERABLE. SOME JURISDICTIONS DO NOT ALLOW THE EXCLUSION OF IMPLIED WARRANTIES, SO SUCH EXCLUSION MAY NOT APPLY TO YOU.

6. Limitation on Liability

EXCEPT TO THE EXTENT REQUIRED BY APPLICABLE LAW, IN NO EVENT WILL LICENSOR BE LIABLE TO YOU ON ANY LEGAL THEORY FOR ANY SPECIAL, INCIDENTAL, CONSEQUENTIAL, PUNITIVE OR EXEMPLARY DAMAGES ARISING OUT OF THIS LICENSE OR THE USE OF THE WORK, EVEN IF LICENSOR HAS BEEN ADVISED OF THE POSSIBILITY OF SUCH DAMAGES.

7. Termination

a. This License and the rights granted hereunder will terminate automatically upon any breach by You of the terms of this License. Individuals or entities who have received Adaptations or Collections from You under this License, however, will not have their licenses terminated provided such individuals or entities remain in full compliance with those licenses. Sections 1, 2, 5, 6, 7, and 8 will survive any termination of this License.

b. Subject to the above terms and conditions, the license granted here is perpetual (for the duration of the applicable copyright in the Work). Notwithstanding the above, Licensor reserves the right to release the Work under different license terms or to stop distributing the Work at any time; provided, however that any such election will not serve to withdraw this License (or any other license that has been, or is required to be, granted under the terms of this License), and this License will continue in full force and effect unless terminated as stated above.

8. Miscellaneous

a. Each time You Distribute or Publicly Perform the Work or a Collection, the Licensor offers to the recipient a license to the Work on the same terms and conditions as the license granted to You under this License.

b. Each time You Distribute or Publicly Perform an Adaptation, Licensor offers to the recipient a license to the original Work on the same terms and conditions as the license granted to You under this License.

c. If any provision of this License is invalid or unenforceable under applicable law, it shall not affect the validity or enforceability of the remainder of the terms of this License, and without further action by the parties to this agreement, such provision shall be reformed to the minimum extent necessary to make such provision valid and enforceable.

d. No term or provision of this License shall be deemed waived and no breach consented to unless such waiver or consent shall be in writing and signed by the party to be charged with such waiver or consent.

e. This License constitutes the entire agreement between the parties with respect to the Work licensed here. There are no understandings, agreements or representations with respect to the Work not specified here. Licensor shall not be bound by any additional provisions that may appear in any communication from You. This License may not be modified without the mutual written agreement of the Licensor and You.

f. The rights granted under, and the subject matter referenced, in this License were drafted utilizing the terminology of the Berne Convention for the Protection of Literary and Artistic Works (as amended on September 28, 1979), the Rome Convention of 1961, the WIPO Copyright Treaty of 1996, the WIPO Performances and Phonograms Treaty of 1996 and the Universal Copyright Convention (as revised on July 24, 1971). These rights and subject matter take effect in the relevant jurisdiction in which the License terms are sought to be enforced according to the corresponding provisions of the implementation of those treaty provisions in the applicable national law. If the standard suite of rights granted under applicable copyright law includes additional rights not granted under this License, such additional rights are deemed to be included in the License; this License is not intended to restrict the license of any rights under applicable law.

Creative Commons Notice

Creative Commons is not a party to this License, and makes no warranty whatsoever in connection with the Work. Creative Commons will not be liable to You or any party on any legal theory for any damages whatsoever, including without limitation any general, special, incidental or consequential damages arising in connection to this license. Notwithstanding the foregoing two (2) sentences, if Creative Commons has expressly identified itself as the Licensor hereunder, it shall have all rights and obligations of Licensor.

Except for the limited purpose of indicating to the public that the Work is licensed under the CCPL, Creative Commons does not authorize the use by either party of the trademark "Creative Commons" or any related trademark or logo of Creative Commons without the prior written consent of Creative Commons. Any permitted use will be in compliance with Creative Commons' then-current trademark usage guidelines, as may be published on its website or otherwise made available upon request from time to time. For the avoidance of doubt, this trademark restriction does not form part of the License.

Creative Commons may be contacted at http://creativecommons.org/.

Index

Lightning Source UK Ltd.
Milton Keynes UK
UKOW012145180712

196238UK00007B/124/P